Organization and Aesthetics

Organization and Aesthetics

Antonio Strati

SAGE Publications
London • Thousand Oaks • New Delhi

SAGE Publications Ltd
6 Bonhill Street
London EC2A 4PU

SAGE Publications Inc.
2455 Teller Road
Thousand Oaks, California 91320

SAGE Publications India Pvt Ltd
32, M-Block Market
Greater Kailash – I
New Delhi 110 048

British Library Cataloguing in Publication data

A catalogue record for this book is available from
the British Library

ISBN 0 7619 5238 1
ISBN 0 7619 5239 X (pbk)

Library of Congress catalog card number 98–75046

Typeset by Photoprint, Torquay, Devon
Printed and bound in Great Britain by Athenaeum Press,
Gateshead

Contents

Acknowledgements

I wish to express my gratitude to my colleagues in the Faculty of Sociology of the University of Trento for their support while I was conducting the empirical research and the theoretical study on which this book is based, and to the scholars who have shared with me the initiatives taken by SCOS (Standing Conference on Organizational Symbolism). My thanks also go to the heads of the organizations who made my empirical research possible, and to the students on my sociology of organization course at the Universities of Trento and Siena. I am indebted to Per Olof Berg, Judith Blau and Antonio de Lillo for their encouragement, to Sue Jones for the opportunity she offered me to write this book for Sage, to Adrian Belton for his marginal notes and his translation of the text, and to Liliana Albertazzi, Alessandro Cavalli, Pasquale Gagliardi and Silvia Gherardi for having read the first draft of this book. However, all responsibility for what follows is mine alone.

Introduction

Music can be heard from the street below. It is sweet music, and it is played well, but it never stops. The walls and windows fail to block it out; they merely reduce its volume. The person playing the music has the right to do so; it is his job. But the two women inside the building at work in the secretary's office are also entitled not to be disturbed. The music is sweet, but the initial pleasure that it aroused has faded, and the pleasant surprise felt by the two secretaries when they first heard it has now changed into obsession. They confide in me their secret wish that the music would disappear, and that the player would disappear along with it.

This, therefore, is aesthetics in organizational life: sweetness and obsession, the feeling of pleasure and destructive desire, the source of conflict, the origin of problems of difficult solution, even in a socially constructed reality (Berger and Luckmann, 1966; Knorr-Cetina, 1994; Schütz, 1962, 1964) like the one described here: on the one side of the wall, two women working in a second-floor office; on the other side of the wall, down in the street, a young musician busking, as he does every day, for the small change given by generous passers-by. This is reality socially constructed by the intentional action (Weber, 1922) of both the young busker and the two secretaries, and it appropriately exemplifies Peter Berger's and Thomas Luckmann's definition (1966: 13) of 'reality' as 'a quality' distinctive of those 'phenomena that we recognize as having a being independent of our own volition (we cannot "wish them away")': however much they may want to, the two secretaries can do nothing to blot the music out. They cannot stop their ears from hearing as they can prevent their eyes from seeing by lowering their eyelids.

The problem, obviously, is not an immediately organizational one. Instead, it is an aesthetic problem, in the precise sense that it concerns a human sensory faculty – namely hearing – and a human faculty of judgement – namely the aesthetic judgement – whereby what we perceive through our senses may provoke pleasure or repugnance, strike us as palatable or disgusting, surprise and intrigue us, or obsess us and pollute our everyday working lives. It is a problem that highlights the importance of also being able to suspend, rather than activate, our sensory faculties and thus no longer hear the sweet melody that haunts us; anaesthetizing our senses, therefore, so that we are no longer aesthetically aware of the reality that surrounds us, or at least mixing our sensory faculties with other sources of aesthetic knowledge so that their sensitivity is blunted.

The two secretaries could turn the radio on, or they could play a compact disc in the computer CD-ROM slot and listen to music which would drown out the music coming from the street. But, the office manager has warned, they are not allowed to transform the office into a discotheque; even less are they allowed to work with their ears plugged. From aesthetic–personal the problem has now become organizational, not because the organization is listening – an organization can neither listen nor hear – but because the two secretaries and their boss have translated the problem into organizational terms. Yet the source of all the difficulty is the essential fact that these women's sensory hearing organs are unable to defend them against the obsessive assault of the busker's music. Their ears are only able to filter the music, thus in some way protecting them against it, but they cannot block the music out entirely. The organization has nothing to do with all this, given that, as said, it does not have ears and cannot hear. The people who work in the organization, however, are indeed involved in this process of hearing a sweet sound, being pleasantly surprised by it, enjoying it, but then coming to hate it, feeling that their acoustic territory is being invaded and violated, finding that their everyday lives are being spoilt by the incessant sound.

The non-human element – to use Latour's (1991) expression – constituted by the busker's music prompted the two secretaries to speak to the office manager to see what could be done. First, they joked about having piped music in the office, but then they took a tougher line, arguing that the organization should protect its employees and not permit them to work in such conditions. The negotiation process now involved the hierarchical relations between the secretaries and their office manager. It centred on the quality of working life within the organization and highlighted the organization's lack of power over the busker's socially sanctioned right to play music in the street. All this, remember, originated from the sound that entered the organization from the outside. The subjects of the process, however, were not the two secretaries alone, but the two secretaries plus the sound, which was an 'actant' which begot further 'actants' (Latour 1991: 122) in the chain-reaction of negotiations, evidencing the 'polymorphous' character of organizational actors and the incommensurable and heterogeneous elements that are connected together (Callon, 1991) in day-to-day organizational life. In other words, the action of the street musician was certainly responsible for the sound. Yet it was not he who caused the secretaries' pleasure or obsession, but the sound he produced, once the two secretaries had perceived it sensorially and judged it aesthetically and, thus, had acquired a knowledge about it.

Aesthetics in organizational life, therefore, concerns a form of human knowledge; and specifically the knowledge yielded by the perceptive faculties of hearing, sight, touch, smell and taste, and by the capacity for aesthetic judgement. The latter is the faculty used to assess whether something is pleasant or otherwise, whether it matches our taste or otherwise, whether it 'involves' us or leaves us indifferent or even repelled. Understanding aesthetics in everyday organizational life requires account to be taken of the non-human elements, of the 'missing masses' (Latour, 1992) which together with human beings constitute the subject of organizational action. But it should also be borne in mind that most of these non-human elements are artefacts. They are therefore products of human action which, although they are very frequently undesired (Merton, 1968), or perverse, should be considered not only in functional terms but also as regards their *pathos*, as Pasquale Gagliardi suggests (1990a): the *pathos* aroused by non-human elements in the members of an organization which also becomes part of the organizational communication process whereby these people have others enjoy their enjoyment, as Hans Robert Jauss writes (1982). Studying organizational aesthetics therefore involves analysis not of something fixed and objective, but of the ways in which both organizational actors and the researcher understand organizational life. And these are forms of knowledge that can be grasped principally in the everyday practices within an organization both of its members and of the researcher studying it.

This brings us to the core of the themes treated in this book on aesthetics in organizational life. They are themes which raise a crucial issue: namely, the deliberate and collective blindness of organization scholars as they have socially constructed their professional and occupational community (Kaghan and Phillips, 1998; Van Maanen and Barley, 1984) on the basis of the research programmes that they have conducted and debated (Reed, 1992), of the theoretical paradigms to which they have referred (Burrell and Morgan, 1979; Hassard, 1993; Scherer, 1998), and of the methodological questions they have raised concerning empirical research (Bryman, 1989; Bryman and Burgess, 1994; Cooper and Law, 1995; Evered and Louis, 1981; Van Maanen, 1979). In fact, most of the research and analysis published in the area of organization theories and management studies describes the following, somewhat bizarre phenomenon: as soon as a human person crosses the virtual or physical threshold of an organization, s/he is purged of corporeality, so that only his or her mind remains. Once a person has crossed this threshold, therefore, s/he is stripped of both clothing and body and consists of pure thought, which the organization equips with work instruments and thus reclothes. When the person leaves the organization, the mind sheds these work instruments and resumes its corporeality, and with it the perceptive faculties and aesthetic judgement that yield aesthetic understanding of reality, but only in the society lying outside the physical or virtual walls of the organization. This phenomenon reflects the separateness that Max Weber (1922) mentioned when describing the ideal-type of formal organization as the distinctive feature of bureaucracy compared with society. It shows that an organization is a reality collectively constructed by 'cyberminds', rather than by the 'cyborgs' described by Donna Haraway (1985, 1991); cyborgs, in fact, are social figures whose corporeality is made up of cyborg and organism, and therefore of a technology whose hardware and software shapes an organism which is not merely biological but a 'refined' body in which socio-cultural codes are inscribed. Cyberminds, by contrast, are devoid of corporeal culture.

In short, one finds in organization theory and management studies the conviction that aesthetics, as a discipline, has nothing to do with organizational life, or at most that aesthetics as a personal/subjective set of criteria have only a limited bearing on it. The prevalent image conveyed by the organizational literature until the mid-1970s, in fact, was that organizations are made up of ideas which meet and merge on the rational level: ideas, therefore, devoid of eroticism, beautiful or ugly sensations, perfumes and offensive odours, attraction and repulsion. Organization theory and management studies depicted organizations in idealized form by depriving them of their earthly features of physicality and corporeality.

This, however, does not correspond to everyday practice in organizations, nor to the use made by their members of aesthetic understanding of organizational life. It does not reflect the need felt by organizations for this kind of understanding, and it fails to take account of the fact that organizations use aesthetics to enhance their products and services, and to create an identity that is immediately communicable to their customers, employees and society at large. It is therefore curious that organization theory and management studies should have developed and achieved social legitimacy by virtue of an idealized view of organizations based on the assumption – not scientifically validated – that aesthetics pertains to society and not to organizational life.

This 'idealized organization' underwent a number of changes from the 1970s onwards, when the attention of organization scholars began to shift to the aesthetic dimension of day-to-day routine in organizations. These changes were in part brought about by a critique against the structural-comparative paradigm and against the excessively rational and reified view of organizational life which ignored the volition of individuals (Zey-Ferrel, 1981), whereas, as James March pointed out (1988: 402), theories of art and criticism permit one 'to see good information engineering not as a passive or manipulative activity in a decision scheme, but as an instrument of interpretation'. They were also changes brought about by a renewed interest in the study of art and aesthetics (Blau, 1988; Zolberg, 1990) which, instead of producing a 'main theoretical perspective', observes Judith Blau (1988: 286, 269), developed on several levels and through various controversies, all of which centred on a view of art as providing 'a unique opportunity for sociologists to investigate the connections between meanings and the social order and the way in which meanings penetrate all levels of that social order, including the level of individuals and that of the entire society'. Again in part, these changes were stimulated by the debate between the modern and postmodern which also involved organization studies (Burrell, 1988; Cooper, 1989; Cooper and Burrell, 1988; Hassard and Parker, 1993), given the emphasis of postmodernism on aesthetics – indeed, the debate on the postmodern is in many respects a debate about art and the aestheticization of everyday life (Calinescu, 1987; Featherstone, 1991; Hutcheon, 1989;

Jameson, 1991; Tucker, 1996) – and which, even when it was argued that modernity had not been replaced by postmodernity but by a 'reflexive' modernity (Beck, 1986; Beck et al., 1994; Giddens, 1990, 1991), saw 'recourse to the aesthetic dimension' (Lash, 1993: 21) as a way out of the dangers inherent in the 'imperialism' of 'an all-conquering reflexivity'.

But the idealized image of the organization has above all been modified by the organization studies which examine organizational aesthetics and which now constitute a strand of studies with its own, albeit modest, tradition of research and analysis, and its own internal theoretical and methodological controversies.

The first studies of organizational aesthetics examined the physical nature of organizations, their concreteness and their 'thingliness' (Heidegger, 1954; Husserl, 1913). These were works by Fred Steele (1973) and by Franklin Becker (1981), of which Jeffrey Pfeffer (1982) has emphasized their refusal to accept purely mental knowledge of organizational life. One of the main conclusions by Steele (1973: 143–4) was that 'the quality of an organization's setting influences the health of the system', but also that, unfortunately, 'the converse also tends to be true', so that 'it is difficult to engage in a healthy design process with an unhealthy system'. The latter will instead tend to choose 'settings which increase rather than reduce its problems'. There must be closer cooperation among designers, consultants and users, Steele therefore argues (1973: 145) and 'a consultant's goal' should be to cooperate with designers in order to 'overcome top management's resistance to change' and set up 'training experiences which will help lower-level employees develop their competence and ability to influence their immediate surroundings in the organization'. Thus, as Pfeffer points out (1982: 270), by focusing on the organization as a physical structure, Steele shows how 'physical settings can assist in organizational development processes'. Becker highlights a set of organizational features which influence the design of physical settings. First, physical design is influenced by the technical requirements of work and power, and by considerations of social control. But it in turn influences (a) the amount of interaction, (b) the affective reaction to job and organization, and (c) interpersonal attraction, competition, cooperation and person perception. Physical design, in fact, concerns such aspects of the organization as size, quality, arrangement, privacy and location. These are aspects with a close bearing on organizational life, and as a consequence, writes Pfeffer (1982: 271), understanding how organizations – as physical structures – 'emerge and get to look the way they do, as well as understanding their consequences, would seem to be an important place to begin to enrich the analysis of organizations'.

These early studies focus on the 'workings' of aesthetics in organizations, and on the possibility of 'managing' them in organizational life. They seek to acquire greater knowledge about aesthetics and about how they can structure the behaviour of organizational actors, while also rendering improvements to the organization's physical structures more remunerative. This is a 'weak' functionalism, therefore, which does not seek to put aesthetics to work in organizations in order to condition the behaviour of their members structurally. Instead, it points out the broad range of influences exerted by physical structures on people in organizations, on the process of organizing, and on the quality of workaday life.

Contrasting with this 'weak' functionalism is the approach used by scholars of organizational aesthetics in order to study the symbols and cultures (Gherardi, 1995; Martin and Frost, 1996; Smircich, 1983; Turner, 1990) constructed and reconstructed by the participants in organizational life. In 1985, a conference on the 'corporate image' was organized by Vincent Dégot in Antibes, France, under the auspices of SCOS (Standing Conference on Organizational Symbolism). Papers presented at the conference, and subsequently published in the SCOS journal *Dragon*, examined the following themes: the organizational identity graphically conveyed by the organization's name (Costa, 1986); the images that circulate internally (Bolognini, 1986a) in or externally (Schneider and Powley, 1986) to an organization and which depict significant organizational events in terms of both the organization's identity and identification with it; and deconstruction of the corporate image in the organizational architecture set in relation to deconstruction of official organizational statements (Grafton-Small and Linstead, 1985). Thus, culture and symbolism were observed in the organization's image, in its logo, in its publicity material, and in its architecture: themes that have become the constant focus for analysis of organizational aesthetics, and which are treated mainly in two collected works (Gagliardi, 1990b; Jones et al., 1988).

Less closely tied to the organization as a physical structure are the studies of aesthetics in organizational life published in the special issue of *Dragon* on 'art and organization' edited by Pierre-Jean Benghozi in 1987 – a theme central to organizational debate as evidenced by the collection of essays edited by Michael Owen Jones, Michael Moore and Richard Snyder (1988). These studies examine the creativity of people who work in organizations, management of organizations by engaging in art-related activities, and everyday organizational practices to do with art. The issue of *Dragon* edited by Benghozi contains three essays (Dégot, 1987; Ramirez, 1987; Rusted, 1987) which illustrate different approaches to the study of organizational aesthetics without referring to organization's physical structures: (a) the gathering of knowledge by means of analogies with art; (b) examination of the beauty of the organization and therefore of aesthetic sentiments and judgements with regard to the organization as a whole; (c) study of how aesthetics are negotiated in aesthetic practices, a phenomenon also researched in cultural studies. These are three studies that directly engage the researcher's point of view and emphasize the importance of his/her aesthetic involvement in the process of gathering knowledge about organizational cultures and symbols. Vincent Dégot proposes an analogy between the manager and the artist, and the situated study of managerial practices. He suggests a number of previously unknown management methods which emerge if the researcher examines managerial practices by analogy with artistic styles and genres.

Ramirez illustrates the beauty of a social organization for those who belong
to it, employing the concept of form (Bateson, 1972; Langer, 1942, 1953)
and showing its influence on aesthetic knowledge of organizational reality,
an argument which he has subsequently developed further (1991). Brian
Rusted shows how organizational decisions about the aesthetics of ceremonies
direct the scholar's attention to the social construction of organizational communication and to the subversion and resistance that undermines dominant
aesthetic practices.

These are the principal features of the organizational aesthetics studied by
the strand of organization studies that concerns itself with aesthetics. It will
have been seen that they are examined in many areas of organizational life:
from management to participation in organizational ceremonies, from the
physicality of work settings to the corporate logo, from the concreteness of
specific organizational artefacts to the insubstantiality of the organization as
a whole. Aesthetic analysis of organizational life is a new area of inquiry in
organization theory and management studies whose crucial contribution has
been to enrich knowledge about everyday organizational life. It is, moreover,
analysis which raises theoretical and methodological issues concerning the
entire corpus of knowledge produced by organization studies, as I have
argued elsewhere (1990, 1992, 1995, 1996a, 1997, 1999) and shall seek to
show in this book.

The linking theme of the book, in fact, is that it is possible to gain
aesthetic, rather than logico-rational, understanding of organizational life,
and that this understanding concerns organizational cultures and symbols as
well as the aesthetics created, reconstructed or destroyed in day-to-day
organizational negotiations. 'Aesthetic' understanding of organizational life,
therefore, is an 'epistemological metaphor' which problematizes the rational
and analytic analysis of organizations because the 'logic' of these analyses
has transcendent features, in that it is 'supposed to have its basis in what is
beyond human conduct and relationships', as John Dewey wrote (1925;
reprinted 1958: 168–9), thereby creating the traditional distinction between
'the physical and the rational, the actual and the ideal'. Instead, it is the lived
experience of people as they act (Dewey, 1934; Strauss, 1993) in organizations that the aesthetic approach seeks to grasp. It does so by means of
that process of evocation which, as Dan Sperber notes (1974; Eng. trans.
1975: 143), 'may be considered as the search for information that allows
the re-establishment of the conceptual condition that was unfulfilled'.
Above all it seeks after empathic understanding of the intentional action of
people in organizations, given that, as Clifford Geertz writes (1973: 13),
although 'finding our feet' is an 'unnerving business which never more than
distantly succeeds', it is 'what ethnographic research consists as personal
experience'.

In Chapter 1 these theoretical and methodological issues are illustrated
through examination of certain organizational artefacts. Discussed are (a) the
falsity, the plausibility and the truth of organizational aesthetics, (b) the participant observation which documents the quasi-objectivity of the qualitative

study of organizations, and (c) the relations between aesthetics and the processes of symbolization engaged in by the members of organizations.

The second chapter conducts detailed methodological analysis of empathic understanding of meaningful action in organizations. The discussion starts with the methodological notes set out by Max Weber in *Wirtschaft und Gesellschaft: Grundriß der verstehenden Soziologie* (1922) – a work devoted to the comprehension of human intentional action – the purpose being to reflect systematically on the issues of method that the aesthetic understanding of organizational life raises for organizational research and theories of organization, to illustrate its theoretical underpinnings, and to emphasize the nuances and provisos which organization studies based on analytical and rational methods have preferred to ignore.

Chapter 3 illustrates the 'connoisseurship' (Turner, 1988) displayed by participants in organizational life. Since this ability is based on the sensory faculties and on the aesthetic judgement, the chapter highlights the similarities between aesthetic knowledge and tacit knowledge (Polanyi, 1962, 1966). Also discussed are the theoretical foundations of the aesthetic approach in phenomenological philosophy, hermeneutics and deconstructivism, as well as its endeavour to gather dialogic and non-causal knowledge about organizational life.

With the importance of aesthetic connoisseurship for the empirical study of organizations based on the aesthetic approach thus demonstrated, Chapter 4 discusses aesthetic representations, especially those which concern the beauty of work and of the organization in which it is performed. Beauty brings out the organizational features that both people and their organizations find significant, while also highlighting the specificity of the organizational understanding based on aesthetic representations.

Chapter 5 examines the body of organization studies that has given rise to the strand of research on organizational aesthetics. It therefore discusses the main issues debated in this area of inquiry, paying particular attention to the empirical research most frequently undertaken, to the organizational aesthetics most closely studied, and to the aesthetic awareness of the researcher who engages in such research.

The conclusions focus on the organization–hypertext metaphor for the ceaseless process of knowledge differentiation in organizations, a process driven by their participants' meaningful action grounded in hearing, sight, smell, taste, touch, aesthetic judgement, as well as logico-rational mental processes. Using the hypertext metaphor in the light of the aesthetic approach, it is stressed, a chaotic and fragmentary patrimony of connoisseurships and artefacts can be viewed in organizational life, and the search for a 'strong ontology', which defines the true nature of organization, can be avoided in order to seek to gather dialogic and non-causal organizational knowledge.

1 Organizational Aesthetics, Experience and Plausibility

For some years I have set the students attending my course on sociology of organization a riddle concerning organizational artefacts. Riddles are a teaching technique often used with children attending nursery or elementary school. Typical ones are the following: 'Which is heavier, a kilo of feathers or a kilo of lead?' 'What colour was Napoleon's white horse?' 'If a cock stands on a roof-top, which side will its egg fall?' These are questions which require guile, and the application of one's own knowledge rather than the mnemonic or factual use of what one knows. A riddle, in fact, is neither a quiz nor a test. It does not require selection of the only correct reply from a set of possible ones, or the reply that is more correct than the others. It is a game without any apparent purpose apart from helping to pass the time. It is a game that children then reproduce by asking each other: 'Riddle-me-ree. What colour is . . . ?'

If one considers the teaching style typically adopted by Italian university lecturers, use of the riddle as a didactic stratagem is highly unusual. Seminars and group work, for example, are common. Less so, but nevertheless widespread – at least as regards organization studies – is discussion of specific topics using video materials or following visits to companies or public organizations. Dramatizations, role-playing or simulations are rare, even when the small number of students attending a course might permit them. The reader will therefore imagine the surprise of the students when I begin a lecture with the words: 'Today we're going to discuss the organizational artefact in more detail than we've done so far. I'm going to set you a riddle. . . .'

The reaction of the students has been generally positive. Confronted with a teaching technique that breaks with the conventional format of the 'serious' lecture and which at the same time proposes a new one, their reaction has usually been a mixture of surprise and pleasure. 'What, a riddle instead of a lecture? That's great. . . .' They ask each other what's going on, they joke among themselves, laugh, jostle, shift in their seats.

Which is fortunate. Because there is a risk that I will not be taken seriously; that the students will treat my lectures as relaxing interludes in the 'true' business of academic study. The riddle, in fact, evokes sensations and memories of infancy, when learning was based on purposive games-playing. In the background to that experience, too, was the institutional organization and process of instruction. But a university is not a nursery or an elementary school. In the latter, riddles constituted the games-playing which enables children to learn how to activate their knowledge and apply it in a given context.

Consequently, to forestall the risk of failure in this transition from the 'serious' to 'serious games-playing' at university, I try to give an aura of formality to the event. I do so by imposing rules on the solution of the riddle. I introduce, that is to say, a second game into the first one:

> You can answer the riddle either individually or in groups. If some students wish to form small groups, that's fine, but the groups must formalize themselves by giving the names of their members. The choice is up to you, but remember that there's a prize for those who solve the riddle, either as an individual or a group. According to by now classical theories in the organizational literature, in fact, your participation will be greatest if you create the prize out of your own pockets. So I'm going to collect the money that you will, I'm sure, so generously disburse and offer it as the prize.

This usually heightens the excitement in the lecture room. Some students go to sit next to those with whom they want to form a group. Others move among the desks collecting the prize money. Others help me to count the money and to compile the lists of group members. But there are also those who fail to join in. They feel at a loss, unable to adapt to the new situation. In these cases my usual strategy is to suggest that they act as observers ensuring observance of the rules, rather than as actors. However, I have never been able to fashion a role which could attenuate the hostility of those against the idea from the outset. Fortunately, these students have always been rare, and moreover not ones able to fill the role of leaders.

Thus, in addition to excitement over the riddle game there is the students' first-person participation in activating the procedures with which to solve the riddle. In their eyes, the success of the new organizational set-up has acquired importance. They are intrigued. They see it is a chance to enjoy themselves. They take the riddle to heart because they see it as marked by an intrinsic extemporaneity. As I have said, their university experience does not comprise lessons based on riddles, but lectures delivered *ex cathedra*. Consequently, they are entirely caught up by this novel opportunity.

Even greater didactic formality is created by my invitation to the students to consider the principles that underlie rules and procedures:

> First, though, we've got to establish some principles about the prize. If someone solves the riddle, they get the prize, they do what they want with it, and everything's fine. But if none of you guesses, what are we going to do with the prize? That's a possibility which you should consider. At least we should agree that the money is a shared asset which (a) won't be handed back (which means that if you don't win, you lose your stake); (b) that it won't be added to other funds that you've pooled (I mean, this money can't be added to your photocopy fund); (c) it's yours. I can't take it, and I can't give it to anyone else. You'll have to decide what to do with it. So it'll be much better if someone wins, to prevent wrangling over what to do with the prize . . .

I then say a few words about the concept of organizational artefact. I outline the meaning of the term, stressing that it refers to numerous things and to many aspects of the organization. It may be something physical or impalpable, ephemeral or enduring, essential or marginal. It may be, that is to say, some object of an organization, one of its underlying assumptions, or one of its distinctive features. It may even be the organization itself. The concept of organizational artefact can therefore be used to refer just as much to the most specific element of the organization as to its most generic one, just as much to its most practical–concrete element as to its most theoretical one, just as much to elements acquired by the organization as to those produced in it. The important point is that any particular organizational artefact 'talks' to us about the organization, It is therefore a notion that should be taken in a very broad sense, even if there is one and only one organizational artefact that matches the requirements of the riddle.

Before specifying those requirements, however, I should explain why I choose to introduce the topic of aesthetics in the everyday lives of organizations in this manner. There are several reasons for my choice, which I give in the next section. I shall then return to the riddle.

Organizational experiences and the evocation of knowledge

My reason for beginning my discussion of aesthetics in organizations by recounting the episode of the riddle on the organizational artefact is that it enables me to highlight the heuristic process based on evocation. Involved here is a form of knowledge that relies not on evidence or proof, but on imagination and intuition. It originates from imagined participation in the organizational situation described. In other words, the heuristic process of evocation involves knowledge-gathering about a particular organizational phenomenon on the basis of experience of that phenomenon. This experience occurs only in the imagination of the subject, but it is lived experience nonetheless.

What have I done, in fact, by telling the story of the riddle? I have given the reader a chance to take a seat in the university lecture hall. I have invited him/her to join the organizational situation described.

Of course, this can only be made possible by the imagination, or more precisely by the images that the reader has formed from my description of that organizational setting. These are images which, although stimulated by what I have written so far, are not absolute correspondences. In other words, they do not constitute the only illustration of the riddle story. Nor, for that matter, is this story illustrated by images that are specific and particular. The reader therefore finds him/herself in a situation in which s/he can, and probably must, create images on the basis of this written text in order to gain an idea of what the text is saying. If s/he has tried to imagine being in the situation described, s/he has done so on his or her own account; that is, with images that are entirely private. The story has therefore only been a pre-text so that the reader can employ his or her own images to picture, for example, the lecture room and the people in it. Paradoxically, this imaginative involvement comes about without the reader having any direct knowledge of the places or the people involved, or of the specific courses of action in the university lecture room where these events unfolded. At this point, two general remarks require making.

The first arises from empirical studies of organizational aesthetics (Strati, 1990, 1992, 1995). These studies have shown that the lived experience of organizational actors is crucial to proper understanding of organizational life. They have not found, in fact, that an organization or a course of organizational action was 'objectively' ugly or beautiful, grotesque or tragic, comic or kitsch. Nor did all informants describe the organization or events in question in aesthetic terms. Those who did so, though, always made reference to their own stock of experiences. On some occasions it was the individual dimension of aesthetic experience that was emphasized; on others, the same experience was referred to as collective, as an experiential heritage shared by a plurality of organizational actors. This happened both when crucial events in the organization's life such as its founding and planning were discussed, and when less critical, more everyday or even routine events were described. This is not to imply that the only method available to study organizational aesthetics is that based on the experiential stock of organizational actors. Indeed, concentration on the aesthetic experience of subjects, the experiential corpus that they rework and narrate, is only one among several ways to conceive and observe aesthetics in organizations. It is a particular theoretical position, one whose foundations will be examined on several occasions in this book.

My other remark relates to the first and takes the argument a step forward: the unfolding within the imagination of aesthetic experience.

Since the reader has had direct experience of university lecture rooms, or has read books, seen films, videos, photographs, or listened to relatives, friends or whomever, s/he can imagine himself or herself in the organizational setting described. However, s/he is not obliged to do so, and may confine him- or herself to a reading of my description of the riddle episode at the level of rational intelligence. But if the reader is willing to immerse him/herself imaginatively in the situation as I describe it, s/he may 'grasp' the capacity of the riddle to alter the dominant schemes of the organization of university courses, namely the lecture or seminar. S/he can 'see' the amused faces of the students and the lecturer as they joshed and joked. S/he can also gain a 'foretaste' of the pleasure implied by the announcement that 'I'm going to set you a riddle'; pleasure that not only involved entertainment but also a minor transgression of the canons of academic organization. S/he can 'observe in first person' that the riddle created a climate of cooperative excitement in the classroom; a particular climate due, of course, to the novelty of the situation, but also marked by a renewed sense of active participation among the students. S/he can 'ascertain' how and to what extent the organization constituted by the course became a source of enjoyment for those attending it, and 'personally assess' the pleasurable expectations of the students, as well as the exhilaration that spread through the room. S/he may 'remain favourably impressed' by the enthusiasm aroused by the idea of a riddle about the organizational artefact.

If one is to gain knowledge about the everyday life of a given organization by drawing on evocative processes, therefore, one must place oneself in the imaginary – rather than factive and physical – position of the participant observer, watching events within the organization without being physically present; in short, visiting the organization without ever physically entering it. All this can be expressed by saying that evocation is nothing but participant observation conducted in the imagination, so that the organizational phenomenon studied is reconstructed by the imagination on the basis of the prompts provided by the text that describes the phenomenon.

The evocative process of knowledge formation, therefore, forces the reader to 'place' him/herself in that lecture room at that Italian university. Only then can s/he begin participant observation of the organizational phenomenon. Once positioned within that organizational setting, the reader 'will see with his or her own eyes', 'hear with his or her own ears', 'move with his or her own legs', 'perceive in person', 'feel emotions', 'form an opinion' and 'draw conclusions' concerning the event.

Of course, all this takes place in the reader's imagination. But the reader does not situate him/herself in the situation solely by dint of logic or rationality: s/he can see, listen, move, and experience pleasure. S/he can perceive, that is to say, with all the senses and, as we shall see later, thereby acquire aesthetic knowledge. For the moment, the point that I wish to stress is that this knowledge-gathering process involving the activation of the sensory faculties unfolds within the imagination. In other words, the aesthetic knowledge of the organizational phenomenon is generated by participant observation conducted on the basis of the imaginative capacity of the knowing subject.

Let us try to reason by absurdity. Let us assume that the reader is willing to explore the organizational phenomenon by evocation, but to do so s/he wishes to use solely his or her capacity for rational thought. Let us consider the riddle situation and attempt to produce a plausible description of the evocative process. The reader is present in that classroom where the others (the students and lecturer) manifest surprise, pleasure, excitement, enjoyment, disorientation, where they jostle, laugh, change places, push and shove, write names on bits of paper, pass among the desks collecting the money, solely in the guise of pure rational thought. S/he does not see the expressions of contentment, but thinks them rationally. S/he does not hear the voices, the laughter, the rowdiness, the noise of chairs being moved, but thinks them. S/he does not smell the odours of paint or of bodies, but thinks them. S/he does not feel the climate of excitement, but only thinks it. The evocations that s/he gathers are only those based on intellectual reasoning. Sensations have no effect, because they require faculties of understanding – those that activate sensory perceptions – which pure rational thought does not possess. Now, to what extent is an evocative process of this kind plausible? It is plausible only to the extent that this reader able to be present as pure ratiocinating thought in a world, albeit imaginary, crowded with bodies and actions, with odours and noises, with emotions and movements, rejects evocation rather than uses it. How can we gain a foretaste of what is 'in the air' in that particular organizational setting if we rely solely on the ratiocinative capacity? We need to deploy the faculty for foretaste prior to actually experiencing what happens, and we should use it at the level of the imagination to prelive the organizational experience. This happens because there is something 'in the air' that evokes prior experience and has us re-live it; prior experience made up of sensations which re-emerge, instead of reasonings that are rationally remembered, and sensations which to be relived must avail themselves of the set of sensory and perceptive faculties, given that rational intellect is unable to revive them.

Let me therefore summarize the concepts relative to the principal theoretical concepts introduced and partially discussed in this section. They concern the interweavings between aesthetics, prior experience and the heuristic–evocative process, and they all relate to comprehension of organizational life. The concepts discussed are those whereby:

(a) prior experience is central to the study of aesthetics in organizations;
(b) the heuristic process of evocation is based on the reader's capacity for imagination;
(c) the reader's imagination employs the perceptive and sensory faculties of aesthetic understanding, rather than only those on which rational analysis is based.

Aesthetics and imaginative participant observation

If one seeks to describe the reader in the light of the arguments set out in the previous section regarding the interweaving of aesthetics, evocation and experience, one comes up with a person capable of knowledge which is simultaneously paradoxical, complex and involving. The reader foretastes, sees, perceives, enjoys or disapproves, feels emotions; in short, s/he forms opinions devoid of rigorous analysis.

This reader will seek a place in the organizational setting while it is being described, and thus observe events from a particular standpoint. Of course, s/he may regard the organization from the same point of view as my own and adopt the same vantage point as my own. But s/he may move away from it in order to look for things that are not yet apparent in the account, asking questions that I have not raised, wishing to see things that I have not noted. In short, s/he can and does act as if s/he were physically present in the context described, and precisely by virtue of the fact that s/he does not conceive of him/herself as present in that organizational situation solely as pure thought and solely with a capacity for pure thought.

A dilemma now arises: what actually happened in the case of the riddle? How can we truly know the changes that it wrought in the organizational context in question? After all, it is this that really interests us. How we imagine the organizational phenomenon, how we interpret events, how we allow ourselves to be influenced by the account, and how we imagine ourselves in the situation: these are secondary matters that can be left until a later stage. In fact, there are numerous possible readings of the organizational phenomenon under examination – at least as many as the people involved in the heuristic process. Indeed, one may hypothesize that certain persons will prefer to have several interpretations of the organizational phenomenon, but this phenomenon must nevertheless remain what it actually is: a single organizational event. And as such it must be described.

But the facts of the matter are different. The two stages of the knowing act – the one relative to how organizational events actually unfold, and the one in which different interpretations of them are formulated – are not so analytically distinct. This is because, first, the evocative process of knowledge-gathering places the reader who uses it in a position which is in many respects the same as that of the scholar. It turns the reader into a participant observer by virtue of his or her capacity to imagine being present at the organizational events. Second, as a participant observer of organizational action, the reader adds original knowledge to the description of the organizational phenomenon described. This is because the reader is obliged to translate my text into comprehensible and familiar images and sensations, but also because s/he is at liberty to conduct his or her own empirical analysis of the organizational events.

It is at the level of in-the-field investigation, therefore, that relations are established between the reader, the unfolding description and its author. Interpretations of the organizational phenomenon already begin to acquire different forms and identities during this first stage of empirical inquiry. If this is the central node in the interweaving of aesthetics, experience and evocation in the knowledge-gathering process, the dilemma of knowing what has actually happened can only be resolved if we acknowledge that the organizational phenomenon studied is multiform. In other words, there is no single organizational phenomenon that corresponds to a plurality of interpretations. There is instead an organizational process which displays features that are simultaneously similar and different; features that are apprehended and illustrated by a plurality of participant observers. Which brings me to my next point.

There is not just one reader. First, there is the author him/herself of the text, but there are various others as well. Although this datum is to some extent obvious, it is nevertheless important because it evidences the complexity of the heuristic–evocative process. Moreover, the plurality of the reader is also the reason why evocation proves to be such a fruitful source of knowledge about aesthetics in organizations. The premise here is that it is not true that a series of relations become established between the reader, on the one hand, and the author or authors of the organizational research study, on the other. Instead, it is assumed that there are a certain number of readers operating within the organizational context being studied. This fact highlights a fundamental feature of the evocative process of knowledge-gathering: a commonality is established among these various hypothetical readers based on the fact that all of them have acquired, by themselves, a specific familiarity with the organizational situation described. Indeed, we can imagine that if they met, they would be able to talk about some occurrence or other without having to retrace all the phases of the organizational event from the beginning. They could exchange phrases like 'Did you see what happened when he told them that they would have to solve a riddle?', instead of ones like 'An Italian university teacher began his lecture by setting a riddle for his students.' They may find the event amusing and joke about it, re-evoking the episode. They understand each other because they know what they are talking about: the room, the people and the events are all familiar to them.

Furthermore, the various readers' familiarity with the organizational event of the riddle is backed by another and much more specific familiarity. I refer to the familiarity which, as I mentioned before, derives from each reader's direct experience of contexts presumed to resemble the one that I have described. Or it is a familiarity based not on direct experience but on films or stories, that is, on texts that others, distinct from the readers and myself, have composed.

The number of subjects to take into account when analysing the heuristic–evocative process has therefore grown larger. Besides the numerous and diverse readers, there are also those imaginary individuals whom they have introduced to the university organizational context. So how many subjects are we talking about? The calculation is difficult, and I shall not attempt it here, mentioning it only to stress a crucial feature of the heuristic–evocative process. Let us return to the university lecture room with which we began. It is not that we have, first, the students with their teacher and the riddle, and then afterwards the account, or the constructed artefact, with its author and reader. In other words, it is not that the relations between organizational actors and the researcher come first, and those between the researcher and the reader – who may be the organizational actors themselves – later. The knowledge-gathering process is not as cleanly defined as this. It is contaminated, so to speak, because of the diverse participant observations by the readers that my text has prompted. And also because of the various ways in which the readers have been introduced to university lecture rooms. It is these introductions, with their diversity, that beget familiarity with the organizational context shared by the organizational actors, the researcher and the readers. It is they that are responsible for the array of sensations, impressions and evaluations that constitute each reader's text; which is a text in its own right, I would stress, not a personal interpretation of the one that I have produced.

The first important conclusion in the matter of knowledge about organizational aesthetics, therefore, is that my text – the one that the readers have read – is neither the only text nor the only true one. Which means that it is not my text alone that has provided the basis for the readers' interpretations of ongoing dynamics in that organization, and it is not my text alone that is responsible for their conflicts of interpretation and their negotiations over the meanings. What my text does, in fact, is provide the stimulus and the template for the constitution of other texts, those that the readers construct on the basis of their participant observation of the organizational phenomenon that I have described. And they do this through the evocative process of knowledge acquisition.

What, then, is the 'true' text of organizational knowledge? Who is its 'true' author? Anyone who describes the organizational process is certainly the author of a text. Anyone who imagines that s/he is directly observing the organizational process is also the author of a text, although it is one based on imagination and not yet written or filmed. Anyone who has taken part in the unfolding of that process in the organization (a student or the teacher) has very probably constructed his or her text about the organizational process – by talking about the event with others, for example. There are then those who have created the texts used imaginatively by readers with no direct and factual experience of university classrooms. These authors are in a rather similar position to the author of the written text insofar as they have provided prompts for the reader's imagination. In other respects, however, their situation is very different, for they are not among those who have conducted participant observation – real or imagined – of the organizational process under examination.

Can one therefore argue that a shared text does not exist? That each author constructs his/her own text about the organizational process in question, and that this text is the idiosyncratic product of its author? In certain respects one can indeed argue as much, but in other respects one cannot. One of the arguments against the conclusions concerns the participant observer's familiarity with the field of inquiry, which constitutes a web of meanings shared by the authors of the various texts. However different the individual imaginings of the university lecture room or the astonished faces of the students may be, it is precisely these processes that engender the familiarity of the various readers with the situation being described.

A shared text therefore exists. But what is it? Whose is it? It is a text in constant formation and de-formation, which constantly shifts from being a shared work to being an individual one. All the authors are fully at liberty to reconstruct it and deconstruct it. Which means that they are not constrained to one single view of the organizational process in question and therefore not obliged to produce one single text.

Asking which is the 'true' text therefore fails to take account of the complex and paradoxical nature of organizational knowledge when seen as a process, when viewed as doing rather than being, when conceived as a social collective construction, and not as something concealed to be brought to light and explained. If we assume that organizational knowledge is a social and collective process, we must 'yield' to the plausibility of diverse texts produced by diverse participants in the knowledge-building process. These texts, therefore, if plausible, all describe the phenomenon in question. Moreover, despite their highly personalized nature, they are all closely interrelated. They possess these features because all of them are based on the evocation of knowledge provided by the aesthetic understanding of organizational life.

The reader now knows why I began this chapter with the episode of the university riddle. I may therefore now resume the description from where I left off; that is, with the clues to the organizational artefact that I asked my students to guess.

Aesthetics and organizational artefacts

When all the students have settled down and are ready for the riddle, we agree a time limit for solving it, usually ten minutes. I then switch on the overhead projector and show the following transparency:

Which organizational artefact in the broad sense:
1. is purchased more often than it is produced
2. goes beyond organizational boundaries
3. is simultaneously material and non-material
4. is individual and belongs to everybody
5. shows up anyone who does not have one
6. is constantly sought after
7. is a metaphor for the hierarchy of organizational levels
8. if flaunted may provoke criticism and invoke sanctions
9. if it shifts, may provoke hilarity
10. homogenizes positions downwards

?

'Power', 'professional expertise', 'organizational culture', 'domination', 'emotion', 'money', are the most frequent answers suggested. But they are wrong. And there are other replies even further adrift from the correct answer. The ones that I have listed at least match a good proportion of the clues, but they do not match them all. What does one notice about these solutions?

1 Each of them comprises an abstract concept.
2 This concept is a theme widely debated in contemporary organizational literature.
3 All these are concepts which pervade organizational life. They concern the organization both as a whole and in its more specific aspects.

What, then, was the correct answer to the riddle? In accordance with the organizational ritual activated in the classroom, one of the students unfolds a slip of paper that I have placed on the desk and reads out the answer: 'This organizational artefact in the broad sense is a chair.'

One can imagine the surprise of the students. 'Nooh! It can't be!' they chorused immediately. 'Come on, it can't be a chair.' In fact, a chair is not generally considered an important element of organizational life. It has not given rise to analysis and debate in the organization literature. The students' bewilderment is therefore entirely understandable. On the one hand, none of them would have denied that the chair is an object present in organizations. Indeed, given their mainly scholastic experience, they would have found it hard to imagine an organization without chairs or other artefacts on which people sit to do their work. The chair was therefore taken for granted. The students could not deny that a chair is useful or even vital, given the fact that they themselves were sitting on chairs! On the other hand, they could not see what such a banal organizational artefact had to do with the study of organizations. And this accounted for their astonished insistence that 'It can't be true', that it was impossible for the answer to the riddle to be 'a chair'. The organizational concept that they had chosen, whether power or culture or skill, was undoubtedly of much greater importance.

My students always fail to solve the riddle, and their reactions to their failure always differ. For example, on the last occasion when I set the riddle, some of them, although surprised and knowing that they had lost, readily admitted that only a chair matched all the clues to the riddle. Others only grudgingly accepted the solution, although they had cooperated generously to ensure the successful outcome of the riddle-based lesson. In other words, for them the chair was only a pretext for more involving analysis of organizational artefacts than a lecture *ex cathedra* could provide. Less generous were those few students who had been hostile to the riddle exercise from the outset, and were now impatiently waiting for the lesson to move on to matters more serious than pointless games-playing. Finally, there were several students, the most combative ones, who refused to accept defeat. Once their initial bewilderment had passed, they counter-attacked and insisted on reviewing the clues one by one, trying to demonstrate for each of them that their solution was a perfect match, if certain minor details were ignored. In short, they tried to show that although they had not guessed the answer, they had by no means lost. But this the other students refused to accept. The competition among groups and individuals still continued, and no one was going to win because they had 'almost guessed' the right answer. It was even necessary to verify whether the chair actually matched all ten of the clues to the riddle. This was duly done in the manner that I shall describe shortly, but first I must point out another aspect to the organizational process activated in that lecture room.

The 'extraordinary' event had now ended. Its disruptive effects on customary university procedure now gradually dwindled and the organizational situation prior to the event gradually re-emerged. We have seen that the construction of the event required the active participation of the students. But its decodification meant that the organizational context of my university course on sociology of organization had to undergo further changes. In many respects it returned to what it had been previously. What persisted, though, was the close attention paid by the students to the success of the lesson and to its delivery. And yet, although they paid close attention, the visibility of the students diminished as their role of protagonists in the organizational process activated by the riddle gradually faded. It was something that could be 'seen' and also something that could be 'heard'.

Until decodification of the riddle, in fact, the students had been visible *qua* actors in the organizational process. Not only had they been essential, from a conceptual point of view, for construction of the organizational context necessary for delivery of the lecture based on the riddle; they had been made visible by virtue of their production of the actions appropriate to it. They were visible when changing places, compiling the list of names, or collecting the prize money. They were visible when laughing, jostling and joking among themselves. When they realized that they had lost, disappointment or resentment was visible in their faces and gestures. As soon as the next organizational stage of decodification had been announced, they were visible as they returned to the seats that they normally occupied during lectures. Some of them did so immediately; others did so in dribs and drabs, shifting in accordance with the pace of change in the organizational context.

Most closely associated with the marked visibility of the students in the course of construction of this organizational context and the flow of its modifications was the noise that they made and the sound of their voices. They could be heard, as well as being seen, while they changed places, and the sound of their voices was audible when they tried to argue their case. And this was before the meanings of the words uttered had been grasped. Sound and noise, movements, grimaces and gesture, prior to being intellectually rationalized and justified, signified search, negotiation and sometimes achievement of pre-eminent positions in the organizational process.

But the organizational context constructed by the riddle lecture was now changing. Profound alterations had occurred in the sense attributable to the organization. New courses of action interfered with previous ones, and they were directed, on the one hand, towards decodification of the riddle and, on the other, towards its legitimation in Italian university organization. The new situation can be described as follows:

1   The students had settled down to listen and ask questions, or to propose different views on what they were being told.
2   The lecturer's principal task was to indicate the meaning of events surrounding the riddle and to set this meaning within the broader context of university teaching, thereby dispelling the impression that it was ephemeral, random, specious or recreational.

However, closer inspection allows more accurate description of the new context in terms of an organizational process. One notes that the organizational setting of the riddle lesson was altered by changes in the following:

1   The *positions physically occupied* by the students as agents of the new courses of organizational action. These were the positions occupied

when 'in study mode'. They also resulted from the students' reciprocal knowledge, and from negotiations over seating conducted since the beginning of the sociology of organization course.

2   The *postures assumed* by the students once they had returned to their places. These postures were very different from the ones to be seen when the students were trying to solve the riddle. They now tended to lean away from the lecturer's podium and the overhead projector. They were also physically less projected towards the others. In general, the students were no longer ostentatiously striving to assert themselves and were instead more composed.

3   *Facial expressions and grimaces, hand and arm gesticulations, body language in general.* The students' expressions, gestures and movements reflected their waning excitement, enthusiasm and enjoyment, their resigned acceptance that they now had to revert to organizational routine, their disappointment over failing to solve the riddle.

4   The *volume of voices and noises*: both gradually lapsed into silence.

5   The *rhythms of these movements, voices and noises*; rhythms which now signalled the end of the game situation and indicated that the organizational actions of these actors were much less diversified. The rhythms in the lecture room were now sequential: one person spoke at a time, there was little movement and no noise. These were rhythms very different from the cadence collectively produced when all the students were speaking at once, all moving at once, and all raising their voices to be heard above the others.

6   The *time taken* for this shift from the construction of an organizational context to its reconstruction in a form more congruent with a university lecture to be tacitly negotiated and realized. Restoring calm after the excitement took time, for it required a change of mood. The time taken to achieve this change differed according to the subjects involved. There were students who could not wait to return to the lecture *ex cathedra*, others who wanted me to continue with the riddle-based format. There were also times which were collectively and formally managed, and those which instead allowed the ongoing experience and the subjective experience of the students and lecturer to prevail.

All these features were observable in the university lecture hall in question. In other words, it was possible to watch negotiation over the value of what is being done and over the meaning attributable to the organizational events. None of this, in fact, happened in the absence of bodies, voices, noises, gestures and movements. This was no encounter here between pure thought and exclusively rational intelligences. Consequently, a description of what happened in that university lecture room when the organizational artefact riddle was set – a description provided so that one can witness (albeit only as imaginative participant observers) the disappearance of lived experiences – requires the formulation of arbitrary interpretations; interpretations, in other words, that are excessive because they distil, sterilize,

conceal and excise a large part of the organizational process as human experience consisting of pleasure, emotion, movement and noise, the exhibition of
personal vitality. These are over-interpretations justified by the theoretical
paradigm of rationality and positivist knowledge. They are, that is to say, the
outcome of a choice made in the ambit of the diverse modalities of knowing
organizations. They result from an epistemological choice and not from
insuperable limits on the human capacity to gain knowledge about quotidian
organizational reality.

I may now return to the organizational artefact constituted by the chair,
proposing arguments in part already set out elsewhere (Strati, 1996a). As
said at the beginning of this section, the organizational context had changed
and the lecture now proceeded in a setting structured more in keeping with
the Italian university tradition. I stress this change because the situation was
at once paradoxical and ironic: the organizational context complied more
closely with the canons of the lecture *ex cathedra*, but the topic addressed
was the chair and its importance and significance for the study of
organizations.

The organizational artefact that is purchased more often than it is produced

This was the first clue to the riddle. The organizational artefact in question –
understood in the broad sense – is usually purchased by the organization
rather than produced by it. There may be cases in which this does not
happen, but the clue states that they are less frequent. A chair fully matches
the specification: organizations do not normally make the chairs that they
require. They may inherit them, or they may receive them as donations from
third parties, but much more often they buy them. They do so by utilizing
the output of other organizations which manufacture and market chairs.
What does this feature tell us? First of all, that a chair is an organizational
artefact, both multiform and multi-purpose, both widely used and complex,
which embodies different organizational cultures and evokes them. Second,
that the artefact 'chair' evidences how profoundly organizations have
permeated everyday life in highly industrialized contemporary societies.

Chairs differ in shape, material, structure, line, style, size, weight and use.
There are chairs designed for private use in the home, and already these are
highly diverse. The chair produced by organizations which cater to the
private market is a chair which depends on its place in the home. One
'domestic' chair differs from all the others according to whether it is
intended for use in the garden, in the kitchen, around the dining table, in the
study, or at the dressing table in the bedroom. Not all homes contain such a
wide range of chairs, but very few of them use kitchen chairs, for instance,
for every possible purpose, especially if they are homes in which chairs are
effectively present in large numbers; homes, that is, located in societies like
those of Europe which consume huge amounts of organizational artefacts.
The chair of the private home is not an organizational artefact except in its
manufacture and sale. But it nonetheless evidences the fact that chairs are

more often purchased than made. Of course, some chairs may be produced by someone in the home with carpentry as a hobby, but they are usually bought from the organizations that market them, or else they are received as gifts or legacies. And whenever possible, a chair is chosen which suits a particular place in the home. On the basis of what criteria?

This question takes us to the core of the problem. Chairs come in different shapes, sizes, materials and weights, but they are always chairs. What does this tell us? That there is a distinctive feature shared by all chairs, namely that they are artefacts produced by organizations for people to sit upon. The chair is the paramount artefact for this purpose, and it is therefore designed, constructed and sold to this end. Being an organizational artefact to be sat upon is the chair's essential characteristic, its ontological determinant.

However, this does not exhaust the range of criteria applied when a chair is chosen for the study or for the garden. It is certainly the main criterion, the one first applied: we are looking for a chair to buy, not a computer or a table or a suitcase. We could of course sit on the table or the suitcase, but this would be at odds with their ontological nature. Can we therefore say that this basic feature of the chair articulates into an array of specific forms and that the same basic conception of the artefact 'chair' is realized in the concrete object? Indeed we can, as we shall shortly see. But this does not solve the problem of the criteria whereby one chair is chosen for the kitchen and another for the living room. The function of being 'that which is sat upon', being useful for this purpose, being definable exclusively as an artefact produced by organizations so that we can have something to sit on, is only the first component in the decision to buy a chair. It is a fundamental moment in the choice because it is preliminary to all those that follow; thereafter this ontological characteristic is taken for granted in the decision process, and the criteria of choice are based on aesthetic knowledge.

What, then, do we look for when choosing a chair? First of all we look for a chair that we simply like, one that aesthetically matches the other artefacts in the room it is intended for. We look for a chair in a particular style, a chair which feels comfortable, one which is not solely an object to sit upon. We look for a chair that will display our good taste. Beautiful or pleasing to look at, pleasant to touch, elegant and solid. Or a heavy chair, in dark wood, suitable for a room decorated in rustic style. We look for a chair that does not creak, and which does not squeak annoyingly when we raise the seat. It is the sensory faculties of sight, touch, smell and hearing that furnish the criteria for choosing a particular chair. They determine our judgements of what is a beautiful chair and what is an ugly one, which chair matches a setting and which clashes with it. Intellectual and rational knowledge – the knowledge whereby a chair is an object to sit on – gives way to aesthetic knowledge, the knowledge that tells us that the chair is a specific artefact that we look at, touch, smell and hear. Consequently, the question as to the criteria applied when choosing a chair cannot be answered in terms of ontological features alone. These may be useful in distinguishing between a chair and numerous other artefacts. But when we decide which artefact to choose, we take this decision on the basis of our perceptive and sensory faculties, because it is through these that we know the chair and pass judgement upon it.

I now turn to the other aspect mentioned earlier: the fact that the chair is an organizational artefact that evidences how widespread organizations have become in contemporary industrialized societies in the course of this century, and how greatly their importance has increased. If we give the appropriate weight to the ontological definition of this artefact and therefore consider it in the broad sense, we can move from the domestic chair to other organizational artefacts designed to be sat upon: those found in offices, cinemas, theatres, airport departure lounges, waiting rooms in train and bus stations, university lecture rooms, restaurants, bars, and so on. In these organizational settings, too, difference predominates. Which amounts to saying that not even in workplaces are all chairs the same. In offices we find ordinary chairs behind the tables, easy chairs behind the desks, armchairs in the rooms set aside for corporate display, chairs of prestige design around the table in the directors' board-room. These are all artefacts that have been conceived and designed for people to sit on. But they are also all of different craftsmanship, structure, style, size, colour, weight and material. Once again it is difficult to argue that they have been chosen purely according to the ontology of the artefact and that the sensory faculties are of only secondary or even negligible importance. If this were the case, we would be able to report the existence of an organization in which there was only one single type of chair – whether in the offices used by management, in those for the rest of the staff, or in the rooms set aside for meetings. Instead, the same process applies in organizations as in private homes: artefacts are chosen on the basis of aesthetic knowledge.

Besides chairs, easy chairs and armchairs, if we consider this artefact in the broad sense we note yet other forms and structures – of which, however, I shall mention only some. Sofas, for example. These may be made of leather, synthetic material or cloth; they may be elegant or functional; they may be huge, comfortable, even grandiose. Stools, too, display a variety of forms. Consider the stools used by piano players or orchestra percussionists and compare them with those used by technical draughtsmen. Again they differ. Stools for drawing boards are higher, they often comprise a metal shaft and have casters fitted to the base. The piano player's stool has a shorter shaft and usually has three legs. They are also very different in appearance. The light colours of the draughtsman's stool contrast with the dark ceremonial colour of the musician's. The materials, too, are different. In the former case, metal predominates and is covered in leather or plastic; in the latter, the metal parts used to raise or lower the seat are concealed. There are car seats, the seats in buses and coaches, those in the driver's cabs of heavy vehicles or machines, in the control cabins of cranes or forklift trucks. These, too, are all of different shapes and materials. Car seats may be wide and comfortable, as in a saloon, or they may be the hard uncomfortable seats of a jeep. Buses have seats made of synthetic materials attached to a single metal base, thus resembling more the seats in heavy goods vehicles than those found in cars. Then there are bicycle saddles, designed to be raised or lowered, and which differ in shape according to whether they are fitted to a push bike or to a sports model, to a woman's bicycle or a man's, to a bicycle manufactured at the beginning of the century or to one manufactured in these final years of it. There are motorbike saddles, and of course there are those used in horse-riding. The latter differ as well, according to the style of equitation. But to leave seats and saddles and return once again to chairs, consider, for example, those used on the beach or beside swimming pools. These are deck-chairs or poolside loungers, which today are mostly made from metal and synthetic materials. At one time, though, they consisted of a wooden structure to which a canvas sheet was nailed and on which one sat or lay. They were heavy, awkward and difficult to carry, compared with their modern-day equivalents, but they were almost indestructible, and with their vivid colours are by now part of the iconography of the Italian and Mediterranean seaside. This last example enables me to move towards some final remarks on the fact that this artefact is more usually purchased than produced. The multiplicity of the shapes assumed by chairs, and the multiplicity of the contexts in which they are used, enable the following conclusions to be drawn.

First, a chair is an artefact specific to the organization in which it is used, and not solely to those in which it is produced. That is to say, a chair is an organizational artefact both because, with its highly diverse forms, it is the product of some organization and because it is a product that the organization assimilates and transforms into a chair which denotes the organization itself.

Second, this organizational artefact is often produced by a plurality of organizations operating in different sectors. Chairs are purchased by some organizations from others; they are commissioned by some organizations from others. Indeed, the production of chairs itself highlights the complexity of this interweaving. On the one hand, there are the organizations that design the artefact; on the other, the materials of which the artefact consists are supplied by organizations with their own distinct productive cultures. Some of them work with wood, others with metals, yet others with synthetic materials or with leather, with textiles, with paints or varnishes. The chair drives the work cultures and production processes of organizations which differ by productive sector and geographical location, by size and by technology, and also in terms of their organizational cultures and occupational and professional communities. This 'banal object' of quotidian organizational reality throws the complexity and diversity of relations among organizations and their cultures into relief. This is especially evident when such organizational cultures disappear. Until a few decades ago, chairs with straw seats closely resembling the one in Van Gogh's famous painting (Hulsker, 1980: 376) were manufactured in Italy. They were made by hand in back alleys, and mainly by women, as can be seen in photographs of those women at work, with their black dresses and aprons, while they sit in the alleyways outside their homes.

Third, the only definition of 'chair' that does not breach the rule of plurality is that of an artefact on which one can sit. This, as said, is its ontological property. Yet it is a definition that requires caution, as we saw when discussing the relationship between intellectual and rational knowledge and aesthetic knowledge. An example may shed further light on the matter. Consider a chair which explicitly connotes the organization to which it belongs and in which it is used: the chair of a Catholic church. This is a simple chair, with four legs, a back and a seat. It is made entirely of wood. It is strong and spare in its outline. The back demonstrates that it has been produced for a religious setting, because it is pierced with the shape of a cross. Although the cross is wide and long enough not to escape notice, it is not blatant. This feature denotes beyond any shadow of doubt the organization in which the chair is used. When this chair is seen together with others like it, in any room whatever and not in a church, the cross-shaped incision proves that the chair belongs to a church, or used to belong to one, or at any rate belongs to a Christian religious organization if not a Catholic one. In other words, the chair does not 'tell' us that we are in a school or an airport. If, on the contrary, we find ourselves in a school or an airport, this particular chair helps us to determine whether we are in a Catholic school or an airport chapel.

The chair does all this with elements that are apparently secondary, decorative and extraneous to its essence as an artefact on which people sit. It does not do so on the basis of its ontology or its *raison d'être*, if we accept the above definition covering the various forms of this aesthetic. The detail of the back pierced with the shape of a cross may appear of only minor importance, but in fact it is not. It reveals that care has been taken over the design of the chair to ensure that it is not just any chair but one that declares: 'Behold, this is a religious organization in a distinct organization setting.' This has important implications for the gathering of organizational knowledge through the study of aesthetics: ontology is not always a great deal of use. Knowledge of some important features of the organization can be gained from examination of the shape of a chair, of its appearance, and not from contemplation of its essence as an artefact on which to sit.

This invites us to look more carefully at chairs, instead of taking them for granted or dismissing them as banal, although inevitably present in organizations. Observing the church chair in close detail, in fact, yields further interesting insights into organizational artefacts. The chair in question has been designed and manufactured so that, if rotated and the seat lifted, it becomes a faldstool. Catholic liturgy requires the congregation to kneel when praying. Most church pews are designed so that the worshipper can use a kneeler attached to the rear of the pew in front; a feature which distinguishes church pews sharply from park benches, for example, which obviously do not have this attachment. The pews in Christian churches therefore allow those sitting behind to kneel. In contrast, the church chair provides the person wishing to kneel in prayer with an individual faldstool, which, moreover, is mobile. Not that it can be moved too far, obviously, but at least far enough to create a private space for individual prayer. What matters most is that the chair is no longer a chair. On some occasions it is an artefact on which one sits; on others it is an artefact on which one kneels. In the former case it is a chair; in the latter it is a faldstool. If we want a general definition, we can call it an artefact which takes our weight, but this definition encompasses numerous other artefacts, from a table to a cushion, from a walking-stick to a bed, from a vaulting pole to a banister.

The ontology of the chair, therefore, does not do justice to the complexity of this organizational artefact. Nor, for that matter, does it account for the complexity of the chair. Chairs are frequently used as tables on which folders, books and printouts are stacked, often as clothes-hangers with jackets carefully draped across their backs. On other occasions, they serve as step-ladders, perhaps with a newspaper laid on the seat to protect them against dirt. The upshot, therefore, is that an organizational artefact should be analysed in terms of its being-in-use, as part of organizational practices activated in courses of action. The church chair is consequently highly indicative. It is made in such a way that it is apparently an utterly ordinary chair, an ontologically exact chair, a chair on which one sits. Made of good wood, brown in colour, with four legs, a broad and slightly rectangular seat, a low back and a cross-shaped incision, nothing reveals its other function as a faldstool. This we discover when we get up from the chair, rotate it, lift the seat, lower it to the floor, and notice the small protruding shelf. We learn about it, that is to say, by watching the chair in use. Or we find out about it from other people who belong to that community or who frequent it. In any event, the church seat carefully conceals its function as a faldstool from those who do not belong to the organization in some capacity.

Of course, its function is evident to scholars interested in the history or design of the chair, or to those who study the organizations of Christian worship. Likewise, its function is well known to the organizations that designed the chair and to those that produced it. However high and solid the walls that organizations construct around themselves may be, there are artefacts like the chair that pass beyond them. This aspect is now discussed with regard to the second clue to the riddle.

The organizational artefact that goes beyond organizational boundaries

A chair is the product of relations among several organizations, as we have seen. A commonplace wooden chair begins in a sawmill – that is, in one of those enterprises often of small size located near woodland and which process lumber, or in one of the larger ones which saw timber into boards of various sizes and values. The timber may also originate from more distant areas and be even more diversified in quality. This is the genesis of the chair, and in certain respects it corresponds to the initial decision to buy a chair and not a cupboard. Cutting down the tree and sawing it into boards – which differ in quality according to whether they are destined for a furniture factory or for one manufacturing boxes for the fruit harvest – are the first and necessary steps in realization of the commonplace wooden chair. But they are not to be taken for granted. There are work cultures associated with tree-felling just as there are work cultures associated with timber-sawing. Skills are involved which are not learnt from books but are the tacit heritage of professional and occupational communities. Organizational cultures are at work which give sense to the quotidian activity of these organizations, and it is these various cultures that give rise to the wooden chair.

However, the wooden chair is also the fruit of the cultures of other professional communities and of other organizations. First, there are the organizations that commission the chair from those that produce it, as we saw earlier in the case of the church chair. That particular chair was not one of our 'commonplace' chairs: neither at first sight, because of the cross carved into the back, nor on closer inspection, because it was a chair that belied its nature as an artefact on which to sit by becoming one on which to kneel. The church chair was therefore intended to constitute one of the organizational artefacts in a place of worship. The organizations that attended to its design and manufacture took account of the organizational culture of the customer. Hence there are other organizational cultures involved in the production of the wooden chair besides those that we have seen as responsible for its genesis, and they constitute the beginning and end of a process which involves a plurality of organizational cultures in the construction of this 'banal' artefact.

Yet this still does not exhaust the account. How many commonplace wooden chairs, instead, do not depend on the organizational culture of a specific customer that commissions them? How many depend on the aesthetic canons of the culture of the professional community of the architects who design them, rather than on those of the organization that commissions them? One may argue that the production of the commonplace wooden chair results from negotiation centred not so much on its ontology as on its aesthetics. In other words, one can argue that the decision that the chair is an artefact on which one can sit is preliminary and essential; thereafter, however, the question of what type of organizational artefact it actually is gives rise to conflicts, power displays and the negotiation of aesthetics among organizational cultures that may differ greatly. Consider the organizations responsible for the design of our commonplace wooden chair. Their work on the aesthetic appearance of the chair is scrutinized not only by the commissioning organization but by other design organizations as well. The aesthetic canons governing the design of commonplace wooden chairs are those proposed and debated within the professional community of designers, in the schools or university departments of graphic design, and in the industrial design sector. The aesthetic canons of the chair are those propounded and illustrated by the design journals, by the interior decoration magazines, by the publicity materials of design organizations. Consequently, the commissioning organization finds itself forced to impose its aesthetic conception of the chair on organizational cultures which are neither of minor importance nor particularly willing to compromise.

The argument so far can be summarized as follows.

First, a plurality of organizational cultures, as well as the cultures of professional and occupational communities, are involved in the design and manufacture of an organizational artefact. The latter, in fact, is the outcome of a process of collective social construction framed by organizations and by the relations that they establish with each other. The artefact is a human product, but only in the sense that it is conceived and constructed in historically specific terms. The first and chief manifestation of this historical specificity is the datum that, in the course of the twentieth century, artefacts have become more and more the work of organizations, rather than of individuals, families or artisan workshops; organizations, however, that we should conceive as organizational – and therefore collective – cultures which arise, fragment, reassemble or decline as the result of the constant learning, invention and negotiation of their identities.

Second, the negotiations, conflicts and power dynamics that centre on the conception, design, manufacture and use of an organizational artefact concern not its ontological properties but its aesthetic features. It is here that organizational identities are at stake. The chair must reflect the organization to which it belongs and in which it is used. It must also reflect the organization that has produced it, as well as the one that has designed it. And these are only the organizational cultures most closely involved in the process of construction and reconstruction of this organizational artefact. Yet even if we restrict discussion to these, we note that the metaphorical arena in which they contend is the arena in which it is possible to touch the artefact, to look at it, hear its noises, smell its odours. Our hands glide over its decorative reliefs, or they stroke its back. We sit easily on the chair, or we find its shape and height uncomfortable. Our backs feel its hard edges or its restful curves. Our elbows rest comfortably or awkwardly on the arm-rests. Leaning on the arms may be relaxing or perhaps, after some time, it may cause tingling or numbness. Our feet rest on a cross-piece, or easily on the floor, or they are prevented from doing so and cannot be tucked under the seat. When adjusted, the chair is noiseless and does not creak. The paint gives off a pleasant smell or it slightly irritates the nostrils. The colour is easy on the eye or it is too dark, too light, too bland. The shape is the one we want: austere and unfussy or baroque and ornate. The chair is in the standard style of the period when it was made, or it is distinctive of the firm that designed it or commissioned it. All these conflicting and negotiated elements, all these attempts to impose an idea of what the chair should be, override the ontology of the organizational artefact.

Third, none of the relations considered so far are confined to the individual organization. The relationship between the organization that commissions the chair and the organization that produces it is not solely a relationship in which money is exchanged for a good; it is traversed by organizational cultures and by the cultures of professional and occupational communities extraneous to these two organizations. Let us return for a moment to the private home. How many organizations does the chair introduce into the home – into the kitchen, the living room, the study, the bedroom, the children's rooms, the terrace, the garage or the garden? From another point of view, how many organizational aesthetics does the chair bring into the home? A modest number, perhaps, but one that is nevertheless significant. It is by means of organizational aesthetics, in fact, that the individual aesthetic of the private domain is expressed. The organizational artefact pervades the home with the organizational cultures that have designed, manufactured and sold that artefact. The exchange of money for the organizational artefact is essential, but it is only a preliminary to the aesthetic canons that permeate the home. These are hybrid aesthetics, the fruit of negotiation and power dynamics, as well as of mixtures among the various organizational cultures involved in producing the artefact. The final aesthetic layer is applied by the person who furnishes the home – on his or her own, with the help of relatives and friends, or following the advice of an interior designer. This renders the result even more composite, and highlights even further that it is not solely a matter of artefacts to sit on.

The organizational artefact that is simultaneously material and non-material

A chair also meets the third requirement of the riddle, namely that the organizational artefact should be both material and non-material. Consider what happens if we draw a chair on a computer screen using computer graphics software. Countless pixels on the monitor represent our chair. We do not notice them, nor do we scrutinize them one by one, as the screen sweep does. We are indifferent to them, in fact, unless we want to adjust their size, number or colours. We never annotate pixel after pixel: what we see, what we read, what we recognize is the image of the chair against a background. Which prompts the following considerations:

1   The concrete object – the pixel – is not considered, because a process of symbolization induces us to recognize a chair drawn against a background on the screen.
2   The chair thus depicted is a chair whose base material is made up of pixels on the screen, as opposed to wood, leather or metal.
3   This chair is a simulation of a chair; it is not a chair. Nor does it depict any particular chair in the same way that a photograph does. A photograph, in fact, like a video or a film, reproduces that particular chair which happens to be before the camera lens. Computer graphics software does not follow this analogic process, not even when cards and software for image digitization yield a photograph of a chair taken with a camcorder or a camera. There is instead a mathematical model at the basis of the visualization of the chair on the computer screen. Thus, by altering a parameter of this model by means of the software, it is possible to adjust the brightness, the size or the colour of the pixels. By contrast, in order

to alter the photograph of a chair – unless one is using a Polaroid film (which can be manually manipulated as it develops by scratching or smearing the surface) – the chair itself, or the lighting, or the setting, must be modified. Consequently, if we prefer to digitize the photographic or video image of a particular chair in order to project it on the screen, the latter must be manipulated using all the graphical effects made possible by compatible software packages. There is no analogue relationship, therefore, between the photographed chair and its reproduction by means of computer graphics. The relationship is instead digital, and whether the chair's image on the screen results from a photograph or whether it is produced by means of a paint program or computer-assisted design (CAD) is of little importance. The chair that we see on the screen is entirely the work of the hardware capability of the computer and of the computer graphics program used.

4   The chair simulated by the computer is two-dimensional, although we perceive it – unlike a photograph or a drawing – as three-dimensional.

The computer-simulated chair provides an example of an organizational artefact that is material and non-material at the same time. What we see depicted on the screen is a composite set of pixels which, by means of a complex process of symbolization, is identified as a chair against a background. Is this truly a chair? If it were, we could sit on it. But if we wished to do so, we would have to get inside the computer monitor. To be able to sit on simulated chairs, people, too, have to be simulated. That is to say, their bodies must also be digitized into a mathematical model compatible with that of the chair and the scenario. Also in the case of the human body, therefore, the principle holds that by changing one of the parameters, that body is modified and its image on the computer screen consists of a pattern of pixels.

However, the simulated chair – on its own against a background, or when it is used by a simulated person – is nevertheless a chair. Symbolization processes ensure that we recognize it as such. In virtual reality, once digitization is complete, the chair is always an artefact on which one sits. Henceforth the materiality and non-materiality of the artefact has no influence on the artefact's ontological characteristics. It follows, therefore, that we cannot use these characteristics to decide whether the context in which we are operating is virtual or otherwise, whether the chair is a simulated organizational artefact or whether it is not.

Yet this distinction is important, for the two contexts are very different. Let us return to the initial situation of drawing a chair on a computer screen, and imagine the digitization process, and specifically the digitization of ourselves sitting on the chair in front of the computer screen. We have thus created the two contexts. Now imagine making yourself more comfortable on the chair, and imagine doing this in the two contexts: the virtual one and the one which, although it is non-material because it is imagined, is not virtual. In the simulated context we change a series of parameters and raise the back-rest to just below neck level, adjusting its angle so that it fits our body more comfortably. We cannot say how we feel following these adjustments. On the other hand, it is more difficult to make these changes to the chair on which we are sitting as we work with the computer, but we can recount the sensations that we feel. Let us return to the virtual world and alter our physique by shortening our legs. We adjust the chair because the back-rest is now too high. We change some of the parameters of the mathematical model, wait for the computer to perform the necessary operations, and see that the screen sweep, pixel after pixel, has simulated us with shorter legs. We now wish to see how we are sitting by looking from beneath the chair, at a particular angle and using particular lighting, and find that all this is possible in the simulated chair environment. But it is not possible in the setting of the chair in front of the computer because we cannot simultaneously sit on a chair and look at ourselves sitting on the chair from beneath it. Even less is this possible if the legs have to be shortened and the back-rest raised and adjusted. The ontology of the chair, however, does not enable us to comprehend the difference between the virtual or non-virtual context in which we find ourselves. If we do discern differences, they are ones due to aesthetic knowledge. They are the differences that we see on the screen, just like the odours that we do not smell or the sensations that we do not feel. It is aesthetic knowledge which merges together the materiality and non-materiality of the organizational artefact.

Here, however, we have taken a step beyond the base definition of the organizational artefact as something at once material and non-material. I have already introduced the materiality and non-materiality of the chair, in fact, when I discussed the chair in the broad sense and considered a variety of organizational artefacts which differed greatly in terms of shape, size and use: bicycle saddles and deck-chairs, office armchairs and seats in the cabs of heavy vehicles, draughts(wo)men's stools and chairs used in Catholic worship. All these seats and chairs are material, but they are also all non-material in their symbolization *qua* chairs. If this were not the case, we would find ourselves dealing with assemblies of materials very difficult to construe: in one case an assembly of pixels on the computer screen, in another an assembly of wood, nails and screws, in another of leather and metal, and in yet another of synthetic materials, wood and metal. If the organizational artefact consisted solely of a physical object composed of different combinations of materials, it would be absolutely impossible to make any sense of it. The artefact, by contrast, is material and non-material at the same time, so that when we see those pixels, or that three-dimensional assembly of different materials, we recognize them as constituting chairs.

We have taken another argument a step further, too. Chairs are both material and non-material for a further reason. In organizations they are used to denote position or status, for example when one is used to indicate the organizational position of chairperson. A chair is an artefact with these features even when it serves to denote the positions of power occupied by individuals in organizations. This is the royal throne, the boss's chair, the chair on which one must never be caught sitting. Likewise it is a chair that provokes a sense of horror – the electric chair – or it is one that causes anxiety, like the dentist's chair, or one that gives pleasure, like the chair that we sit on to relax. A chair is a simultaneously material and non-material artefact in its connection with organizational structurings and events. The dentist's chair is both a physical organizational artefact and a symbolic artefact constituted by our image of it and the emotions that this image arouses. The same applies to the chair on which we must never be caught sitting. It is not the materiality of this chair that matters but its non-material connotation of untouchability. As regards the chair used for relaxation, given the pleasure that it promises, one notes the non-materiality of our mental image as we imagine for a moment that we are sitting on it. This is the chair of our desires, therefore, like the chair occupied by the head of an organization and which some of its members so earnestly covet; to be sure, these are material organizational artefacts, but at the same time they are symbols and sources of power in an organization.

The organizational artefact that is individual but belongs to everybody

Save in exceptional cases, two people do not usually sit on the same chair, neither on the driver's seat in a car or a tractor nor in the armchair behind the president's desk. They may alternate in their use of a chair but they do not occupy it simultaneously. This also applies to a university chair: it is not assigned to two or more persons at the same time, although everyone may aspire to it.

On the other hand, no one is refused a chair. If someone enters an office and there are chairs available, s/he is invited to sit down. 'Available' means unoccupied. In fact, we do not invite the person who has just entered to sit on a chair already occupied by someone else, because this would mean that the person already seated would have to give up their place for the new arrival. We can also take a metaphorical approach to the matter, where by 'chair' or 'place' is meant the position occupied in the organization. What, therefore, does this fourth requirement tell us as regards the organizational artefact?

First, the chair specifies the position acquired in the organization: the position of forklift driver in a warehouse if we are talking about the seat on that kind of vehicle; the position of the person presiding over a meeting if the chair belongs to the chairperson; that of university professor if the reference is to an academic chair. Of course, this is not the only way to signal the positions occupied by people in organizations, but it nevertheless emphasizes that an individual has temporarily or permanently acquired a place in the organization. Consider a room in which it is not possible to hold a meeting because there are not enough chairs to go round, or there is not enough space for a sufficient number of chairs. Consider an airline flight which we have been unable to book because all the seats have been taken. These are only two examples, but they are of relevance to the life of an organization. Decisions have to be taken in both instances. Booking a place on another flight may mean that a meeting has to be postponed. If the room is too small, some of those summoned to the meeting may have to be excluded, or it may be necessary to split the meeting into two if another room can be found, or to look for another room with a sufficient number of chairs for everyone.

Second, the chair is prescribed by organizational ritual and ceremony. Chairs are important in encounter rituals, for example. Invitations are made to sit down, to take a place at the table, to sit and talk for a moment. Encounters that take place standing up, perhaps in the corridor, do not have the same flavour or the same legitimacy. The board of directors of an organization would never hold a meeting standing up because this would preclude serious discussion. Decisions taken 'on the hoof' are like fast food eaten standing up: they are not good for the health. Organizational ritual dictates the use of chairs in these cases – for sitting, for talking, for discussing, for deciding. Whether the meeting involves two people or the entire organization, whether the purpose is to communicate impressions or to take decisions, whether the atmosphere is confidential or formal, organizational ritual prescribes that these actions should be performed while sitting. This is even more evident on the occasion of organizational ceremonies, for instance the presentation of an award to deserving employees: only those receiving the award and the person presenting it stand up, while there is an unwritten rule that the audience must remain seated.

Third, whatever its specific form may be, the artefact 'chair' is both individual and belongs to everybody, because it is the property of the organization and not of any individual. However, this does not apply to all organizations, for there are some organizations in which people are forced to procure their own chair should they need or want one. There do exist organizations in which every individual owns his or her own chair, but in many other cases it is the organization itself that provides chairs, so that the person does not own a chair but merely uses it in order to stay in the organization. Here the organizational artefact evidences the variability, mobility and substitutability of the persons who sit upon it. Whether these are visitors, customers, users or members of the organization, they are all individuals who only temporarily occupy the chair *qua* organizational artefact.

The organizational artefact that shows up anyone who does not have one

The fifth requirement of the organizational artefact is that it should focus attention on anyone not using it. This is precisely what the chair does. Those standing up are especially visible in organizational settings, which, as we have seen, usually require everyone to sit in their proper place. Those who wish to emphasize a point at a meeting or a university lecture get to their feet, as if this gesture will make their argument more intelligible. Negotiation is therefore involved which operates on two levels: the first concerns the attention of others; the second, which is equally important, concerns placing of oneself on display. The chair highlights this process by being momentarily not in use but at the same time available for use. This does not only happen in organizational contexts which involve teaching or training. The act of rising to one's feet to speak is an extremely common ritual in a wide variety of organizational contexts. Consider a trade-union assembly. A speaker from the audience is usually invited to stand up so that she or he can be seen while speaking. Consider the formal dinner that concludes an event in an organization. The person who makes the closing speech, and the person who then thanks those responsible for the success of the event, get to their feet to speak.

The act of rising from one's seat, and therefore the non-use of a chair, is part of the ritual of placing oneself on display and calling attention to oneself in predominantly formal organizational contexts. In informal organizational settings, in fact, it is more difficult to resort to this ritual; even more so if only a few people are present. But even in this situation, more force, importance or emphasis can be given to one's words by rising to one's feet. The action, in fact, accentuates that change is in progress. The physical raising of one's body emphasizes that one is changing position in the organizational context. First, rising to one's feet shows that one is leaving one's place but not ceding it to anyone else; second, albeit only for a moment and in a specific setting, one places oneself on display by not using a chair.

The organizational artefact that is constantly sought after

Again this applies to the chair. If we fail to find a chair, in fact, we may be excluded. Consider the situation of arriving slightly late for the general meeting of the organization for which you work. The room is already full and all the seats are taken. The meeting has already begun and the chairperson is speaking. You scan the rows of chairs in search of an empty seat, indicating your intention to sit down with eye movements, raised eyebrows and hand gestures. As you do so, you keep an ear on what the chairperson is saying in order to grasp what is going on. You engage in two simultaneous actions, therefore: following the chairperson's words and searching for a seat.

But all the seats seem to be taken and a chair becomes the object of search. If you find one, you will cease to be on display, given that in this situation – unlike the one described above of the momentarily and deliberately unused chair – visibility is at odds with the organizational situation. As long as you remain standing, you highlight the shortcomings of an organization which is unable to accommodate all its members by providing a sufficient number of chairs. Your failure to find a chair, therefore, is irksome to both yourself and the organization.

It is even more irksome if you ask for help in finding a seat by means of eye contact, eyebrow-raising and shakes of the head when the meeting has already begun. On the one hand, you try to listen to what is being said; on the other, you interfere with what is being said by looking for a place to sit and by asking the others present to help you. The two activities are not similar, nor are they coordinated and cooperative. Moreover, they interfere with the meeting. The speaker must regain his or her audience's attention, the person looking for a seat must pay attention to what is being said, and those helping him or her must do likewise. The latecomer may even disturb the meeting by leaving the room to find a chair in some other part of the organization, bringing it back to the meeting room, putting it in position and finally sitting on it. Other late arrivals may follow his or her example and leave the room to fetch chairs. For a number of minutes, therefore, proceeding in parallel with the meeting is an organizational course of action which those involved deem important: the action of procuring a chair outside the meeting room and bringing it back. Those who arrive even later, noting as they search for a seat that the room contains chairs of different shapes, or that the chairs have been arranged in a pattern which differs from that of the chairs usually in the room, or prompted by the example of the others who have gone off to fetch chairs from somewhere else, do likewise, thereby constituting an organizational routine, although one that is parallel to the meeting and obstructs it. Now, what is it that allows all this to happen while the meeting is formally in session? It is the fact that a chair is an organizational artefact which is part of an organization, of its rituals, of its ceremonies, of its formal activities. Without a chair we are excluded from taking due and legitimate part in events and actions important for the life of the organization.

Of course, such behaviour during meetings is not permitted in all organizations. Not all organizations would allow these comings and goings by latecomers who enter the meeting room, fail to find a seat, leave the room, return with a chair perhaps different from those already in the room, place it alongside the others – perhaps asking those already seated to make room – sit down, and finally participate in the meeting by listening to the speaker. The noise of doors opening and closing, of chairs being moved and placed in position, the whispered enquiries if a seat is free and the muttered replies, the bustle of people moving, bringing chairs into the room, asking the others to make space, and finally sitting down, apologizing, expressing thanks: all these actions disturb and distract both speakers and listeners. Yet there is a further factor present in these organizational contexts in which such behaviour does not incur formal sanctions, or is otherwise not impeded, but is considered inevitable or at least tolerated. I refer to the pretence that, in terms of the organizational event in progress, everything that concerns the search for the chair is in fact not happening. Or if one prefers, although it is happening it is not part of the organizational reality, as if it were something that is and must be extraneous to the meeting and to memories of it. One notes this when reading the minutes of the meeting, which make no mention of such incidents even though they usually punctiliously record the names of those who leave a meeting while it is in session. The stir caused by the latecomers with their chairs, the shifting of the chairs already occupied, the energy devoted to finding a place, none of these are part of the organization's ordinary routine. In other words, chairs are rigorously excluded from organizational events; an exclusion which also concerns chairs as metaphors for membership of the organization. In the Anglo-Saxon universities, the chair denotes the academic position of greatest prestige and power, the full professorship. Gaining a full professorship usually entails an extra workload which diverts energies from research and teaching. A career, in fact, is 'made', and in all organizations it must be specifically constructed; but in all organizations, on the other hand, the pretence is made that this construction is not part of everyday working practice.

The conclusion, therefore, is that the search for a chair is behaviour instigated by organizations. It is instigated by the simultaneous celebration of principles of organizational collaboration – 'Let's sit around a table and examine the problem' – and principles of organizational competition – 'Sooner or later that job will be yours'. Of course, organizations do not always have all the chairs necessary to accommodate everyone who works for them, so that somebody will be perforce excluded. Yet observation of chairs yields a somewhat bizarre image of the organization as an ambit where, on the one hand, everyone is in search of a place, while, on the other, nobody stably occupies the place that they have. One notes in this image a constant milling around of people who get up from one chair and sit down on another, as if participation in the life of an organization were based on a constant endeavour to change places.

The organizational artefact that is a metaphor for the hierarchy of organizational levels

The chair signals specific levels of the organization. In this case, too, its shape, structure and materials, how it is made, what it looks like, how it smells, convey information. The chair of the head of an organization is usually not a commonplace chair made of wood, nor is it a kitchen chair, nor the seat in the control cabin of a crane. It is usually an armchair or a heavily upholstered easy chair; in other words, a chair which indicates the organizational level of its occupant and not solely the organization for which s/he works. I begin with the latter point.

A number of deck-chairs arranged in rows on a beach denote the presence of an organization engaged in the business of summer tourism. Wooden chairs attached to each other in rows, dark in colour and with seats that can be lifted when no one is sitting on them, or when nothing heavy like a coat or a handbag is placed on them, tell us that we are in a cinema, an organization where people gather to watch films. But neither type of chair guarantees that we are in the ambit of the organizations with which they are normally associated. The deck-chair may be in someone's private garden; the row of cinema seats may be in the home of someone who finds that kind of furniture to his or her taste. There are obviously fewer of these chairs and their arrangement involves a certain amount of decontextualization. Moreover, even if the chairs are located in a cinema, we could very well be sitting on them not to watch a film but to listen to a lecture, or to take part in a trade-union meeting or a political rally. As I have pointed out on several occasions, the chair is an organizational artefact that goes beyond organizational boundaries. Yet it is always an artefact connected with the organization in which it is customarily used: cinema seats are distinguishable as such by virtue of aesthetic knowledge, and in this respect they are very different from the deck-chairs on a beach.

Bearing this in mind, we may analyse the chair within organizational boundaries to show that it exhibits traces of the organizational level at which it is found. This is made possible by aesthetic knowledge and not by the ontology of the chair. Hence, although it is possible to sit on any chair whatever in an organization, its shape, colour and smell indicate which level of the organizational hierarchy its incumbent occupies. Our sensory faculties tell us that we are in the managing director's office, or in the administrative offices, or in the reception rooms, or in the cafeteria. Although it may be the case that in organizations managers sit on plain chairs while the president sits on a heavily upholstered easy chair, this should not be taken to be an organizational principle valid for all organizations. One cannot formulate general rules to be applied indiscriminately. In other words, just because we note the presence in a room of an ordinary office chair we cannot deduce that we are not in the president's office but in his secretary's. We can only do so when we have observed the chair more closely in its being-in-use in the organization, although the organizational artefact has, of course, already provided us with some clues.

Imagine that you are visiting a medium-sized organization for the purpose of research. This is the first time that you have entered the organization's premises and you note that the switchboard operator is seated on a particularly elegant chair, one that you have already seen in a specialist furniture shop. You know that it is a particularly expensive item and that it is the work of an extremely well-known firm of designers. You cannot look at it more closely because you have been ushered into the secretary's office, where all of those present are seated on comfortable leather armchairs. Here, however, you do not have time to test the softness of these chairs before you are told that the managing director is ready to see you. As you walk along the corridor, you glance briefly into the offices occupied by some of the managers: all of them contain folding wooden chairs, like those usually found in the garden or at the tables of a terrace-bar, with metal splats and stiles, all of them old and rather dilapidated. The person accompanying you is a guard who occasionally doubles as a porter. He does not have an office of his own, but sits at a low table with a few papers, a telephone and a settee, in the corridor leading to the managers' offices. You enter the managing director's office. He gets up from his folding wooden chair, takes one of the three stacked in a corner, opens it and invites you to sit down. As you do so, the seat creaks. Perhaps, if for a moment you abandon your intellectual and rational knowledge of the ontology of the chair, you ask yourself: 'What sort of organization have I ended up in?' Your question is based on the assumption that the chair is a metaphor for organizational level, so that the more expensive chair made of finer materials corresponds to a managerial organizational level, whereas a plainer, more austere one corresponds to a more routine and hierarchically lower organizational level. Now it is true that the organization that I have described does not exist; but the fact that we find it implausible shows immediately that the organizational chair, in terms of its shape and quality, can be credibly associated with the power, prestige and hierarchical position of the organizational level at which it is used. What conclusions can we draw, therefore?

1 The chair is an organizational artefact whose shape and quality denote hierarchically ordered organizational levels.
2 This hierarchy concerns offices and not the people who work in them.
3 As far as the ontology of the chair is concerned, the hierarchy of organizational levels is a nonsense extraneous to the chair's explanatory capacity.

The organizational artefact that, if flaunted, may provoke criticism and invoke sanctions

This is the eighth component of the riddle and it highlights the ethos of the organizational artefact – that is, the set of ethical values embraced by the organization and with which the chair must also comply. The chair meets this criterion as well, and first of all, as a metaphor for the hierarchy of organizational levels, because it symbolizes an organizational source of power and prestige.

If power, prestige and hierarchy are features of an organization and not of individuals, the chair *qua* organizational artefact embodies them in its aesthetic and manifests them by means of this aesthetic. As long as the chair does not constitute an organizational niche in which it lives on rent rather than producing, its visibility provokes neither criticisms nor sanctions. The ethical codes of organizations, like those of professional and occupational communities, set limits on the chair's self-display. These limits are determined by the processes of organizational negotiation that concern, as we have seen, the shape and workmanship of the chair, not its essence as an artefact on which one sits. The aesthetic of the chair, in fact, does not constitute its visibility.

The point, therefore, is that when the visibility of prestige and power becomes their ostentatious display, this shift does not always come about in the absence of criticism, complaint or derision. Some of these constraints are applied to the search for personal power that exploits the opportunities offered by the formal organization, and they express criticisms and sanctions which derive from organizational and professional codes of ethics. These are the criticisms that, when applied to a particular person, describe him or her roughly as follows: 'There goes someone who's after the boss's chair.' This is an expression which not only criticizes the organizational action of the person concerned, but also sanctions such action by attaching a derogatory label to it. The organizational artefact of the chair is part of the saying and it is well defined in aesthetic terms. This is not any chair, but the chair that denotes a high position in the organizational hierarchy. Thus, although searching for a chair for oneself in an organization is judged positively, setting out to acquire the boss's chair is condemned, thereby indicating a dimension of the organization's ethos: if the chair is flaunted rather than straightforwardly occupied – if the chair is used for self-advertisement rather than for participation in the organization's activities – then this behaviour is stigmatized as an abuse of what the chair can and does contribute to the organization. The ethos of the organizational artefact therefore highlights the following:

1   By means of a chair, individuals can acquire positions of power which they relinquish only reluctantly, given that they are occupying the chair for personal rather than organizational ends. The flaunted chair is enslaved by the persons that occupy it, rather than being itself what people serve.
2   Ostentation of the chair, and the criticism that this provokes on account of the ethos of that particular organizational artefact, translates the chair from a metaphor for positions and organizational levels into a metaphor for the entire organization. In other words, the chair is an artefact able to symbolize the organization as a whole. In fact, the ethos of this artefact sanctions those individuals who seek to use the organization to achieve power, and wish to flaunt this power rather than place themselves in the service of the organization.

The 'banal' features that dispel remaining doubts as to the identity of the organizational artefact

These are the last two clues to the riddle. They enable the organizational artefact to be identified unequivocally. At the same time they refer to features usually considered too trivial to include among those that typify the artefact. Yet the answers to these two final clues have usually cut short the argument between myself and the students about whether power, culture or expertise might equally be solutions to the riddle. The value of these two criteria, in fact, is precisely that they assign to this apparently 'banal' or 'unimportant' artefact the decisive position that it actually occupies in the knowledge-gathering process.

The first clue states that if the organizational artefact slips or shifts, its occupant may tumble to the floor and provoke derision. The extraordinary fact is that on these occasions laughter may overcome cultural and linguistic barriers. If a person who falls to the floor because his or her chair has moved, or because a joke has been played on him or her, or because s/he has been clumsy, the outburst of laughter provoked by the incident does not seem to be culturally mediated. It is as if this particular being-in-use of the chair itself constructs the hilarity.

The second feature is that the chair homogenizes positions downwards, in the sense that people become physically shorter when they sit down. In this case, a chair is purely and simply an organizational artefact on which one sits. One notes, therefore, that this apparently 'banal' characteristic is the one that highlights the ontological properties of the chair.

From this derives a general point concerning knowledge of organizational artefacts: they are not easily confusable. They are not confusable pragmatically because a chair is not an artefact identical, equivalent or similar to the artefact, for example, of organizational power or domination. A chair is a chair, so that if someone removes it when we are about to sit down, everyone laughs. Likewise, it homogenizes us all downwards. And yet pragmatic and intimate knowledge of this organizational artefact does not afford certainties, but instead paradoxes and ambiguities which – as we have already seen and shall again see in the next section – stem above all from the rational definitions of the organizational artefact based on its ontological properties.

Organizational aesthetics and symbolizing processes

This section brings the first chapter to a close. In it I shall discuss the construction and reconstruction of the daily life of an organization through processes of both aesthetic understanding and symbolic construction. I shall do so by examining some of the organizational artefacts described.

One of the artefacts examined at length in this chapter has been the didactic organizational artefact based on the riddle. If considered in the abstract, the university organization in which the episode occurred was always the same. But if observed in the practice of organizational action, the routine didactic organization, at the beginning of the two-hour lecture, was first changed and redefined as ephemeral didactic organization by means of the riddle, and then restored to its original form as the lesson drew to a close. If we draw on pragmatic rather than hypothetical–abstract knowledge of organization, therefore, we note that during the two hours of the lecture the organization was repeatedly translated into some other organization by means of ongoing processes of construction and destruction, of deconstruction and reconstruction, of creation and memory.

However, on the basis of epistemological options very different from the one that underlies the argument of this chapter, there is nothing to prevent the riddle from being viewed solely as an ingenious *ad hoc* device to give some 'zip' to the lecture. After all, those attending it always remained the same, and so, too, did the organizational space, the hours and the institutional norms. These are dimensions that, if observed from a certain distance and from a long-term temporal perspective, are altered little by the *ad hoc* didactic device. The same applies to power relations in that organization. On close inspection, in fact, the power of the lecturer remained invariably the pivot of organizational action, and, paradoxically, the more the students became the protagonists of construction of the artefact of the riddle-based lecture, the more this became evident. One may argue likewise concerning the organizational ethos. Not only did the new didactic organization conserve the previous ethos centred on the importance of university learning, but in its own way it also celebrated it.

However, one cannot fail to observe that something changed in the organization of those two hours of the university lecture, and that it changed because of aesthetics. This is true of both the epistemological options mentioned. But whereas one of them emphasizes the value of organizational knowledge for the subjects operating in that context, and for those who set about studying it as researchers, the other prefers to view it as a sort of didactic sham. The latter option denies the evidence, however, and in doing so sets a precise limit on the domain in which organizational theories have legitimate value.

In fact, even if one views organizational aesthetics merely as a device used to facilitate the students' learning, it was not merely window-dressing. It wrought changes in the activities of the students by redefining the task to be performed so that the organization of the riddle-based lesson could proceed and be successful. It gave rise to secondary formalized structurings where the students formed groups, separated or displayed their individuality; in other words, it gave rise to specific organizational sub-levels. It altered the dependence relation between students and the already-defined organization and assigned the former the role of participative managers in the new organization. It modified the spatial and temporal dimensions of the two-hour lecture, increasing opportunities for movement within the organizational space and enabling the actors to structure the temporal cadences of their organization interaction. These and other changes were not embellishments intended to add style and beauty to the organization as it appeared at the beginning of the lecture. Modest and insignificant though these changes may have been, they concerned organizing; they did not merely decorate the already-organized.

The first and most important conclusion of this chapter is therefore that aesthetics in organizational life are a driving force of organizing, not a *maquillage* of the organization. Organizational aesthetics drive organizational actors on opposing sides, as we saw with regard to the enthusiastic, uncertain or hostile reactions of the students. Aesthetics induce subjects to imagine themselves as living in the organization before it has been brought into being. In fact, the riddle-based lecture was foreseen as interesting by some students and as a waste of time by others. All this came about in their imaginations. It was an experience imagined prior to the experience constructed and reconstructed in the course of the riddle-based lesson. The experience that subjects acquire from their sensory faculties and from their socially constructed aesthetic judgements is a *conditio sine qua non* of organizational life.

The second conclusion concerns the fact that whatever information organizational aesthetics yield for subjects, they do so by means of continuous processes of symbolic construction, deconstruction and reconstruction. An example is provided by the translation of the organizational meanings of activities, time and space as evidenced by the ephemeral artefact of the riddle-based lecture. As I have emphasized on several occasions in the course of this chapter, the meaning attached to the riddle differed from one subject to another, just as it acquired different nuances according to the organizational actions performed. Put otherwise, without a symbolization process which gives meanings and values to the organization, the organization as translated in the course of the riddle-based lecture, both while the riddle was being solved and while the initial organization was being restored, would not have been either collectively constructed or collectively deconstructed. Indeed, the symbolization process is an activity which constantly engages the collectives that beget organizations – as we saw regarding the money prize to be awarded to the individual or group guessing the answer to the riddle. Nobody solved the riddle, and the heap of coins lost its symbolic value as a prize but retained its value as an organizational asset. However much the money's loss of symbolic meaning *qua* prize may have been an effect foreseen by the subjects of organizational action, it required the organization that possessed the money to deconstruct and reconstruct its symbolism before it could be put to use.

Symbolization processes also create organizational memories. The riddle-based lecture was an ephemeral organizational artefact of limited duration. But the subjects who took part in the construction of that didactic organization may then have translated it into a much more enduring artefact on the basis of their remembered aesthetic experience of it: it was beautiful, it was ugly, it was a waste of time. Today, therefore, it is an aesthetic experience subject to constant reconstruction according to the occasion, and according to the will and above all the pleasure of the subjects concerned when they recall the episode; and likewise if it becomes part of the organizational stories that characterize that university faculty. In each case, the organizational memory focuses less on the details of the organization activated by the riddle than on its symbolism for the subjects actually involved in solving it, and for those who have subsequently heard it talked about.

One also observes this phenomenon in organizational documents, specifically in those that concern an explicit aesthetic endeavour to transmit an organization's culture. I refer to iconography, sculpture and architecture; in short, to the visual culture of a particular organization. The organizational documents produced with regard to visual cultures exhibit the relations between subjects and artefacts that the organization finds of especial importance. Visual documentation depicts persons and things placed in relations which are sometimes only outlined, which sometimes are purely random, but which on other occasions are intentional and even ostentatiously paraded; ostentation which the aesthetics of visual cultures emphasize to counter the disappearance and oblivion of the organization.

The portrait is a visual document of undoubted importance in identifying which relations between people and objects are deemed important by organizational memory. Whether it is a painting, a photograph or a film clip depicting a single individual or a group, the more a portrait is official, the more it gives prominence to the organization's predominant values, to the activities that it most celebrates, to its heroes, to the personages that it turns into lay or religious cult figures. The portrait does this on the basis of the relation between the symbology of the person depicted and the objects surrounding him or her in the picture. In some portraits one of these artefacts is a chair which, when foregrounded in the iconographic composition, meaningfully encapsulates the organization's symbology. The aesthetics of the chair enable the viewer of the portrait to grasp the overtly displayed values of power, ability and wealth, and the introspective ones of simplicity, modesty and intimacy.

Consider the portrait of Federico, Duke of Montefeltro, which hangs in the Palazzo Ducale in Urbino, Italy. Between 1476 and 1477, Federico commissioned from the Spanish painter Pedro Berruguete an official portrait that would also celebrate his military prowess. The duke is therefore painted wearing armour. Thus accoutred, and presumably greatly weighed down, he sits reading a book; an act supposed to symbolize the value that Federico set on the humanistic qualities. This value is also celebrated in the portrait of the Madonna attributed to Raphael frescoed on one of the walls of his home, again in Urbino. The Madonna sits on a chair of dark wood, with the child Jesus in her arms while she reads a book. The chair is beautiful in its simplicity and fits well with the overall composition of the picture, just as Federico's richly decorated chair is an integral part of Berruguete's portrait of him.

But it is not always the case that such pronounced emphasis is given to the chair as artefact. Indeed, sometimes it is kept out of the visual field altogether and is not included in the iconographic representation. There are paintings, photographs, postcards, frescoes and films that document this absence. To remain in the sphere of official portraiture and the display of military prowess, I cite the photograph of the samurai warrior taken by the Japanese photographer Hikoma Ueno in 1865 (Colombo et al., 1979: 30), which portrays the samurai bearing his weapons and seated on what is probably a cushion. But this seat does not explicitly belong to the iconographic representation of military gifts, of power, of wealth or of reputation. Nor do other chairs.

What do we deduce from this? That visual cultures illustrate not only that chairs have different values in different societies and organizations, but also that in some civilizations, societies and organizations this artefact is an element which serves to identify individuals, so that the persons-with-chairs in these organizations and societies are distinguished sharply from persons-without-chairs. For that matter, how many chairs appear in even the most recent films set in Japanese private homes? Take erotic iconography (Kronhausen and Kronhausen, 1968–70), for example. One notes that in European images the chair is an integral part of the rooms depicted, almost as if it were included as an actor in the eroticism of the iconography. But this is not so in Japanese images, where chairs are rarely depicted except for purely decorative purposes.

It should be pointed out that these features do not depend on a general difference between Europe and Japan or between West and East. Nor does the decision to insert and emphasize the non-human element constituted by the chair in the image, or the decision to exclude it, derive from the aesthetics of visual cultures in Europe or Japan. Confirmation of this point is provided by another Japanese photographic work. In this case, the iconography emphasizes the chair precisely as an artefact-in-use in an organization. In the 1970s Ikko Narahara, a Japanese photographer, took a series of photographs of Buddhist monks belonging to a Zen sect founded in twelfth-century Japan. These celebrated photographs were taken in the Sojiji temple of Tsurumi (Colombo et al., 1979: 118–19). In one of them the monks are shown as they meditate seated with their legs folded around a small cushion, thus making what they are sitting on invisible and only presumptive. Here and there, however, cushions can be seen because no one is seated on them. Indeed, to one side of the temple there is a whole row of unoccupied cushions. The photograph thus seems to be emphasizing not only the relation of this non-human element with the Zen monks in their organization, but also that the seats are there to symbolize the places that belong to other worshippers, or that they have been set aside for those who wish to take part in this activity of the organization. The photograph is ambiguous: it does not reveal whether those seats are individual or whether they belong to everybody. Nevertheless, as far as my discussion of the organizational artefact is concerned, those small round cushions are seats-in-use in that organization.

Visual cultures therefore reconstruct the connection between the person and non-human objects in organizational life in terms of aesthetic knowledge. They do so by highlighting the symbology relative to the features deemed distinctive of that connection, and by documenting the being-in-use of the artefacts regarded as symbolically important in an organization – those, that is, that assign a specific configuration to the organizational actor. Take, for example, the filmography relative to the conquest of the American West: saloons with chairs around the tables, sheriff's offices with a chair behind the desk, the sheriff seated outside his office with a gun in his arms, cowboys seated on their horse-saddles, and, on Sundays and during funerals, on the pews in the church. The Native Americans, by contrast, are represented as belonging to 'chair-less' societies and organizations: they sit on the ground for their meetings, and they ride bareback. Their teepees, even those of the chiefs, are devoid of chairs. If particular value is given to the 'banal' artefact of the chair in the analysis of organizations and societies, by an irony of fate we may see a general distinction drawn between organizational actors constructed and identified as 'persons-with-chairs' and those others who are defined as 'persons-without-chairs'. Besides this somewhat provocative conclusion, there is another one, more modest and covert, which concerns the fact that aesthetic understanding of organizational life construes the organizational actor in terms of the connection between people and non-human elements. It is this relationship, so specific and different from case to case, that the aesthetic knowledge of organizations brings so emphatically to the fore, and in so doing draws on the knowledge-gathering faculties of the human senses.

In this regard, I stress that the sensory faculties referred to by the aesthetic approach to organizations are not so much the faculties innate to human perception as the educated and sophisticated ones developed by processes of social and collective construction. This is principally because aesthetic judgements have their own history; they are fashioned by complex social negotiations and they are much less immediate than is commonly believed. But it is also due to the fact that the social construction of the aesthetics that underpin this approach to the study of organizations is, as we shall see from Chapter 2 onwards, a complex, ramified and haphazard phenomenon. In other words, the qualification 'aesthetic' to this approach requires further elucidation, given that the definitions of aesthetics are many and often conflicting. Before moving on to the next chapter, however, I wish once again to stress the unreliability of intellectual and rational knowledge of organizations, and I do so by making a final remark concerning the fact that ontology does not suffice to gain thorough knowledge of organizations.

What the aesthetic approach seeks to show is that the ontological features of an organization yield knowledge about it that is neither accurate nor exact. Consider chairs again. Chairs are not artefacts on which it is possible for everyone to sit, in all civilizations, in all epochs. In other words, the ontology of the artefact is not self-evident. Not only is a chair not always a chair, because we can place the most diverse of objects on it, or use it as a step-ladder or a faldstool, as we have seen in this chapter, but a chair is not universally and invariably interpreted, understood and used as an artefact on which to sit. In India, for example, the chair is not principally viewed in these terms. On the contrary, it is primarily a 'support base' and only occasionally 'an artefact on which to sit'. Consequently, when travelling by train in India one meets numerous passengers who prefer to squat on their heels rather than use the seats in the compartments. Or at Indian cinemas, one finds that after the audience has sedately watched the film from their wooden seats, during the interval they relax by leaving their seats and squatting in the aisles. This is not an observation of minor importance, for it shows that a considerable number of people in the world do not conceive a chair as a seat merely because it has been defined as such by rational knowledge. These people are aware of the ontology of the chair as an artefact on which to sit, but they prefer to ignore this intellectual datum and they refuse to comply with this rational prescript.

After the foregoing discussion, which has raised serious doubts as to whether knowledge of the ontological properties of organizational artefacts, and therefore also of organizations, is *the* higher form of knowledge about them, we may now move to the definition of aesthetics and its categories, beginning with the methodological questions raised by the aesthetic approach as regards organization theory.

incomplete

2 Aesthetic Knowledge of Organizational Action

In Chapter 1, I discussed the pervasiveness of organizational aesthetics and the way in which subjects make constant recourse to the aesthetic knowledge of organization. Although my intention was to emphasize the importance of the aesthetic faculties of organizational actors, this did not rule out discussion of the ontological and ethical features of organizational life. Indeed, on several occasions, the *ethos*, *logos* and aesthetics of organizational life were examined in terms of their interweavings, diversities and paradoxes as they shape organizational knowledge. Nothing emerged from the analysis to suggest that aesthetics as a form of organizational knowledge should be ignored, even less abandoned. On the contrary, it became plain from examination of the relations among ontological, ethical and aesthetic characteristics that the latter are an important 'engine' of organizational life.

In this chapter I shall consider the theoretical and methodological implications of the study of organizational aesthetics. Much has already been said or implied on these matters in the course of the first chapter. In organizations, subjects either attribute an aesthetic connotation to an organizational event or phenomenon, or they disclaim it. When individuals interpret organizational life, they employ their perceptive faculties and aesthetic sensibilities to decide whether it is ugly, grotesque or repressive, or whether it is pleasant, attractive or beautiful. They thus express an aesthetic judgement which some members of the organization accept, others reject, others dispute, and yet others counter with their own opinions. This was noted in the first chapter when I examined the conflicts and negotiations that underlie the definition, redefinition, affirmation, diffusion and even repression of organizational aesthetics: intentional behaviour, meaningful action, a complex pattern of organizational interaction.

Meaningful social action is therefore a fundamental concept for the aesthetic interpretation of organizations. It is for these reasons that I return to the first great methodological debate on cultural sciences, the so-called *Methodenstreit* of the beginning of this century, and to Max Weber, whose methodological and theoretical ideas also concerned the artistic and emotional empathic analysis of intentional action. This latter theme, in fact, is the link that ties the aesthetic study of organizations to the questions of method treated in Weberian sociology. Part of the 'basis for certainty in understanding' social action, Weber writes (1922; Eng. trans. 1978: 5), 'can be of an empathic or artistically appreciative quality'. Now, as I shall seek to show in this chapter, the methodological issue of empathy is one of the theoretical foundations of modern aesthetics and constitutes a major contribution by aesthetics to the autonomy of the social sciences from the natural sciences. I shall also illustrate the importance of the methodological question of empathy for the aesthetic understanding of organizational life.

Choosing between paradigms and aesthetic considerations

To return to Weber, I hasten to point out that he certainly preferred the intellectual, rational and causal analysis of meaningful action to its empathic understanding. He always gave secondary importance to the empathic understanding achieved by imagining oneself in the place of a person whose purposes, motives and meanings one wishes to explain. His principal aim was to provide a causal explanation of intentional action in order to formulate causal models and verify them. Inquiry into meaningful action, therefore, was not for him a question of imagining and understanding moods and the emotional context in which such action unfolds, however important they might be. Instead, reasons, meanings and emotions were to be imputed to social action within a theoretical framework used to predict courses of action and to compare them with the actual behaviour of social actors.

One can discern an aesthetic influence on Weber's theoretical and methodological choice in favour of causally based, rather than empathic or artistic, intellectual understanding. To be sure, this was a choice also determined by the need to combat the psychologistic vitalism that circulated in various disciplinary areas of European culture at the beginning of this century. But aesthetic considerations can be seen in the close connection established by Weber between the individual and the moment when s/he is 'objectified' in a social fact by his/her action. And they are also apparent in the *pathos* that Weber imputed to objectivity and to fecund operativeness, without thereby reducing the weight of subjectivity, or of individual responsibility, or of ethics. The individual is anchored in action which produces ascertainable effects. It is this '*pathos* of objectivization' (Bodei, 1997: 52–3) that gives sense to a reality in itself bereft of sense and which displays the aesthetics of Weber's paradigmatic choice.

I believe that his preference stemmed from aesthetic considerations in the sense given to the expression by Thomas Kuhn (1962: 152–8) when discussing why a scientist may prefer one paradigm to another, or abandon an old paradigm for a new one. There is no doubt that the capacity of a scientific approach to solve problems is a crucial factor in its selection, especially in paradigmatic conflicts among scientists like Copernicus, Galileo or Einstein. And thus it was for Weber in his endeavour to establish whether forecasts based on causal explanatory models correspond to the real actions of social actors. But, Kuhn writes, to see

the reason for the importance of these more subjective and aesthetic considerations, remember what a paradigm debate is about. When a new candidate for paradigm is first proposed, it has seldom solved more than a few of the problems that confront it, and most of those solutions are still far from perfect. (1962: 155)

'Fortunately', Kuhn observes, there are also aesthetic considerations to be made on such matters, those that appeal to the sensibility of the scholar and attract him/her by virtue of their aesthetics.

These are the arguments, rarely made entirely explicit, that appeal to the individual's sense of the appropriate or the aesthetic – the new theory is said to be 'neater', 'more suitable', or 'simpler' than the old. (1962: 154)

Aesthetic considerations can sometimes be of decisive importance. This is not to argue, Kuhn points out, that the decisiveness of some form of mystic aesthetic permits one paradigm to triumph over its rivals. Yet the fact remains that Einstein's theory is still able to attract scientists by virtue of its elegance, and that although aesthetic considerations 'often attract only a few scientists to a new theory, it is upon those few that its ultimate triumph may depend. If they had not quickly taken it up for highly individual reasons' (1962: 155), the new theory that proposes itself as a candidate for a paradigm might not have received the elaborations necessary for it to win endorsement and legitimation from the scientific community as a whole. On this matter, Michael Polanyi observes that the sense of intellectual beauty functions in the scientific community as a criterion with which to distinguish between facts that are demonstrable in science, and are of scientific interest, and those facts which instead are not:

Only a tiny fraction of all knowable facts are of interest to scientists, and scientific passion serves also as a guide in assessment of what is of higher and what is of lesser interest; what is great in science, and what relatively slight. I want to show that this appreciation depends ultimately on a sense of intellectual beauty; that it is an emotional response which can never be dispassionately defined, any more than we can dispassionately define the beauty of a work of art or the excellence of a noble action. (1962: 135)

Also founded on aesthetic considerations is the epistemological option that gives priority to aesthetic understanding and awareness of the 'sensible' in organizations. The *pathos* of objectivization should be contrasted with the '*pathos* of the sensible'. Preferred to causal understanding – no matter how aesthetically attractive it may be – is empathic or artistic understanding, with its distinctive features of playfulness and mystery. The choice is determined by the fact that it is the knowledge of the 'sensible' in the study of intentional action that most sharply distinguishes the social sciences from the natural sciences and their methods of inquiry and explanation. For Weber, too, however, lived experience and empathic understanding highlighted this distinction.

This choice, which has its aesthetic roots in the *pathos* of the sensible, should therefore be examined in the context of a methodological dispute that has traversed the social sciences ever since they first split away from the natural sciences. One current aspect of this methodological dispute is the divide that separates those social scientists who seek to interpret and understand intentional action from those who instead prefer heuristic strategies based on explanation, evolutionary theory and the insights of the biological sciences. The cleavage between the two approaches to social action is profound, and as far as the aesthetic perspective adopted in this book is concerned, it is ineradicable. I shall illustrate it further by returning to an aesthetic sentiment mentioned on several occasions in Chapter 1. I refer to pleasure.

Jean-Pierre Changeux has written (1994: 43–6) that, without indulging in over-imaginative speculation, it now seems legitimate to formulate a hypothesis on aesthetic pleasure that can halt the progressive 'decerebralization' (Changeux, 1994: 16) of the social sciences. Wired into the brain, in fact, are three different evolutions: that of the species, that of persons, and that of cultures. Unless the action of these evolutions is taken into account, the contemplation of a work of art cannot be intellectually grasped, and even less can its creation be understood. The decerebralization of the human sciences implies that investigation of the brain has no relevance to history, language and thought, which are viewed as processes entirely independent of such investigation. But pleasure, Changeux contends, should indeed be studied in terms of its relation with the brain, because the hypothesis that pleasure activates sets of neurons, and that it does so in a coordinated manner, seems plausible. Studies of the brain indicate, in fact, that it is the coordinated mobilization of neurons located at different organizational levels of the brain (that is, which link the forebrain to the limbic system) which generates aesthetic pleasure.

Although certainly of great interest, this sort of analysis involves an epistemological option and a set of assumptions on aesthetics which are greatly at variance with those considered in this book. Nevertheless, it does show how deeply philosophical aesthetics and theories of art are imbued with the evolutionary paradigm and the naturalization of intentional action that springs from it.

By contrast, the understanding of aesthetics in social action is not grounded in the belief that it is possible to account for aesthetic pleasure by locating it in a particular interweaving of the brain's organizational levels. Once we have stated – and we are still not certain on the matter – that aesthetic pleasure is the result of neuronal activity between the frontal lobe of the brain and the limbic system, have we really understood how or why the riddle described in Chapter 1 aroused pleasure in my students? In what way does this 'cerebralization' of pleasure explain the decision of the students to play an active role in constructing a different organizational form for the lesson on the organizational artefact? The two sets of notions and arguments are very distinct.

And yet the evolutionary and biological account of pleasure does raise an important point, although it is one very different from Changeux's arguments because it does not provide an explanation but prompts rational and aesthetic considerations. If the frontal cortex is damaged or malformed, dramatic consequences may ensue, and not only because the person concerned is unable to feel pleasure. The idea of such damage arouses sentiments of an aesthetic nature because we feel a shocked compassion for the victim and we sense the tragedy in his or her life. Consequently, the gulf between the two ways of defining the intentional action problem is unbridgeable. In the case of aesthetic pleasure, both the interpretative and the biological–evolutionary paradigms construct their subjects of study, but they do not furnish juxtaposable hypotheses. They do not complete each other, so that even when they are considered jointly, they indicate completely different manners of acquiring knowledge about meaningful action.

This is a theoretical and methodological dispute which, according to Luca Ricolfi (1997: 38–9), can be expressed in terms of the two founding myths of social research: that of adequacy and that of objectivity. These two myths express the social sciences' hard-won independence from the natural sciences, but they also replicate the controversy that has surrounded the social and collective construction of the various and conflicting identities of the social sciences. Weber's ideas have contributed to both myths, because they concern as much the quantitative and structural-comparative analysis of intentional action as its qualitative analysis (Schwartz and Jacobs, 1979: 17).

In this dispute the proponents of the independence of the social sciences from the methods of the natural sciences argue that account should be taken of the complexity of social phenomena, that the points of view of social actors should be respected, and that the non-arbitrariness of scholarly interpretations should be guaranteed. These scholars have preferred, that is, to make a clean break with the natural sciences, assigning primacy to the 'social' specificity of their fields of inquiry and to their criteria of validity. Understanding, hermeneutics and the supremacy of the subject of study have thus been set against the explanation, positivism and the primacy of method advocated by those admirers of the hard sciences who fashioned the myth of objectivity. This controversy, Ricolfi observes (1997: 38), has been dismissed by some methodologists as misleading and indeed artificial. Yet, however indefensible it may be on logical grounds, it takes account of styles of research and analysis now deeply rooted in the scientific community as alternative forms of knowledge, as I shall illustrate in my discussion of aesthetics and the understanding of organizational action in this chapter.

The *pathos* of the 'sensible' and intentional action

In the course of Chapter 1 I repeatedly employed the tools of empathic and artistic understanding of intentional action. That is to say, comprehension of meaningful social interaction in organizations was yielded largely, but not always, by:

(a)   intuition, imagination and analogy;
(b)   imagining oneself acting as if occupying someone else's place, or adding one's own presence, again by means of the imagination, to those of other participants in organizational life;
(c)   doing all this in order to grasp the aesthetic aspects of organizational action.

This knowledge-gathering process lacks the *pathos* of objectification mentioned above with reference to Weber. This is not because intuiting, imagining, drawing analogies or placing oneself in someone else's shoes is alien to the experience of organizational actors. Nor does it imply that aesthetics is unable to anchor the individual in action, or to emphasize the moment at which subjectivity is objectified in some organizational entity, activity or performance. In other words, the *pathos* of objectification is not lacking because aesthetics are unable to produce ascertainable effects or social facts. It is lacking because causality is not the criterion used to explain meaningful organizational action – not even in Weber's subtle, complex and elaborate terms.

Organizational aesthetics refer to intentional action, in the sense that they consist of what social actors make happen or, conversely, prevent from happening, or even allow not to happen. Davide Sparti (1992: 24–5) provides a cogent example of the fact that actions, in general, do not consist of what happens to social actors. He points out that each of us at this precise moment is travelling eastwards at around 1200 kilometres per hour. But can this circumstance whereby each of us is being moved by the rotation of the earth be described as our action? It is certainly something that we do; indeed, it is something that we are doing now. However, this action lacks a fundamental requisite, namely that of being 'intentional'. And because it is not intentional, it cannot be considered an action, for there is no category of generic action which enables us to distinguish between intentional and unintentional action (Wright, 1980). Moreover, we may add, this action also lacks the fundamental aesthetic requisite of being knowable through the perceptive and sensory faculties. However, the scientific datum that we are travelling eastwards so rapidly and incessantly may inspire an aesthetic judgement on this particular idea of being-in-action. That is, we may find ourselves fascinated by the idea itself of moving at such speed without sensing it, and judge it fantastic, grandiose or beautiful. This is an intriguing paradox of aesthetic knowledge, because it focuses on the importance of imagining an action compared with directly experiencing it, as noted in Chapter 1 during discussion of imaginative participant observation. This chapter focuses on an aspect of even greater importance: the relationships between the intention of the action and aesthetics, and the ways in which we are able adequately to grasp and illustrate the intentionality distinctive of the social behaviour of organizational actors when we adopt an aesthetic approach.

The basic assumptions shared by empathic and rational understanding

Weber's methodological and theoretical notes contain a number of basic assumptions which are shared by interpretations that employ the criterion of causality and by those founded on the reliving of the experience of intentional action. The first of these assumptions is that knowledge about the intentional action of social actors lacks objective truth. However much one may insist on causal and rational explanation in one's study method, for Weber this explanation is not based on 'belief in the actual predominance of rational elements in human life' (1922; Eng. trans. 1978: 2). Indeed, nowhere does Weber assert that rational considerations determine intentional behaviour. On the contrary, he stresses the danger of generalizing rationalist interpretations of social action. Although people's actions may be rationally motivated, they may equally be based on irrationality, myths, aesthetics, affectivity, or even tradition. There thus arises that plurality of different motives from which the scholar is not always able to select the one that actually triggers certain actions. And for this reason it is not possible to gain objectively valid and correct knowledge about meaningful action:

> Every interpretation attempts to attain clarity and certainty, but no matter how clear an interpretation as such appears to be from the point of view of meaning, it cannot on this account claim to be the causally valid interpretation. On this level it must remain only a peculiarly plausible hypothesis. (Weber, 1922; Eng. trans. 1978: 9)

Causality does not entail truth, therefore; it instead depends on the meaning of human action. This is the meaning intentioned by the actor, whether as regards a certain event or as regards an intellectual construct. But it is meaning that does not comprise metaphysically established truth or objective correctness. It is the meaning that the scholar is able to grasp by taking account both of the subjectivity of the persons who construct it and of the connotations added to it by the attitudes of others. The motives of which individuals are aware, and which they adduce as responsible for their intentional action, often conceal the various motivations and repressions that are the real driving force of their action. Even the sincerest testimonies are consequently of only relative value in causal explanation. Moreover, people's actions are often driven by conflicting impulses, and the relative influence of the various meaning referents involved can only be approximately established when interpreting the causes of action. Furthermore, actions which may strike the scholar as equivalent may be induced by sense connections that are very different for the subjects concerned.

All this demonstrates the complex nature of understanding and interpreting. There is a broad spectrum of intended meanings – ranging from rational calculation to emotional, aesthetic and affective states – to be grasped. Hence Weber does not believe that the 'rational understanding of motivation' is the only form of knowledge able to interpret the intended meaning complexes of social action. Although he may prefer such knowledge, he emphasizes that there are two ways in which meaningful action can be studied:

> All interpretation of meaning, like all scientific observations, strives for clarity and verifiable accuracy of insight and comprehension (*Evidenz*). The basis for certainty in understanding can be either rational, which can be further subdivided into logical and mathematical, or it can be of an emotionally empathic or artistically appreciative quality. Action is rationally evident chiefly when we attain a completely clear intellectual grasp of the action-elements in their intended context of meaning. Empathic or appreciative accuracy is attained when, through sympathetic participation, we can adequately grasp the emotional context in which the action took place. (1922; Eng. trans. 1978: 5)

There is therefore a distinct interweaving between intellectual and empathic understanding, an interweaving which is not solely determined by the complex and opaque nature of the subject of inquiry but also arises from the following methodological assumptions:

1 Both forms of knowledge furnish the bases for interpretative certainty.
2 Neither of them claims scientificity, objectivity, exactness, correctness, validity, or truth.
3 In order to understand meaningful action, one must identify its intentional orientation (Weber, 1922; Eng. trans. 1978: 7, 24–6). Of the four ways in which social action can be oriented – 'instrumentally rational', 'value-rational', 'affectual' and 'traditional' – only the first is strictly rational. In the case of value-oriented social action, in fact, the determining factor is 'a conscious belief in the value for its own sake of some ethical, aesthetic, religious or other form of behavior, independently of its prospects of success'. Examples are 'the pursuit of beauty', 'honor', 'personal loyalty', sense of duty, pity or 'some cause'. Value-orientation may stand in various relations with instrumentally rational action. Very seldom, in fact, is social action exclusively oriented in one way or another. Nor are these the only possible types of orientation. From the point of view of end-directed rationality, 'however, value-rationality is always irrational', and *a fortiori* when the value to which action is oriented is posited as absolute. The 'affectual' type of social action is 'especially emotional' and determined 'by the actor's specific affects and feeling states'. Strictly affective behaviour only just falls within the definition of meaningful action, because, according to Weber, it is more a reaction to stimuli than an action engendered by motives of various kinds. The same applies to the 'ingrained habituation' that determines the 'traditional' orientation of social action. Of course, when Weber speaks of aesthetics as determining the orientation of social action, or of affective states, he does so in order to identify a causal explanation of

action. However, writes Alessandro Cavalli (1969: 72–5), here emerges the dualism of Weber's methodology and the ambiguity that it engenders. In the case of value-rationality, in fact, understanding is a-causal because it involves the adjustment of meaning to the value and not the causal adjustment of means to ends. This dualism in rationality – causal and a-causal – is flanked by a dualism between the ethics of responsibility and the ethics of intention. The former characterizes the rational action that takes account of its possible consequences. The latter induces the actor to intend his/her action as manifesting adherence to certain values, rather than view it as a means to an end. Moreover, contrary to Weber's preference for rational explanation, one may legitimately argue that both value-oriented and affect-oriented action significantly involve empathic understanding. And this is true of 'traditional' and 'instrumentally rational' action as well. There is nothing that prohibits self-identification with an acquired habit of others or with their purposive use of expectations to achieve rationally established goals. These are not experiences alien to social actors and which cannot be relived in order to be understood.

4 Neither form of knowledge enables formulation of conceptual schemes universally accepted by the scientific community. In both cases, the underlying assumption is that scholarly interpretations are ineluctably subjective. Scientists are just as much human beings as the subjects whose actions they strive to understand. It is interpretation, or, in other words, the production of meanings and the use of symbolic and abstract representations, that enables scientists to carry on the business of science. And it is precisely this feature that they share with the human beings whom they study.

However, rational understanding and empathic or artistic understanding are not equivalent; even less are they of the same value. This is because of the following:

1 Even though emphasis on empirically founded knowledge is the feature shared by the two forms of interpretation, it is also the feature that distinguishes them. Empathic knowledge gives great weight to subjectivity and to the ability to imagine oneself in the situation in which an action is taking place. It is therefore rooted in experience, as far as it is possible for the latter to be lived in a person's imagination. This is not objective experience, nor does it demonstrate the truth of meaningful action. But, as we have seen, it is a feature shared by the two kinds of knowledge. Instead, what distinguishes between them is the construction of the ideal-types that are employed by rational interpretation but which are entirely absent from empathic understanding. However much Weberian ideal-types may be the product of drastic choices, and however much they are merely imaginative constructs, according to Remo Bodei (1997: 52–4) they are objective both because they are intersubjective and

because they operate scientifically on the basis of causal nexuses. This is not a question of cause–effect determinism, since Weber denied the existence of absolute causality, just as he denied the existence of absolute indeterminism, of the preponderant role of chance, of human freedom to decide and to act. The issue is instead the meaning and predictability of human action. Hence Weber's 'understanding sociology' studies individual actions as much as historical events, proceeding by causal inferences, decomposing phenomena in order to imagine them, perhaps shorn of some of their premises, reconstructing them in unreal manner on the basis of 'if' and 'but', and establishing the extent to which some element or other is able to bring about their objectification.

2   The study of both rational and irrational phenomena involves a process of detachment and abstraction from reality, rather than one of convergence and immersion. The intention is to impose order on reality through the construction of ideal-types to be used in interpretation of that meaningless universe to which the intentional action of social actors imparts sense.

Basic assumptions on the subject and method of understanding intentional action thus both merge together and distinguish 'explanatory understanding' and knowledge 'of an emotionally empathic or artistically appreciative quality'. Weber's crucial achievement, writes Cavalli (1969: 73), lay in his use of causality to render scientific knowledge into historical knowledge, because without verification of causal connections, history can never be science but only literature or, at best, art. But this is not to imply that understanding coincides with causal explanation, since Weber's method can be used to acquire non-causal knowledge. The fact is, Cavalli further points out (1969: 71), that the notion itself of understanding (*Verstehen*) is very far from being defined with rigour, although the literature on the subject is huge and ramifies through philosophy and methodological theory in the social sciences. In short, there are conflicting opinions on this interweaving of rational understanding and empathic knowledge in Weber's method (Abel, 1953, 1967; Baar, 1967; Chisholm, 1979; Collingwood, 1946; Coser, 1971; Dray, 1957; Hempel, 1942; Martin, 1969; Outhwaite, 1975; Schwartz and Jacobs, 1979; Scriven, 1971; Stewart, 1956; Van Evra, 1971; Wax, 1967). Predominant, however, are those who argue, like Davide Sparti (1995: 44), that Weber sharply distinguishes understanding from empathy, and thus rejects every metarational and psychologistic–immediatist implication of understanding and interpreting. In this chapter, instead, it is the importance in Weber's sociological thought of empathic or artistic knowledge that is emphasized.

Empathic knowledge in aesthetics and in the social sciences

Weber's principal concern in assigning weight to empathic knowledge was to distinguish sociology from the natural sciences. In this endeavour he was closely influenced by the philosopher and historian of culture Wilhelm Dilthey, to whom Weber largely owed his concept of *Verstehen*. He was also influenced by the philosopher and psychiatrist Karl Jaspers, for whom the workings of the mind could only be comprehended by empathic knowledge (Coser, 1971: 245–7). Both Dilthey and Jaspers argued that a distinction should be drawn between explanation and understanding. Dilthey sought to provide a speculative foundation for what he called the 'cultural sciences' (*Geisteswissenschaften*) and which subsequently came to be known as the human sciences. The distinctive themes that emerge from the 20 volumes of his collected writings (Dilthey, 1914–36) are his opposition to positivism and his search for a scientific method which differed from that of the natural sciences, although he acknowledged that the latter had theoretical significance. Dilthey argued that explanation of human action was not constrained to purely extrinsic knowledge because, in this case, the investigating being coincided at least in part with the investigated being. In other words, writes Franca D'Agostini (1997: 304), the investigating being 'belongs' to the history and society that it is engaged in studying and describing. And in a certain sense it 'creates' the historical–social world that it seeks to illustrate. Dilthey therefore held that the subject belonged to its context and that it took part in the constitution of its 'objects of experience'.

These objects are not only texts. Sculptures, musical notes, gestures, economic systems or institutions are equally things that belong to the world of the mind. They are the fruit of lived experience (*Erlebnis*) and they require interpretation. Dilthey thus extended the range of hermeneutics, the philosophical tradition of textual interpretation that had taken its name from Hermes, the Investigator, and which was developed as an independent discipline during the Renaissance and the Reformation. Friedrich Daniel Ernst Schleiermacher (1959) has emphasized that Romanticism viewed interpretation as a part of human existence, and thus anticipated contemporary hermeneutics by influencing Dilthey's philosophy of life and his contribution to the discipline. Bodei points out (1997: 62–5) that the Ego described by Dilthey is not monolithic: it instead resembles a fabric woven from a thousand threads. By means of *Verstehen* – the 'understanding' typical of hermeneutics – the self is able to reactivate appearances as inert symbolic universes and to live lives parallel to its own as if it were endowed with several biographies.

Verstehen is therefore the device that releases people from their isolation. We understand the meaning of human action on the basis of dynamic connections and in relation to purposes and values. We are enabled to do so by a process of inner experience which revives these values and purposes, and then deciphers and reconstructs them. It is a process, moreover, which frees us from the necessity of having directly lived the experience or emotion that we wish to understand. But such understanding is not available when we study insects, for example. We cannot relive and re-experience the lives of insects, and consequently we are obliged to formulate rational explanations of their behaviour.

This introduces the important difference in subject-matter that I stressed earlier when discussing the dispute that gave rise to the social sciences and the aesthetic understanding of organizations. Once this difference of subject-matter had been established, in fact, the difference of method naturally followed: if causal explanation was the method of the social sciences, then understanding was the procedure used by the social sciences. It is such understanding, Dilthey maintained, that prevents inner experience from being impervious to historical mediation, and history from being an inexorable objective process devoid of the individual mediation of meaning. He developed an interpretative procedure which yielded singular and non-generalizable results, and he pointed out the myriad individual initiatives that give sense to ever more rigid economic and political organizations. In other words, people's lives are manifest in an infinity of different modes which evade pre-established formulas. Consequently, Alberto Izzo observes (1994: 132), Dilthey was obliged to criticize both Hegel's idealism and Comte's positivism. Both doctrines displayed a faith in history as necessary progress which moves through stages that are equally necessary. Conversely, Dilthey examined people in their concrete situations, together with the history of these situations and of the actions and artefacts that constitute them, independently of any metaphysical presupposition.

Aesthetics are ideal for this sort of inquiry, Dilthey observes (1914–36, Vol. VI) in *Die Einbildungskraft des Dichters: Bausteine für eine Poetik* (1887) and *Die drei Epochen der modernen Ästhetik und ihre Aufgabe* (1892). 'Poetic', he writes (1887; It. trans. 1995: 742–5), is the term we use for the nature that enables us to enjoy vitality. 'Poetic' is the action of an art form which tells us of its vitality. Poetry is above all the nourishing, strengthening and awakening within ourselves of this vitality, this energy of the life-sentiment; a sentiment that resonates in images, in music, in words, because it is the content of all poetry. It is an experience which can only be entirely appropriated through reflexivity, by being set in relation to other lived experiences, because it can never be expressed in thought or ideas. It is thus that lived experience is understood in its essence – that is to say, in its meaning.

Not only are poets able to grasp this meaning; they are able to reproduce it. They view the world intensely and in their own terms; they hear it with finely tuned ears, they feel the intensity of sensations, they record sensory perceptions in images. But above all they vividly reproduce the psychic states that they have directly experienced, as well as the psychic states of others and their interweavings. The poetic imagination freely fashions experience and its reproduction beyond the confines of reality. Aesthetics thus enable us to pass from lived experience to the concrete and productive plane of the cultural sciences, to extend the compass of our inner experience, and to link it with a wider historical and spiritual dimension, but without lapsing into subjectivism or relativism (Franzini and Mazzocut-Mis, 1996: 89).

Stefano Zecchi and Elio Franzini (1995: 815) inform us that Dilthey – like Husserl and Scheler – had read and discussed Theodore Lipps's book *Ästhetik* (written between 1903 and 1906), which assigned central import- ance to the concept of empathy (*Einfühlung*). No art – wrote Lipps in a subsequent work on empathy (1913: It. trans. 1977: 190–1) – can transform into an occasion for joy what on the contrary causes repulsion and intimate disapproval. But art is able to extract whatever is human from the repulsive and enables us to perceive therein the life, the force, the will, the work – in a word, the activity – that arouse echoes within us. What we empathize with, therefore, is life-as-force, inner work, tending, realizing (1913; It. trans. 1977: 179–80).

We therefore do not empathize with what we perceive with our senses. If I feel threatened by a thunderstorm, I can neither hear nor see the activity of its fury and menace, but only feel them within myself. But the fury and the menace reside in a sensible object, which means that I find myself in a sensible object, that I feel myself in it. That is to say, I possess myself, I find myself, I feel myself in it. This is empathy. In its more general sense (1913; It. trans. 1977: 184), the term means that, if I grasp an object mentally, I accomplish an activity in it or I fulfil my self as if I were part of that particular object. In some cases this comes about without conflict between myself and my natural tendency to self-fulfilment, on the one hand, and the activity that is elicited or engendered in me by the object, on the other. But there are situations in which I am both attracted to an object and repelled by it, which is a situation of negative empathy. But if I am not only in a harmonious situation of positive empathy, but also fulfil myself in a sensible object which is distinct from me, then I feel the enjoyment of my objectified self which constitutes aesthetic enjoyment.

Lipps developed these arguments on empathy within a broader conception of aesthetics that took the name of 'scientific aesthetics'. Lipps (1897), in fact, conducted experimental studies of great interest, most notably his investigation into the optical and aesthetic impression yielded in the percep- tion of geometric visual forms. In perceiving, what is essential is not the perception in itself but its meaning for us from some point of view. Aesthetics, Lipps claims (1903–6), is a psychological discipline, because founded in the object is an act of aesthetic evaluation, an act which can only be accomplished in a consciousness. Proof that empathy is a singular fact, observes Lipps (1913; It. trans. 1977: 180–1), and that it represents the fundamental concept of modern aesthetics, is provided by the finding that my consciousness can be connected with or belong to something that is sensibly perceived.

Einfühlungstheorie stimulated a debate that was vital for the development of aesthetics (Scialpi, 1979: 82). According to Gianni Vattimo (1977: 35–6), it was the theoreticians of empathy, and Lipps especially, who did most to transfer the arguments of philosophical aesthetics to the human sciences. The enhanced status of the humanities wrought changes in the programme pursued by the scientific aesthetics of Lipps in particular, and by an aesthetics which closely interwove with the methods and theories of the social sciences in general. As Vattimo writes, many of the issues addressed by nineteenth-century sociologism and psychologism became themes specific to sociology, psychology, ethnology and cultural anthropology. At the same time 'the endeavour to give scientific definition to the laws that govern art concentrated in the disciplines that study language', namely linguistics and semiotics.

The methodological question of empathy was an integral part of the foundations of both modern aesthetics and the social sciences, as distinct and independent from the natural sciences. Although causality-based 'explanatory understanding' was preferred, empathy was central to the *Methodenstreit* of the early years of this century. This debate was part of the wide-ranging endeavour to redefine science and philosophy which involved historicism, neo-Kantianism, logical empiricism, neo-idealism and the sociology of Max Weber (D'Agostini, 1997: 24). And empathy has continued to be part of methodological controversy ever since, with its stress on the following theses:

1   Knowledge about the human world – from society in general to the artefacts produced in it, from organizational life to the aesthetic experience of the individual – is sharply distinct from knowledge about nature by virtue of its subject-matter and method.
2   Comprehension is the legitimate procedure of the social sciences.
3   'Irrational' motives as well as end-directed calculation, habits as well as aesthetic considerations, emotions as well as values, constitute human action and must be cited in explanation of intentional behaviour.
4   All social phenomena and events are unique and irrepeatable phenomena and events to which the subjects concerned belong and which at the same time they create.

Debate on the concept of empathy in the second half of this century has centred on its operationalization as a method and on its scientific validity. The concepts of *Verstehen* and *Einfühlung* have often been treated as synonymous with 'understanding' (Van Evra, 1971: 381). As Howard Schwartz and Jerry Jacobs stress (1979: 19), numerous scholars have assumed that the term *Verstehen* denotes a form of sociological analysis which seeks to undertake empathic appraisal. They have thus associated the concept with Weber, for whom, they believe, empathic understanding was the principal goal of his inquiry into intentional action. As a consequence, the notion of comprehension has been framed in terms of empathic understanding, and a wide range of meanings have been attached to the concepts of both *Verstehen* and understanding:

> Both terms refer to the act of comprehending the subjective or mental factors involved in human behavior, such as meaning, insight, evaluation, motive, attitude, Thomas' 'definition' of the situation', and Znaniecki's 'humanistic coefficient'. (Abel, 1967: 334)

Therefore, as Abel indicates, other scholars besides Weber have been associated with the methodological issue of empathy. Indeed, writes Murray Wax (1967: 323), 'an international galaxy' of outstanding and well-known scholars like 'C. H. Cooley, P. Sorokin, R. M. MacIver, M. Weber, as well as Dilthey, Jaspers and Rickert [. . .] not only favored but purportedly used' this methodological procedure. Must one therefore conclude that empathic understanding is scientific knowledge of meaningful action? The answer is 'no', because the 'operation of *Verstehen* does not, however, add to our store of knowledge', wrote Theodore Abel (1953: 687) in what many consider to have been the funeral oration for empathic knowledge, although he later stated that he considered the operation of *Verstehen* to be 'the chief source of hypotheses in sociology' (1967: 336). It is probably for this reason that the methodological question of empathy continues to be a matter of scientific controversy. Nonetheless, it is highly regarded as the theoretical source of working hypotheses, and of insights which provide the basis for subsequent empirical research, thereby providing access to the context in which the analysis is conducted.

Roderick Chisholm, too, has developed a stance favourable to empathic or intuitive understanding. The point is, he writes (1979: 243), that it is not just a matter of having a rich source of hypotheses; we must also be able to justify them. Consequently, we must develop epistemological principles which allow us to state that intuitive comprehension furnishes justified hypotheses about the mental states of others, so that

> in addition to the principles of inductive and deductive logic, and to the principles of perceptual evidence and the principle of mnemic evidence, there are also principles of evidence which are such that, in application to one's perceptually and mnemically extended evidence base, they will justify certain propositions about other minds. These principles will refer to the phenomenon called *Verstehen*. (1979: 241)

Hypotheses, therefore, are not consequences 'deduced' from a body of evidence; nor do they arise from the application of 'inductive' logic. They are justified by principles of evidence which are just as valid as the epistemic principles of deductive or inductive logic. In short, empathy is a method that furnishes the scholar with intuitions that are not merely plausible but actually true.

No matter how plausible or true the knowledge produced by empathic understanding may be, it is nonetheless confined to the ambit of hypothesis formulation (Hempel, 1942; reprinted 1994: 50). These hypotheses must subsequently be verified by research methods other than those of empathy. Empathic understanding may consequently be of value to research – by providing truth-justified hypotheses or solely by yielding 'intuitive grasp' – but it must always be followed by 'non-intuitive verification before it can be called knowledge' (Van Evra, 1971: 381). Thus empathic understanding is transformed from the autonomous method for comprehension of social action defined by Max Weber into a useful first or preliminary stage in the scientific analysis of intentional action. Empathy is accordingly entirely subordinate and functional to research methods based on the scientific verification of hypotheses and on the objective and universal control of procedures for the gathering and processing of the data used in the study of meaningful action. It would in fact be wrong also

> in cases of high initial plausibility, that the method used to produce the hypotheses (i.e. the 'method of discovery') *is taking the place of verificational methodology.* If, for instance, the hypothesis were such that it could in principle neither be verified nor proved false, then no matter how initially plausible it might have been, it could not attain the status of scientific knowledge. (Van Evra, 1971: 380)

In support of his argument Van Evra develops a delicate topic, that of the ideas that arise in the course of scientific research. This is especially illustrative of the reasoning behind Van Evra's ideas and of the analytical precision of his distinctions and classifications applied to meaningful action, which stems instead, in my view, from an array of opaque motives that resist division into classes and categories. However much ideas in science may be generated by beautiful intuition, they are not part of scientific thought by virtue of their beauty:

> It's tempting to think that the beauty of Schrödinger's intuition was enough to warrant calling the equation scientific knowledge. But while beautiful, the equation *could not* have become part of the corpus of scientific knowledge if experimental corroboration were never forthcoming. In that case, the beauty would have been entirely deceptive. [. . .] Empathy, in other words, is not a 'fine provider of knowledge', nor can it produce 'sure signs' for science. (1971: 381)

At issue is not the transposition of aesthetics to a different domain inappropriate to them, namely the domain of scientific proof. The point is that one may say – paraphrasing – that although research hypotheses may arise from empathic understanding, empathy does not give them heuristic value. Just as the beauty that generates the intuition of a scientific equation has nothing to do with science, so the empathy that generates the intuition of a research hypothesis has nothing to do with the social sciences.

Fortunately, not all scholars have subscribed to this sharp distinction between empathic understanding and causal explanation; a distinction which, as we have seen, should not be expunged from methodological questions concerning the study of intentional action. There are scholars who have instead insisted on the specificity of the heuristic value of empathic understanding and on its autonomy. The neo-positivist theses of the proponents of the scientific verifiability of hypotheses and the controllability of research procedures have been criticized as excessively self-referenced. That is to say, they have been attacked for being based on research assumptions that in fact belong to their particular methodologies of analysis (Scriven, 1971) – criticisms advanced by Van Evra as regards both aesthetics and empathy.

Advocated instead has been the autonomy of *Verstehen* from attempts to subordinate it to other methodological procedures and to obscure its knowledge-producing potential.

I have already discussed these matters, but I must dwell on them further in order to emphasize the heuristic route opened up by the autonomy of empathic understanding, the completeness of this route, and its irreducible difference from rationalist and positivist methods in the social sciences.

Murray Wax (1967) considers four different meaning levels of *Verstehen* in order to study social action: the extracultural level, the intracultural level, the level of interpretation and the level of interpersonal intuition. He claims (1967: 324) that only the intracultural level is appropriate and truly useful. This is certainly not the view advanced in this chapter, in which I emphasize that the other levels proposed by Wax are important and appropriate as well. Nevertheless, it has the merit of recasting the debate on the comprehension of intentional action. Wax's arguments presuppose the complete extraneousness of the knowing subject from the culture and language of the subject whose intentional action is being studied. What, therefore, are these four meaning levels in comprehension that range from extracultural to interpersonal intuition?

The extracultural level is based on the inferences that can be drawn from the elementary needs and sentiments of another person, or from more complex forms of transaction and agreement involving empathy and sympathy, given the impossibility or great difficulty of accessing another person's culture and language and making proper use of them. However, it is the second level of *Verstehen* which, as said, Wax regards as the most appropriate. It is also the level of closest interest to us here, because it is via the intracultural level that the difference and autonomy of the knowledge yielded by *Verstehen* is brought out. At this level, understanding of a person's intentional action is based on familiarization with his/her everyday life. *Verstehen* thus becomes comprehensible in its essential features

> if we shift the emphasis from such incorrect uses as 'applying the operation of *Verstehen*' and consider instead *the acquisition of Verstehen*, namely socialization, either the primary socialization into one's native culture, or the secondary socialization (or resocialization) into an alien culture, or – yet more tenuously – vicarious socialization. (1967: 327; emphasis added)

Understanding is therefore a process, and essential to this process is socialization and the learning of languages and symbolic systems, as regards their formation as well. The most salient examples are provided by research based on participant observation – ethnography and ethnomethodology – given that the researcher spends a period of time socializing him/herself to the culture of the natives and learning its essential features. The aim is to see matters from the insiders' point of view, something very difficult to achieve when scientific tools like the questionnaire are used and quantitative analysis is conducted.

Verstehen should therefore not be viewed as an 'operation', nor as an 'instrument', but instead as socialization to the culture that constitutes the research setting and also as a form of learning. Socialization and participation are also of great importance to interpretation – the third level of *Verstehen*. Once again the aim is to gain empirical knowledge of the actors' point of view, thereby enhancing insights with the sociological meaning of recognition of an implicit model.

The last level of meaning that attaches to *Verstehen* – that of interpersonal intuition – is the 'product of a confusion embedded in sociological tradition'. Wax dismisses it as 'incorrect' (1967: 324, 331). This is the type of knowledge that one person may gain about another by means of inter-subjective understanding. Wax declares also that interpretation (the third level) should be kept distinct from the first level, which is the one most replete with empathy. He then discusses the close interweaving of these four levels of meaning of *Verstehen*, and contrasts *Verstehen* as an autonomous form of knowledge with the positivist and structuralist methodologies that scholars 'impose on the society, utilizing their theoretically-driven conceptions of the requirements of a social system' (1967: 330), with the result that 'the reader of their reports seldom finds that via their pages he is encountering people who perceive the world differently than himself and the authors' (1967: 328).

Yet the fourth level of *Verstehen* – that of interpersonal intuition – as well as the first level of extracultural comprehension between people not wholly alien from each other by culture and language, are by no means of secondary consequence. Besides Max Weber, the American sociologist Charles Horton Cooley, amongst others, has stressed the importance of these two levels: they are important if one wishes to affirm and illustrate the difference between understanding and the other methods employed in the study of intentional action.

At the beginning of this century, but working entirely independently of Weber, Cooley stressed that the subjective meanings attributed to their actions by actors should be studied, at least in part, via internal or sympathetic understanding (Coser, 1971: 311). Knowledge of human beings, argued Cooley (1930: 290), is founded on our ability to comprehend the motives and origins of human action by means of a sympathetic relationship which in its most manifest expressions may also be called 'dramatic' in that it gives rise to the visualization of mental states. By sharing the mental states of other persons, by undergoing an emotional or intellectual process similar to theirs, through communication and contact with their minds, we develop knowledge that is an 'originative mental synthesis'. Herein lies the possibility of grasping the significance of people's social lives, and at the same time the difference between this kind of understanding and the knowledge we have of a horse or a dog. Richard Brown (1977: 144–5) adds the following emphasis to a quote from Cooley (1926) in order to underline the subtlety of the understanding of intentional action envisaged by Cooley in his description of the autonomy of understanding and of the central role played therein by empathic understanding:

> There is, no doubt, a way of knowing people with whom we do not sympathize which is essentially external or animal in character. An example of this is the practical but wholly behavioristic knowledge that men of much sexual experience sometimes have of women, or women of men – something that involves no true participation in thought and feeling . . . Put rather coarsely, *a man sometimes understands a woman as he does a horse*; not by sharing her psychic processes, but by watching what she does.

Theoretical presuppositions of the empathic understanding of organizations

I have so far discussed the heuristic value of empathic understanding in both aesthetics and the social sciences. I have also described the connections between aesthetics and the study of human and social action; connections evident since the beginnings of the social sciences. We may now turn to consideration of empathic understanding in the study of organizations, and with particular reference to the aesthetic approach. The empathic understanding of intentional action essentially requires the researcher to place him/herself in the shoes of the social actor studied; only subsequently will s/he seek to describe the latter's action. This process presupposes active willingness, knowledge-gathering methods, definition of the empathy situation, the architecture and style of accounts, and an option for the dominant character of the knowledge process. These various aspects are now discussed in detail.

First, *the willingness of the researcher* to place him/herself in the shoes of the organizational actor. This cannot be taken for granted, as if it were a formal act, because it entails the researcher's readiness to gather lived experience through his/her imagination. In other words, the researcher must be willing to gain experience of social action which, in our case, unfolds in organizations or in the relationships that these establish with other organizations or with society at large. This active willingness has two principal aspects:

1 *Self-immersion* in the organizational action being studied, which is the most general feature of empathic understanding. This implies that the researcher's willingness is not due solely to an ability to formulate intellectual, rational and objective interpretations. S/he does not formulate hypotheses that are only thought, no matter how accurately, but lives and experiences them through feelings and emotions. Thus ruled out is the objective and neutral detachment of the social scientist, who cannot remain aloof from the ongoing event or action, because self-identification with another person in order to understand his/her intentional action entails involvement in personal experiences as well.

2   Activation of the researcher's *perceptive or sensory faculties*. The researcher seeks to gain direct experience of whatever aesthetically motivates the intentional action of others. His/her readiness to do so becomes active because it does not obfuscate his/her capacity for aesthetic sentiment or his/her faculty of aesthetic judgement, nor does it attenuate his/her ability to feel emotions or to conduct intellectual reflection.

Second, the *knowledge-gathering methods* distinctive of empathy. Through the joint use of these methods the researcher inductively infers the multiple combinations of social and personal motives that best illustrate the intentional action of the organizational actor. There are four of these methods, and although they are often used jointly, this does not have to be invariably the case. What matters is that the inductive, rather than deductive, character of the inquiry should remain paramount whatever combination is selected. These methods are as follows:

1   *Self-observation.* The researcher observes him/herself whilst placing him/herself in the shoes of another person. S/he observes the sensations provoked by the action, the motives that induce it, the judgements that can be made about it. The researcher thus notes and describes the moods aroused in him/herself, the emotions felt, the lateral thoughts that arise, the aesthetic attraction of a particular course of action, its management or closure. These annotations reveal how the researcher interprets him/herself in the details of action and in the various organizational times of the action. The procedure is analytical because it is intended to capture the various nuances rendering that particular action distinct from others of a similar kind, so that it is possible to illustrate the complexity of intentional action. It is by means of self-observation, in fact, that the qualitative data essential for empathic knowledge are produced, and their accurate annotation is crucial for proper understanding of intentional action in organizations.

2   *Intuition.* Without intuition it is impossible to gain empathic knowledge of the intentional action of the organizational actor. The researcher must activate his/her intuitive capacities in order to assume the role of the organizational actor. This s/he does by utilizing the signals that, in his/her opinion, manifest the moods, impressions and assessments of the organizational actor. Some of these signals activate the researcher's intuitive capacity, but not all of them. Indeed only certain signals are a source of intuition for the researcher, and it is on these that s/he concentrates in order to intuit the organizational actor's cognitive, emotional and aesthetic states and thereby gain the requisite intimate and personal experience. As said, without intuition there is no empathic knowledge. To which I would now add that this presupposition is a further reason for the partial, fragmentary and specific nature of empathic understanding.

3   *Analogy.* Like the previous method of intuition, analogy enables the researcher to establish a dynamic relationship with whatever the organizational actor thinks and feels, and hence with the intentional action under

examination. The researcher is thus able to recognize the signals indicative of the aesthetic–emotional states of the organizational actor. S/he is also able to go beyond resemblances and tap into the familiarities that place him/her at ease in the process of empathic knowledge-gathering. Moreover, analogy enables the researcher to hypothesize the existence of signals that manifest the organizational actor's states of mind as well as his/her cognitive states. Analogy is a rich source of qualitative data for the study of organizational life. By means of analogy, in fact, the researcher can hypothesize what the actor is thinking, what sensations s/he is feeling, and what others sensations s/he may be about to feel in the course of the organizational action. By means of this method of knowledge-gathering, the researcher can also hypothesize meanings of the organizational actor's action of which the latter is not aware.

4 The *reliving of experience in the imagination*. This is the chief source of qualitatively rich data for empathic knowledge. The researcher uses his/ her intuitive faculties, employs analogy, or relies on a combination of the two methods, to place him/herself in the shoes of another. S/he observes him/herself in this role and describes intentional action with its complex array of motives to him/herself and to others. The empathic method enables the researcher to recognize moods, thoughts and aesthetic sentiments closely connected with the intentional action of the organizational actor. But in order to understand such action, s/he must act it out or reactualize it. By reliving the experience in the imagination as an experiential and not intellectual process, in fact, the researcher is able to create the qualitative data necessary for empathic knowledge.

Third, *definitions of the situation of empathy*. The situation is defined in three different ways. The first of them is 'hard', the other two are 'soft':

1 *Hypothesis verification.* In this definition of empathy, hypotheses about the motives for the intentional action of the organizational actor undergo empathic verification. By means of intuition, analogy and relived experience, the researcher verifies which combination of motives is able to explain intentional action in organizations. There may be many of these combinations. Some of them will be confirmed, others will be deemed of lesser significance, and yet others will be judged extraneous to the organizational action under examination. For this definition of the empathy situation, the coincidence is postulated between the researcher and the organizational actor – that is, between the observer and the observed. It is a coincidence, however, that highlights the reversal of the relation between the knowing subject and the subject of the intentional action. Although the situation is defined in terms of increasing self-identification with the Other, the researcher attributes to the organizational actor what s/he in fact feels and thinks. A paradoxical situation thus arises: whereas the observer coincides with the observed, in reality the latter coincides with the former. This is the 'hard' definition of the empathy situation,

because although, on the one hand, it assumes the rigorous verification of the hypothesized knowledge, on the other, it also assumes that empathic understanding is the more rigorous, the closer the coincidence between observer and observed.

2   The *sharing of experience*. In this case the researcher posits his/her empathic knowledge on the condition that s/he has already lived an experience and found him/herself in a situation. This therefore is to postulate not the coincidence, but the analogy of the situation with others found to be similar and familiar. This type of definition of the empathic situation is thus very different from hypothesis verification, since the researcher who uses it presumes not that verification will be forthcoming, but that plausible descriptions of the intentional action will be produced.

3   *Imaginary participant observation*. In this case, although the researcher uses intuition and analogy, s/he does not necessarily and solely place him/herself in the shoes of the organizational actor. S/he may choose to do so, but this is only one of the options available. Besides self-identification with the organizational actor, s/he may choose to 'flank' or to 'shadow' the latter. In other words, the researcher may adopt several points of observation on the intentional action, but always ones based on his/her imagination. Thanks to the latter, as in the two previous definitions of the situation of empathic knowledge, the scholar participates in the intentional action. The feature that distinguishes imaginary participant observation from other methods is that the researcher is not obliged to identify him/herself with the author of an action, whether by coincidence in order to verify hypotheses, or by analogy in order to describe the plausibility of the emotions, sensations and thoughts experienced. The researcher's imagination enables him/her to assume the semblance of another person: from the organizational actor to the conductor of participant observation of his/her action, from that of some other subject involved in the intentional actor and deemed important by the organizational actor to those who watch from a distance or distractedly. Like coincidence and analogy, imagination places everything that can be thought or felt regarding intentional action on the plane of 'lived in the fantasy'. Without obliging the observer to share the standpoint of the observed, and conversely without obliging the observer to place him/herself in the shoes of all those who participate in the action, this situation enables the researcher to consider the organizational action from several points of view, however incomplete and fragmentary they may be.

Fourth, the *architecture and the style of the description*. The description of the knowledge yielded by the empathic methods discussed above may, in many respects, be considered a genuine method of empathic knowledge-gathering. At the same time, however, description is not usually regarded as being able to generate empirical data, and it is therefore not a method of inquiry. This dilemma is ever-present in the case of empathy, with its ambiguity and paradoxes. In the course of description of the knowledge yielded by combinations of the four methods described, qualitative data are constantly created. Reconstruction in the imagination – which is the memory store of knowledge about the social action – is able to generate further information. Description is not prior to the production of the qualitatively rich data necessary for empathic understanding. But the 'artisanship' (whereby a sensation is related to a thought, a topic is addressed before rather than after, a certain sensitivity or elegance is recounted, implicit emphasis is added on the basis of aesthetic considerations) involves a continuous process of revision, re-reading, re-comprehension, re-argumentation. Although not always, this is an active process of reconstruction of lived experience in the imagination. In this sense, constant re-analyses of the architecture of a text are not solely the outcome of theoretical reconstruction via the continuous definition of the categories or subcategories used to expound the meaning of one's inquiry. In the case of empathy, they may also be a method to create the relived experience relative to the intentional action under examination. In empathic knowledge, description cannot be considered as if it were 'the perfect and universal tape-recording' or the 'photographic plate of a single type'. Whatever is written, shot for a film, composed into words and images for a book or a video, recorded for an audiovisual display, is the product of the constant re-examination of personal experience. But this experience does not reside in the memory, fixed, immobile and sedimented as if the process of empathic understanding of the action has unexpectedly come to a halt. Description evokes the experience, sharpens its focus, and, according to the method used and the definition of situation selected, adds detail and argument. Empathic organizational knowledge therefore neither envisages nor prescribes the existence of a sharp caesura between the production of qualitatively rich data and the communication of the knowledge acquired about intentional interaction in organizations. On the contrary, a cleavage of this kind is as unsuited to knowledge production as it is unjustified by the essential features of the empathic process. This is borne out by the fact that the aesthetic features of the description may influence the architecture of the arguments that it describes. These are aesthetics founded on personal stylistic canons, on those that apply in the professional and occupational community concerned, on those cited or manifested by the imagined users. On the basis of both personal aesthetics and those affirmed or imposed by other individual or collective subjects deemed to be important, the description is embellished, emphasized and transfigured. These various processes have the undeniable power to render the description dramatic, incisive or persuasive, or alternatively impersonal, neutral or aseptic. The aesthetics of the description may be diverse or contradictory but they are nonetheless aesthetics. In the case of empathic knowledge, the conscious decision is taken to illustrate how the lived experience that undergoes reconstruction is still sensible life in organizations. In its architecture and style, therefore, the description must strive to recast the *pathos* of organizational life, its sensuality and allure, and not to emphasize a detachment and a distance that have never existed.

Fifth, the *choice of the feature dominant in the knowledge process*. The dominant features of empathy are essentially the following:

1　*Cognitive*. If this is the dominant feature, attention concentrates on thoughts, reflections and conjectures. The inquiry focuses on the cognitive states of the organizational actor. The researcher seeks to understand the inner reasons for the intentional action, formulating hypotheses about which particular combinations of personal and social motives may provide clues for the understanding of organizational interactions, so that persuasive interpretations of the intentionality of the action are forthcoming. The researcher draws on his/her sensitivity and talent to relive the cognitive states of the organizational actor. These are abilities that differ from the intellectual skills employed by rational inquiry into the inner causes of organizational action. They are based on empathic identification with the Other, rather than on an attempt to reason in the same way as the Other. It is only the emphasis on the reflections and thoughts of the organizational actor, in fact, that distinguishes this procedure of empathic understanding from the emotional and aesthetic methods. Also cognitive empathic understanding of organizational life is based on definition of the empathy situation, on the researcher's willingness to use his/her imagination, on the architecture and style of the description.

2　*Aesthetic*. Unlike cognitive empathy, aesthetic empathy does not principally concern itself with the organizational actor's cognitive state. Other states intersect or interweave with the latter, and they are equally important. I refer to the aesthetic states that words and images are only able to suggest, rather than explain; states like those evinced by expressions such as 'How beautiful!', 'It was enchanting', 'It touched me profoundly'. These are aesthetic–sensory states of mind aroused by wonder and sensuality. So, too, are shock and amusement. Interpretation of intentional action based on the evocation of what is unsayable and ineffable thus replaces interpretation which persuades because it is able to dramatize the reasons for intentional action. Such evocation draws on the sensory faculties of the observer and the observed but also on the social and collective construction of aesthetic judgements. Consequently, it is not thought-dominated motivations that are re-experienced but raw impressions, pointless reflections, ordained judgements, irresolvable paradoxes, random distractions, nonsensical choices. In short, relived in aesthetic empathy are all the elements of intentional action that cannot be translated into cognitive states without being radically distorted. The principal purpose of empathic understanding, therefore, is to evoke, and thereby grasp, not only the persuasive, plausible or well-motivated elements of intentional action, but also those that are unexplained, unforeseen or incongruous. The intentionality of action therefore acquires further elements, takes on nuances, and emerges in more multi-faceted form. In a word, it becomes more 'human'.

3   *Emotional.* In this case, empathy fixes on emotional states, immersing itself in them before they are translated into cognitive processes. These are experiential states distinct from and simultaneously interwoven with the aesthetic–sensory states of aesthetic empathic understanding, but they are distant and distinct from the states privileged by cognitive empathy. Comprehension of the inner determinants of intentional action is based on the ability to tap into the emotional states experienced by the organizational actor as the action unfolds, so that they can then be relived. Anxieties and ill temper, frustrations and satisfactions, anger and displeasure, feelings of gratification and self-fulfilment, pride in one's work and a sense of possessing the material and non-material setting of one's workplace: all these make up the complex array of emotional motives that the researcher sets out to relive in order to understand organizational action.

The route followed by empathic understanding (Table 2.1) begins with the researcher's self-immersion in the role of the Other and the activation of his/her sensory and aesthetic faculties in order to gather qualitatively rich data from self-observation, intuition, analogy, relived experience and, often, the construction of the architecture and the definition of the style of the description. This is flanked by a choice which defines the situation of empathy; a situation which may involve hypothesis verification, previous experience of the phenomenon or one similar to it, or the imaginary participant observation whereby the researcher does not only assume the organizational actor's viewpoint but adopts others by means of which, albeit fragmentarily, s/he can experience, observe and analyse intentional action.

TABLE 2.1 *The components of the empathic understanding of organizations*

The researcher's willingness to empathize	Identification with the Other
	Activation of perceptive or sensory faculties
Knowledge-gathering methods	Self-observation
	Intuition
	Analogy
	Reliving the experience in the imagination
Definition of the situation of empathy	Hypothesis verification
	Sharing experience
	Imaginary participant observation
Architecture and style of the description	Open text
Dominant aspect of the heuristic process	Cognitive
	Aesthetic
	Emotional

In describing empathic understanding, I have emphasized that it yields a form of inductive knowledge. As an independent and self-sufficient route to knowledge, empathic understanding operates outside the theoretical framework of deductive science (Baar, 1967: 339).

Empathic understanding, moreover, does not require either linearity or sequentiality. For example, the four methods described above can be used in various combinations, rather than in sequence, with one adopted first and then another. As regards description, I have shown that this is integral to the production of empathic knowledge; it does not remain on its margins. The definitions of the situations of empathic knowledge are not mutually exclusive, nor do they mesh with each other, nor should they be adopted jointly.

In outlining empathic knowledge of intentional action in organizations, I have depicted a process that is non-prescriptive and non-normative, although some of its essential features have been analysed in a certain amount of detail. I have discussed the dominant characteristics of the empathic knowledge-gathering process in terms of the heuristic strategy preferred by the researcher. This strategy may be cognitive, so that everything that is known empathically is set in relation to thought. Or it may be aesthetic, so that the sensory faculties, aesthetic judgements and feelings are an integral part of knowledge production. Or it may be emotional, so that the researcher places him/herself in someone else's shoes in order to empathize with the emotional states of the organizational actor.

This book deals with empathic understanding that prioritizes the aesthetic strategy. This is a specific and partial method, especially if compared with the more general one described when I illustrated the components of the empathic understanding of organizations. It ties intentional action to the aesthetic knowledge of the subjects concerned, and on this basis describes meaningful action in organizations. This, though, is to reverse the relationship between empathic and causal understanding as set out by Weber and debated in the *Methodenstreit* mentioned at the beginning of this chapter. It is a method centred on the fact that the dilemma between causally based objectification, on the one hand, and the reliving of the organizational actor's experience, on the other, is far from being resolved. It is the significance and force of this dilemma that drives the aesthetic understanding of organizational life. As I have sought to show, and shall continue to do so in the following chapters, such understanding is very distant from, and indeed at odds with, the causal understanding and the *pathos* of objectification so distinctive of analyses of intentional action.

3   The Elusiveness of Organizational Aesthetics

In the previous chapter I stressed the value of empathic, as opposed to causal, understanding for the aesthetic comprehension of meaningful action in organizations. However, using the concept of aesthetics in order to give distinctive characterization to an approach to the study of organizations does not mean that such study must be univocal and standardized.

It is advisable at this point to establish what is meant by 'aesthetics', both in philosophical terms and as regards theories of art and studies of creativity. As we shall see in this and in the next chapters, philosophers have always been divided on the definition of aesthetics. And in the course of this century especially, the debate has been joined by anthropologists, psychologists, semiologists, sociologists, art critics, and also by artists themselves. Thus, on the one hand, the definition of aesthetics has a long history behind it, with its origins in eighteenth-century philosophy and its roots extending to Ancient Greece; on the other, organizational aesthetics are socially and collectively constructed by subjects in organizations. I begin with the latter, and in so doing must return to the organizational artefact of the riddle discussed in Chapter 1.

Aesthetics as difference in feeling

The construction, deconstruction and redefinition of the organizational artefacts examined in Chapter 1 highlighted the importance of the negotiation of aesthetics. It was also pointed out that a distinctive feature of organizational artefacts is the negotiative process whereby aesthetics are affirmed or denied. Accordingly, organizational aesthetics do not constitute an imaginary terrain of peace, harmony and love. On the contrary, I have repeatedly stressed that they are subject to social conflict in organizations, to the violence of corporate cultures, to the power of the dominant coalitions in organizational life.

The memory of the aesthetics of a particular organizational artefact provides vivid evidence of this. There are some aesthetic connotations of the artefact that persist in the experience thereof which subjects remember having had in the organization. By training their memory upon this artefact, they bring out what I shall call 'dominant aesthetic features' or the 'dominant aesthetic' in their experience of it. These features represent the aesthetics affirmed and transmitted by the negotiations conducted over time among diverse organizational actors until, in many cases, they are taken for granted. That is to say, it may be taken for granted that an organizational artefact, no matter how ephemeral, arouses some aesthetic sentiments rather than others in subjects who harbour memories of it.

This happened with the artefact of the riddle. When I proposed it to my students I did so on the assumption that there was a shared organizational aesthetic concerning the artefact. I took for granted not only that the riddle possessed its own aesthetics but also that some aesthetic qualities were distinctive of it and predominated over others. And this proved to be the case. None of the students asked me: 'A riddle. But why?' They were immediately amused or offended by the idea; an outcome, however, that could not come about in every context and situation. In fact, the organizational aesthetics of the riddle were immediately explained to the reader, an action which would have been out of place in an Italian lecture hall.

What I wish to stress is that, first of all, in some social and organizational contexts it is inadvisable to take the organizational artefact for granted in terms of aesthetic knowledge of it, whereas in other contexts it is appropriate to do so. This is undoubtedly a consideration of fundamental importance for the aesthetic understanding of organizations. It emphasizes that aesthetics should not be examined on the assumption that they are objectively and universally true.

Second, I wish to emphasize that those aesthetics, in that specific organizational context constituted by the Italian lecture hall, were taken for granted to ensure the success of the course of action that had been activated. In other words, there was presumed agreement as to the dominant aesthetics of the artefact in its experiential reconstruction in the memories of the members of the organization. Consequently, mention of the artefact almost automatically triggered its reconstruction and reliving in memory. Assumptions about dominant aesthetics were taken for granted by virtue of a process of aesthetic empathic understanding. Indeed, it was precisely the aesthetic form of organizational knowledge – which is learnt and reconstructed through organizations and lived and relived through organizational artefacts – that was used to manage organizational processes and to create new organizational artefacts. As regards the riddle, the aesthetics exploited to intrigue the students were those of enjoyment and play for the purpose of learning. These aesthetics were not shared by all the students, as we have seen, but they were distinctive of the artefact even when it was decontextualized from its customary setting of the nursery school and reconstructed in that of the university. They were aesthetics dominant in the riddle, but they were not so in the artefacts of infant education.

Every organizational artefact may thus be characterized by distinctive dominant aesthetics which are unseen but activated and utilized in the management of organizational life. We saw good examples of this in Chapter 1 during my discussion of chairs: these objects differ in their aesthetics, which are taken for granted and are therefore unseen because of their diverse dominant aesthetics, and they are used differently because of differences in aesthetic feeling.

The experience of difference, observes Mario Perniola (1997: 154–5), signals the abandonment of the concept of identity around which Aristotelian logic rotated, and of the concept of contradiction which constituted the core of Hegelian logic. Difference means 'non-identity', Perniola writes, and starts from and operates within feeling. This is impure feeling, for it is imbued with the ambivalences of lived experience, which are impossible to recompose into a coherent and unitary representation because of their irreducibility to identity. Rather than being a concept analogous to the logical notion of diversity or to the dialectic one of contradiction, for the aesthetic understanding of organizational life difference means the following:

1 *Exploration of intentional action in organizations.* This comes about through feeling and it modulates between terms asymmetrical with respect to each other. Aesthetics highlights the difference of feeling in organizations, not by employing logical aesthetic explanations but by allowing the existence itself of difference to emerge with its paradoxes, incongruities and inaccessible or non-existent explanations.

2 *Experience of the obligation to organizational conflict.* Not only is this impossible to eliminate or avoid, it cannot be resolved by means of the dialectic that sets one position against the other and derives therefrom a higher organizational order. Aesthetics emphasizes this conflict and its irreducibility in the quotidian life of organizations, in strategic decisions and micro-decisions, in the artefacts produced or reconstructed in organizations. These are dominant aesthetics with respect to others in organizational artefacts and in the memory that reconstructs the organizational actors. There is the irreducibility of 'I don't like it' or 'I don't feel so' compared with the reasonableness of the 'I don't understand' which asks for clarification and hence persuasion.

3 *The living and reliving of the manifold characteristics of intentional action in organizations and of their specific and individual nature.* Aesthetics emphasizes that the plurality of feeling in organizations should not be conceptualized in terms that frame it in the speculative and theoretical schemes of relativist interpretation. This denatures the character of difference, superimposing on it the multiform manifestations of the truth and uniqueness of the organization.

4 *The merging and close interconnection of reified human feeling and the 'thingly' dimension which appears to be endowed with its own sensibility.* The difference of feeling in organizations does not exist over and above the 'thingliness' of organizational artefacts, whether material or impalpable. The phenomena and events that occur in organizations are not the synthesis of some speculative and ideal procedure. They are 'things', and aesthetics renders them knowable in their being-different by observing their actual use in the day-to-day routine of an organization.

The difference of feeling revealed by aesthetics is thus an essential theoretical premise of the aesthetic approach to organizations: not because difference is presupposed by it but because aesthetics brings the difference of feeling to the fore.

Difference in feeling and existentialism, hermeneutics and deconstructivism

The Italian hermeneutic and existentialist philosopher Luigi Pareyson (1954, 1971) has formulated the problem of dealing with the inexhaustible process of irreducible differences that concerns aesthetics by stating that reality is completely independent of thought. Interpretation of reality, no matter how authentic it may be, can never achieve definitive truth. An infinite process is set in motion whereby there is always a further truth, which is present in its entirety.

The human person, argues Pareyson in his writings on existentialism (1943), should be conceived in terms of the living self, in those of the freedom of the self, and in those of the irreducibility of the subject to a formal beginning or to an ontological instance. The 'person' is concrete; it is the incarnation of the body and it is participation in existence. There is a gap, an extraneousness and an attrition in this hermeneutic account between the thing and the subject who interprets it, although the subject always participates in the thing to be interpreted (D'Agostini, 1997: 301–2). Hence, also reality and its truth can only be understood by means of interpretation. Consequently, truth is not objectifiable; it can only be attained through a personal formulation and within the ambit of the individuality of this formulation.

For Pareyson, difference is the self-reference that constitutes the person, and a person simultaneously belongs to and participates in the existence of the sensible experiences with which s/he is involved. According to Pareyson, 'truth', 'thing', 'work of art', 'text', are only 'appeals' to which the 'person' may or may not respond. His position is therefore at odds with that of Heideggerism, and with the hermeneutic ontology of Gadamer, observes Franca D'Agostini (1997: 319). Pareyson did not approve of the Heideggerian oblivion of the concreteness of human existence, of the living and carnal being of the person. And he also rejected the deresponsibilization of the self in the interpretative process that Gadamer envisaged. This is evident in his writings on aesthetics.

Starting from a point of view rooted in the hermeneutics of Wilhelm Dilthey and Schleiermacher, in his book *Estetica* Pareyson describes interpretation as reconstruction of the process underlying the text to be interpreted. Every human operation is formative, he states (1954: 23); whether it concerns thought or action, every human operation 'forms' something. For example, when we frame and solve a problem, we perform 'movements of thought' and by means of an 'act of invention' discover the most appropriate of these movements and formulate them. Forming means giving shape, and it involves the interpretative activity of the person and the re-proposing of difference. The works of thought or practice are determined and specified, while the manner in which they are to be realized is simultaneously also in the process of being invented. The theory of formativeness thus establishes a relation between forms and persons: persons interpret forms that have been generated by an interpretative process which is inexhaustible in concrete and thingly terms; they do not do so by means of theoretical abstraction. Interpretation is made possible by a person's refashioning of the formative dynamic that has given rise to a particular form.

According to Franco Restaino (1991: 226), Pareyson endorsed Dewey's contention that aesthetics concerns the entire complex of human experiences. Dewey (1934) developed a pragmatic—naturalist theory which argued that aesthetic experience is not an exceptional aspect of human life. Nor is it confined to the aesthetic objects produced by what are conventionally regarded to be 'the arts'. On the contrary, aesthetics are a distinctive feature of human experience which modern society has muted with its distinctions and circumscriptions. There is an artistic element in every human work, Pareyson writes. In every field of human endeavour there is a fundamental aestheticism grounded in people's spiritual lives, and to restrict aesthetics to art is to perform a crude and artificial 'amputation'. Art is something else. Every operation is formative, but the artistic operation 'is "formation", in the sense that it deliberately sets out to form' (Pareyson, 1954: 23). That is to say, art is pure formativeness; it is forming for the sake of forming. This is so because an artistic operation involves a process of invention and production performed only for oneself, and not to produce works which are practical or speculative, or of some other kind. However, art requires a 'material to form' (1954: 27), something within which to give existence to form. Otherwise pure formativeness would be abstraction rather than concreteness, determinateness and singularity. Art needs 'material', but this material should not distort pure artistic formativeness into common formativeness. The distinctive feature of the artistic operation, in fact, is the intentionality to form for the purpose of forming.

The understanding of intentional action as discussed in Chapter 2 – and not just when it is directed towards artistic creation – therefore rests on the following principles:

1 Aesthetics are part of the entire array of human experiences in everyday organizational life. They concern every area of human endeavour, from the practical to the speculative.
2 Art does not coincide with aesthetics. One may observe the art of organizing by watching managers at work, or the art of entertainment by watching musicians or actors perform. One may observe a mechanic as s/he pursues his art of tuning a car engine, or a designer at his/her drawing board engaged in the art of designing a car body. In Pareyson's terms, all these are arts distinguished by an 'of' which ties them to a particular activity. They are not intentional actions performed purely for their own sake, like those of the artist.

3   The need for material and the difference described by Pareyson highlight the 'sensible' component of the understanding of intentional action in organizations. We have already met these features in Chapter 1, where thingliness and difference were shown to be distinctive of the various organizational artefacts examined. A chair, for example, is always concrete and different, not merely because of its shape or its material structure, nor because it symbolizes different organizations and societies. It is concrete and different by virtue of its being-in-use – that is, by virtue of the endless sequence of interpretative acts that render it into a 'particular thing'.

Hence, there is no 'original' that can be grasped by means of interpretation. There only exist substitute meanings which arise in the context of a chain of deferrals, as Jacques Derrida observes (1967a: 227–8). One must therefore not subject differences of signification to a 'system of sense' (*système du sens*), thereby claiming absolute mastery of them, even if this mastery is only formal (1967b: 401). The attention of the knowing subject should instead focus on the level of difference (*différance*) made up of irreducible differences and polysemies (1967b: 428). Consequently, difference does not consist of a dialectic of opposites which starts from the postulate of identity. Rather, it consists of a labyrinthine interplay of deferrals, allusions and repetitions, the referral of signs to themselves and to others, duplication and simulacrum. It is only these elements that are amenable to interpretation, for, on the one hand, the original object is already a web of interpretations and transcriptions (1967b: 314) while, on the other, although every interpretation draws forth and reveals, it also simultaneously hides and obscures. Describing, therefore, is to 'deconstruct' this chain of deferrals and deferments, but without ingenuously presupposing some kind of metaphysics of difference, as if there existed a teleological principle which imposed order on differences and polysemies (1967b: 291).

The theme of metaphysics brings us to arguments examined in the next section. Here, by way of summary I would stress that when an approach to the study of organizations is said to be 'aesthetic', this means that the researcher concentrates on elements of distinction and difference in organizational life. These elements reveal the elusiveness of organizational aesthetics, because there is no 'organizational aesthetic reality' to be interpreted and there is no 'organizational aesthetic original' to be grasped. Aesthetic understanding is therefore focused and situated knowledge precisely because the subject of study itself suggests methods of inquiry and analysis which yield insights so closely attuned to lived experience that it can be relived in the imagination. This is the crucial feature of the aesthetic understanding of organizational life: a form of knowledge tied to experience and immanence, to nuances and details, to the sensible and worldly, to the construction and reconstruction of lived experience.

Aesthetics as the finiteness of knowledge

One discerns in the birth and growth of aesthetics in the eighteenth century the sensible experience, immanence and finiteness that arise from the constraints of the concrete world. This is not to suggest that no philosopher and scholar of aesthetics has ever sought to frame the subject in a metaphysical and transcendent context. But since its origins as a modern discipline, aesthetics has tended to confine itself to the specifically human and tangible sphere in which phenomena only exist in relation to persons and in so far as phenomena constitute lived experience. This is because aesthetics has always taken everything relatable to the 'sensible' as its subject-matter.

Aesthetics does not involve the writing of poetry to sing the praises of the Christian God, the erecting of churches to transmit His precepts, or the frescoing of walls to celebrate His word. Aesthetics does not recount paradise, inferno and purgatory because it is the hereafter that gives meaning to the earthly experience of individuals. This is art, not aesthetics. Aesthetics, to cite the Greek verb root *aisth* (feel), is the knowledge yielded by the sensory organs (Barilli, 1995: 16). Thus aesthetics is utterly distinct from the divine that gives meaning and value to human sensible experience. Aesthetics is the sensibilities activated to help the human observe, just as 'anaesthetics' (Marquard 1989: 9, 11–12) is the means whereby the sensory faculties are blunted, and one of these means may be art. It is possible to observe, in fact, the transformation of sensibility into insensibility stimulated by art, the aestheticization of quotidian reality by decoration, hedonism and the dominion of illusion. These are ways to 'anaesthetize' organizational actors and thereby render them insensitive and entirely unable to comprehend organizational life. Aesthetics, by contrast, involves an effort which activates the sensory faculties and sharpens their perception of physical phenomena. One must therefore take account not only of what is aesthetic but also of what is 'anaesthetic' and which dulls, even if temporarily, the sensory faculties.

Aesthetics views humans as the 'subjects' of their sensible experiences, both experiential and cognitive. The realm of the sensible is entirely independent of all those meanings that are not legitimated by the finite, imperfect and socially constructed human faculties. It is the domain of everything that can be recognized as extra-rational in human experience. Thus, by positing the validity of human values above and beyond the cosmic orders of religion, philosophy and politics, at the level of knowledge about human and social extra-rational phenomena, aesthetics raises a challenge analogous to that of Cartesian scientific method in the seventeenth century. Indeed, it was the study of the extra-rational without searching for teleological explanations that marked the eighteenth-century intellectual upheaval attendant on the birth of aesthetics.

Still today, human beings are distinguished from animals by their ratiocinative faculty: by their intellect, therefore, not by their sensibility.

Eighteenth-century aesthetics not only placed itself outside the domain of theology but also broke with the social construct of the human person who was such by virtue of being able to think. In other words, it was no longer the intellectual faculties alone that made an individual into a 'subject'. This was because aesthetics enabled the sensory faculties that yield understanding of sensible experience to become part of the social construct that defines the features distinctive of human beings. In this respect, aesthetics reflected the radical change that affected every field of learning in the eighteenth century (Ferry, 1990: 35). The point of view of the human person finds legitimacy in the finiteness of his/her knowledge of the sensible. When the aesthetic study of human action won its independence from theology and metaphysics, a phase of human history came to a close, and with it a cultural paradigm.

All this means that it is possible to study and understand human action in terms of its sensible finiteness, and not in those of its end-directedness. Human action 'becomes' whatever sight, hearing, touch, taste and smell – that is, the sensory faculties – enable us to perceive. It becomes the smelling of a perfume or the feeling of a sensation very different from a jarring screech. Or the neat arrangement of one's work instruments which is pleasing to the eye and the mind. Or the intimate sensing of one's partner's skin by touch and odour as one explores it with one's eyes. It is human experience acquired for its own sake, not in the name of religion, science or ethics. The caress given by the parent to the child does not have to signify anything; neither do the purity of love, the goodness of a gesture, the truth of a natural relationship. The mother's caress may possess its own *pathos*; it may signify beauty, it may arouse emotion, indeed it may paradoxically both elicit and transmit it. In the same way, the worker does not neatly arrange his/her tools for the purposive end of working more efficiently or because the act arouses a feeling of attachment to the organization. On the contrary, the aesthetic quality of the action resides in its being-in-use within the organization, rather than in its being tied to the purposes of the organization or being functional to it.

Finiteness, aesthetics and phenomenological theory

A similar view to that outlined above was propounded by Edmund Husserl (1913); and it was developed in his lessons on passive synthesis (1920–6) which concerned the original constitution (*Urkonstitution*) of the 'thing', observes Liliana Albertazzi (1989: 137). The starting-point of his phenomenological theory was the specificity of every material object, and its central intent was to 'describe' the tight network of acts of experience that connect with the perception of sensible reality.

A sound, for example, has the nature of being a sound in general, and therefore of belonging to a particular 'region' of sensibly perceivable empirical objects. Furthermore, it has the nature of being a particular sound because it possesses specific material and temporal properties – such as duration, volume, timbre or pitch – which distinguish it in space and time.

With these stratifications of meaning and in this particular form, the sound impacts on our sensory faculties. It is not an objective and mathematizable entity, nor is it an exclusively mental one. Instead it is a bundle of qualities which require activation of the sensory faculties by the knowing subject; a subject who in turn has his/her own body which moves spatially and temporally, and who operates not in isolation, but as a living self surrounded by other corporeal subjects which perceive the same sensible reality.

The knowing subject of Husserl's phenomenology always stands in an intersubjective relation with other subjects, and accurate perception of the world is founded on their reciprocal adjustment of shared knowledge judgements. The subject is thus related to a community of subjects, and it is in the realm of intersubjective relations that the objective nature of phenomenological description is formed. This objectivity has nothing to do with a presumed realistic or reified world. It is instead constructed by intersubjective processes whose principal referent, writes Elio Franzini (1991: 51), is the corporeal subject, the aesthetic body.

Phenomenological description must be able to grasp these various layers of meaning, because it is they that yield knowledge about the surrounding world. These layers become more complex, the more complex the 'thing' that we perceive, but they inhere in the specific sense of its 'being-in-the-world'. Take the case of visiting a seaside resort that one does not know, suggests Stefano Zecchi (1978: 3). I have known boats, beaches and the sea since my infancy, and they constitute the essential reference points of an image of 'seaside landscape' which is already part of my lived experience. I can therefore relate this unknown seaside resort to an image that enables my consciousness to recognize it. However, the place also has features that differ from my previous experience and which attract my attention. The image of the seaside landscape relived in my memory is replaced by a new image incorporating those different features that have attracted my attention. My image of the seaside landscape has 'something' new that I seek to interpret on the basis of what I now see and feel. That 'something' of the resort which has attracted my attention is lived in sensible experience. In other words, according to the philosophical method of phenomenology (Husserl, 1913; It. trans. 1965: 300 and 84):

(a) everything that is called an 'object' is an object that belongs to consciousness;
(b) whatever the world and reality are or may be, they must be represented by the consciousness through the senses;
(c) the fundamental corporeality of all reality explains sensible perception and sensory experience.

None of this justifies the sharp distinction drawn between object and consciousness by Cartesian rationalism with its *ego cogito*, and by modern rationalism with its objectification of reality and its relativization of the subject. Phenomenology aims to describe the quality of things themselves;

not, however, in an abstract or metaphysical objectivity but in their specificity as objects of experience which are intentionally addressed by experience. Knowledge is therefore founded on the acts of experience, and its 'description' reveals the specific qualities of thingliness. This is a sensible process constituted in the subjective acts themselves and in their immanence, just as happens in aesthetics when it is defined as a theory of sensibility that goes beyond art. Imagination, memory and perception, therefore, as the foundations of knowledge of the 'sensible', are studied not by means of positivist factualism, but by returning to things themselves. One may therefore legitimately claim, observe Elio Franzini and Maddalena Mazzocut-Mis (1996: 124), that the genesis itself of phenomenology was radically 'aesthetic'.

This close association between phenomenology and aesthetics was pointed out by Husserl himself in a letter of 1907 to the poet Hugo von Hofmannsthal. Husserl wrote that phenomenological theory is closely akin to aesthetics in pure art, except that phenomenology is a 'view' adopted in order to make statements about the philosophical sphere. But the artist adopts the same stance towards the world as the phenomenologist: s/he observes it in order to gather knowledge about nature and human beings which will furnish material for his/her creations. As s/he contemplates the world, it becomes a phenomenon. The existence of the world is a 'matter of indifference' (1907; It. trans. 1985: 205) to both the artist and the phenomenologist, because all knowledge is constituted in subjective experience. At the same time, however, all knowledge captures the objectivity that inheres in that world.

This, therefore, is the paramount problem of the possibility of knowledge; this, therefore, is the enigma that must be addressed. Knowledge is based on the relationship between consciousness and whatever it is that one has consciousness about. Hence, on the one hand, the real object-in-itself does not exist independently of consciousness of it, and, on the other, there is no consciousness-in-itself which is not consciousness of some 'thing', or, put otherwise, consciousness that is not intentional.

In the theory of intentionality that Husserl derived from Brentano's conceptualization – but which differed from the latter, as we have seen, in that it was the projection of consciousness towards something external so that the intentioned object was always immanent to consciousness – the contents of intentional consciousness refer to the entire sphere of subjective experience, from representations to judgements, from volitional acts to emotional and aesthetic ones (Zecchi, 1978: 3–4). None of this, writes Husserl (1907; It. trans. 1985: 204), assumes that any form of existence is pre-given. Thus, every reality, even the reality of one's own self, becomes pure phenomenon. If no form of givenness is admitted, we are obliged to observe and investigate in a purely visual and purely aesthetic manner. This is not to imply that we can proceed no further than quasi-knowledge. On the contrary, it means that knowledge can be acquired which is authentically intuitive and self-evident without going beyond mere phenomena and assuming that they comprise transcendent existence.

Thus the crucial problem for phenomenology is learning how to see and how to feel. This obliges us to forgo obviousness and the imposition of meanings of 'things' by habit and tradition. Seeing and feeling become the capacity of consciousness to translate an individual and empirical intuition into an essential intuition of the permanent forms in whatever it experiences. The body itself of the conscious subject is important for this purpose, because all the meanings of experience are involved in the specificity and operationality of the body. Knowledge itself is rooted in the body as its locus. The empathic understanding which – as we saw in Chapter 2 – enables me to experience another's body as similar to mine, and which yields a qualitative analogy with that other body, grasps humanity's being-in-the-world, especially if the qualitative relations presented by the object do not confine it to a causal knowledge relationship (Franzini, 1991: 54).

Aesthetics as finiteness of organizational life

The aesthetic understanding of organizational life emphasizes finite and concrete sensible experience. The qualification 'aesthetic' given to the approach highlights its paradigmatic break with the view of organizations as entities dominated by human intellectual and ratiocinative capacities, while all the other faculties have sense only if they are subservient to these capacities or are controlled by them. By contrast, the qualification 'aesthetic' seeks to shift the scholar's attention to the sensible aspects of organizations, to the construction, redefinition or repression of sensible experience, to experience relived in the memory.

With its roots in the eighteenth-century rejection of the thesis that humans are distinguished from animals by their rational capacity, in the phenomenological philosophy of the early Husserl, in the deconstructionism of Derrida, and in the hermeneutic and existentialist thought of Pareyson, the aesthetic approach seeks after the 'sensible' in intentional action within organizations, while at the same time problematizing the exclusively mental knowledge of the intentionality of such action. One discerns, therefore, a direct connection with the humanist, rather than scientific, philosophy which regarded logic as a discipline of concept rather than calculus and which relied on interpretations, constructions and descriptions instead of the results yielded by the exact and natural sciences. Especially evident is the view that aesthetics and the theories of art are the philosophical foundation of this approach to the study of organizations – which, however, is not to dismiss them as metaphilosophy, but instead to acknowledge their value as antithetical to the entirely mental, and often entirely rational, knowledge of intentional action. Also involved here is the ethical shift in philosophy that took place during the 1980s and 1990s (D'Agostini, 1997: 9–10), as a result of which inquiry now concentrates on the 'practical sphere' and thus emphasizes the failure of the conception of philosophy as metaphysics, providing ethical legitimization for such principles as pluralism and contextuality. It was an ethical shift directed at the understanding of organizational phenomenological topics and which challenged the imperative of the applicability of organizational knowledge.

Finiteness – as the qualitative feature assigned by aesthetics to the study of organizational life – is also antithetical to the so-called 'goal paradigm' in organization theory. This paradigm, argues Petro Georgiou (1973: 291–2) is so deeply rooted in our consciousness that it now constitutes a truth rather than a theoretical construct. This is because the core of organization studies has always been a conceptualization of organizations as the means with which to achieve ends. Citing Edward Gross (1969), Georgiou observes that there is general agreement that organizations are distinguished from all other systems by the dominant presence of an end; a goal which should be studied in order to gauge how and to what extent it is achieved by organizations, but which is never called into question or contested. As a consequence, like a Procrustean bed, the goal paradigm fits all new organization theories to itself, and absorbs counter-paradigms in organization study regardless of their explanatory potential. The Greek root *organon*, which evokes the idea of instrument, and the fact that the concept of paradigm highlights the act of faith performed by those who adhere to it, make the goal paradigm something profoundly different from a theoretical construct which can be discarded when it has outlived its usefulness. Is it possible to conceptualize organizations independently of the goal paradigm? Georgiou (1973: 299–300) argues that this is indeed possible, if we view organizations as:

(a)   not endowed with personalities;
(b)   not constituted by depersonalized individuals;
(c)   not able decisively to influence those who devote their energies and labour to them.

Georgiou thus proposes a counter-paradigm which enables us to overcome the view of organizations as means to achieve ends and according to which organizations are the product of the interactions among the persons who belong to them. In other words, he proposes a reversal of the relationship between individual and organization, where greater weight is given to the former than to the latter. This reversal of emphasis also characterizes other approaches to the study of organizations which, during the 1970s, proposed themselves as alternatives to structural-comparative analyses and to those centred on structural contingencies (Zey-Ferrel, 1981).

Georgiou bases his counter-paradigm on the theories of Chester Barnard, who considered organizations to be instruments of cooperation, incentivation and distribution. The aesthetic approach, too, draws on Barnard's ideas, in particular those of cooperation and the reciprocal dynamics between the formal and informal organization. There thus emerges a vision of the organization as founded mainly on subjects who are volitional, capable of cooperative intentional action, and able to choose. If one observes the direction or effect of their activities, writes Barnard (1938: 86), one may deduce the 'common purpose' of the organization. The goal is therefore the product of their organizational action, in accordance with the principle that a vague desire to associate with others is not sufficient for formal organization. For this to come about the will to cooperate must prevail, and for this to happen the cooperation must pursue an objective, in other words the organization's purpose.

> Hence, an objective purpose that can serve as the basis for a coöperative system is one that is 'believed' by the contributors (or potential contributors) to it to be the determined purpose of the organization. The inculcation of belief in the real existence of a common purpose is an essential executive function. It explains much educational and so-called morale work in political, industrial, and religious organizations that is so often otherwise inexplicable. (1938: 87)

This emphasis that individuals must be persuaded of the existence and sense of the organization's common purpose entails recognition that an organization is not an objectively given reality which transcends the intersubjectivity established in everyday organizational life. The common purpose must instead be constructed and reconstructed as a shared belief. This is one of the principal activities that must go on within organizations if they are to benefit from the will of individuals to cooperate. Persuasion also highlights the irreducibility and plurality of the personal motives that induce people to cooperate. Barnard points out that it is often assumed that common purpose and individual motivation are identical, or that they should be so. But this is not always the case:

> Individual motive is necessarily an internal, personal, subjective thing; common purpose is necessarily an external, impersonal, objective thing even though the individual interpretation of it is subjective. The one exception to this general rule, an important one, is that the accomplishment of an organization purpose becomes itself a source of personal satisfaction and a motive for many individuals in many organizations. It is rare, however, if ever, and then I think only in connection with family, patriotic, and religious organizations, that organization purpose becomes or can become the 'only' or even the major individual motive. (1938: 89)

Indeed, people interact, maintain contact, and come together 'without any specific "joint" purpose' (1938: 114). No matter how accidental or how organized such behaviour may be, it involves interactions which alter the experiences, knowledge and emotions of the persons concerned. Over time, it gives rise to mental states and habits which evidence the social conditioning and construction of experiences and memory. Barnard refers to these interactions and aggregate forms when he describes 'informal organizations', pointing out that '[t]hough common or joint purposes are excluded by definition, common or joint results of important character nevertheless come from such organization' (1938: 115).

Above all, such organizations generate customs, cognitions, social norms, ideals, folklore and institutions. They precede the constitution of formal organization and create the conditions for it. Informal and formal organization are therefore interconnected from the moment when the organization is created. It is an interweaving that persists even after the organization's demise and which formal organization seeks to perpetuate. The dynamics between them are driven by reciprocal dependence and reciprocal reaction (Barnard, 1938: 286). In fact, whilst formal organizations are necessary for order and coherence, informal organizations are essential for the vitality of the organization and for the integrity of the individual, because they safeguard the sentiments of independence, personal integrity and self-respect in organizational life.

In conclusion, the aesthetic approach to organization emphasizes that the sensible experience of the people who belong to an organization is not relative or functional to its purposes. Nor do organizations represent the symbolically higher order that enables us to give meaning to and explain the lived experience of the individuals who belong to them. I made this point when discussing the difference and plurality of feeling in organizations, and also when describing the reasons why aesthetics broke away from the grand theories of end-directed rationalism. Aesthetics distinguish and separate the human being from any explanation based on end-directedness, whether of a divinity, a great truth or, indeed, an organization. Aesthetics also emphasize the finiteness and the importance of the human mind's dynamic connection with sensible experience.

Aesthetics and tacit knowledge

When I discussed aesthetics as the finiteness of organizational life, I also defined a set of theoretical principles which, as we shall see, underlie the topic treated in this section, namely the relationship between sensible experience and the so-called 'tacit knowledge' of organizational actors. The notion of tacit knowledge was first developed by the Hungarian philosopher Michael Polanyi (1946, 1962, 1966, 1969) to define the knowledge that individuals are able to put into practice, but are unable to say how they do so. The importance of the relationship between aesthetics and tacit knowledge resides in the fact that it highlights the elusiveness of organizational aesthetics. In order to illustrate this relationship I shall relate an incident that occurred while I was conducting research.

I was attending a department meeting of a manufacturing organization as an observer. There were sensitive matters on the agenda and I had been asked not to use a tape-recorder, not to be seen taking notes, and not to make my presence felt. I sat at the end of the second row, next to a large window, almost as if to symbolize my simultaneous presence and non-presence at the meeting. Through the window I could see three workmen stripping the roofing tiles from a small building. Both distracted and attracted by the racket from the building, my attention increasingly focused on the workmen. 'What idiots! Just look how they're working. And if someone slips and hurts himself?' The workers had apparently ignored every safety precaution, although the roof sloped steeply and the building was two storeys high. In truth, there were some ropes, but nobody seemed attached to them. Nor did any of the three workmen attend to the safety of the others instead of working.

The meeting proceeded, and I followed it as closely as I could. But every so often my attention wandered back to events on the roof. I was struck by the movements of one of the workmen. Although plump to the point of obesity, he moved up and down the roof with surprising agility. He was obviously in charge because he was gesticulating orders to the others. If he saw that one of his workmates was doing something wrong or had not understood, he went to help him, hanging onto the rope with one hand to descend the roof, hauling himself up with the rope to ascend, on some occasions even grabbing the chimney stack. Once he had reached the other workman, he took over, almost pushing him out of the way. I also gained the impression that his was the most satisfying, most difficult and most demanding job. All three workers, however, were intent on removing the old tiles from the roofing timbers. They then took the stripped materials and threw them down to the yard below. As the debris hit the ground, it made a variety of thumps and crashes, all equally annoying, and all of which disturbed the meeting.

I was struck by the fact that as the three workmen dismantled the roof, they were in a literal sense removing the ground from beneath their feet. I was also struck by the speed at which they worked, as if they had been overcome by a destructive frenzy. They must have taken particular pleasure from throwing down the largest pieces which made the loudest noise. But I did not feel that they were competing against each other, only that they wanted to get the job done as quickly as possible. What I still could not understand, though, was why they never slipped nor even put a foot wrong. Above all, I was astonished by their recklessness in not moving more carefully or working more slowly: there was the steep slope of the roof; there was the physical effort required to rip free the old roofing materials; there was the dexterity required to ensure that the material thrown away landed in the yard below, and not on a workmate or on the roof itself.

When the meeting had finished and we were going off for lunch, I stopped in the yard to exchange a few words with the roofing workers, who were now sitting among the debris eating their sandwiches. I spoke to the stout man who seemed to be the leader and asked him: 'But how do you do it?' He laughed, the others joked and nudged each other. He then stamped his feet and, as if he was speaking for all of them, told me that the secret lay in feeling the roof through your feet as if they were fastened to it. You have to set your legs firmly, not make a false move with your upper body, and pay close attention to noises, because they tell you what is happening. You should keep your hands as free as possible, because you are not climbing the roof, you are up there to work.

Over the next few days I talked to the workmen on several more occasions while they took their lunch breaks in the yard. The topic was always the same: how they had learnt to move about the roof with such confidence, and what someone going up on a roof for the first time needed to know. 'You mustn't be afraid of heights,' one of them said. 'No,' the leader corrected him, 'it's no use being unafraid of heights if you don't feel the roof with your feet. And that's something you must learn the very first time, because afterwards it's too late.' They laughed. But when they realized that I had not seen the joke, they explained that there were lots of things that were in fact taught to a novice: he was taught to climb a ladder like a bear, looking up and never down, and using at least one hand to grip; he was taught not to bend with the slope of the roof but always to counteract the slope, holding his body as if he were leaning on the air between himself and the roof; he was taught to recognize good handholds to grasp while working, or to grab if he momentarily lost balance, but to beware of false handholds which would not take his weight; he was taught to listen to the noises given off by the roof because they told him how the work was going and whether he was safe; he was taught always to watch his workmates.

This was quite a lot to learn, I admitted, but it was too vague. How can you be safe on a roof merely because you 'feel' that your feet are attached to it, 'hear' noises that you have never heard before, 'smell' previously unknown odours because they act as warnings, 'lean' against the air and not 'feel' afraid. I accepted that the novice was taught to 'see' good handholds, but the body angle to assume when on the roof was unclear, because the base features of the correct posture were left to individual 'feeling', and therefore depended on the direct relationship that the novice established between his body and the roof. The reply was blunt: 'Once you're up there, you feel immediately if it comes naturally to you.' If not, 'you'd better find a different job.' And then, declared the leader, 'you see immediately' if someone knows how to stand on a roof. All the rest comes with time, but not the knowledge of how to stand on a roof, because that is something that 'is taught badly'. It is something that 'must come by itself', without getting it into your head that you cannot do it or that being on the roof only means 'being in danger'. 'There's something beautiful' about working on a rooftop, he said, looking at me closely to see if I understood. 'There's fresh air up there, and you can see everything down below.' These are sensations which those safely working down in the yard 'never feel', he added, while the others nodded in evident satisfaction, although I cannot say whether they did so because they agreed or because their leader had chosen fine words to express the thought.

I shall dwell no further on my conversations with the roofing workers, for these short notes about 'working on a roof' have already brought us to the core of the organizational features examined by the aesthetic approach. Even only preliminary study of the roof-stripping organization brings out several characteristics of its organizational life: for example, knowing how to lean against the air, the beauty of an organizational activity conducted amid personal danger, the feeling of being attached to the roof. Are these not features which shed significant light on that organization?

Of course, they may appear even superfluous when considered in terms of the goals of that organization. Its goals, in fact, did not transpire from the description provided by the three workmen of the characteristics required to work for their organization. It is also true that I did not explicitly ask about organizational goals. I instead asked how they managed to do what they did, and no reference was made to organizational goals in their replies. Obviously, this is not to imply that such reference would not have been made if I had talked to other members of the organization, or if investigations had been conducted in organizational contexts different from the one discussed here. What I merely wish to emphasize is that the subjects of empirical research only rarely talk primarily about goals when asked to describe their organization, unless they are specifically prompted to do so.

This is an important point, and it obviously has a polemical bearing on the goals paradigm discussed in the previous section. It will also be noted that the three workmen made no mention of other organizational themes like the success or the survival of the organization. Did I phrase my questions badly? I do not think so, in view of what the workmen described as the absolutely vital aspect of their organization, a requisite essential indeed for its very survival: namely 'knowing' how to move properly on the roof while stripping it. Hence, if one tries to stand in the shoes of those workmen, imagining oneself working in their place or alongside them – thereby seeking to acquire empathic understanding of the meaningful action of those organizational actors – further light is shed on the crucial importance of that knowledge and its associated skills for that particular organization, for its success, its profits, its survival. In short, one acquires important insights into a good number of issues considered central by the theory of organization. However, to restrict discussion to the organizational as described by the three workmen, I note that it is an organization which:

(a)   requires of its workers that they should be able to stand on rooftops with their arms free to work;

(b)   recruits its workers on the basis of their ability to implement this knowledge of theirs;

(c)   trains its workers in many aspects connected with this skill, but not in its principal aspects: indeed, none of the workmen made mention of any sort of training in 'rooftop work practices';

(d)   is able to assess whether its workers actually possess the skill when it is put to use in ongoing organizational activity;

(e)   assigns groupwork the task of improving the skill, which remains part of the knowledge stock of the individual worker, not of the organization;

(f)   bases its distinctive feature – that of being an organization which strips and lays roofs – on the activation of its workers' sensory faculties in order to apply their skill.

The foregoing discussion of roof work cannot be dismissed as irrelevant to aesthetics on the grounds that it does not concern the organization's publicity, or the elegance of its work-clothes, or the beauty of its machinery and tools, or the elegance of its customer relations, or the refinement of its logo. Aesthetics, in fact, as defined by the aesthetic approach and as discussed in previous chapters and sections, involves the activation of the perceptive faculties and a capacity to make aesthetic evaluation of intentional action in organizations. Under this definition, organizational aesthetics closely interweave with the tacit knowledge of individuals. That is to say, they are bound up with the type of knowledge that members of organizations are able to put into practice but which at the same time evades analytical and detailed description by either these subjects or the researcher.

More than any other, it was the workman's statement that keeping oneself steady on a roof can only 'be taught badly' which clarifies the matter. This phrase expresses the head-worker's awareness that telling the novice what posture to adopt on the roof can only be a minor step, because the real point is that one must 'feel by oneself', 'understand by oneself', in short one must 'know by oneself' what to do. Feeling, understanding and knowing are intermeshed, and they merge into their being-in-use within the organization. Here there is no explicit description that can tell us more than the feeling that one is able to do a particular thing because one's sensory faculties have been activated, and because one is aware of being personally able to accomplish that action. There is nothing mystic, unfathomable, inexplicable or esoteric in this, only the consideration that people are able to know and operate with the distinctive sensory faculties of their own bodies. The *pathos* of the knowledge of the 'sensible', awareness of what one is sensibly and perceptively able to do, and the implementation of one's know-how, therefore underpin the abilities of people who work in organizations and/or on their behalf.

Practice of skills, aesthetics and personal knowledge

The members of organizations use skills that they are unable to account for, in the sense that they are more able to apply them than to describe them. Even when they try to describe them in detail, as in the case of the roofing workers, there is an area that remains obscure and which concerns how these skills are put into practice. However much detail is given, it seems that what counts most in the practice of skills remains 'unsayable'. In order to illustrate the concept of tacit knowledge in the putting-to-use of skills, Michael Polanyi cites examples like keeping afloat when swimming, or maintaining one's balance while cycling, or playing the piano. These are examples of relevance to my topic because they involve the activation of a perceptive faculty, while the person concerned has a body and acts together with some non-human element, such as the air that the swimmer breathes while moving through the water, or the bicycle that the cyclist rides, or the keyboard that the pianist plays. In other words, they are examples which do not neglect the body by extolling the mind, but on the contrary are designed to show how meaningful action comes about by virtue of the physical and sensorial capacities of human bodies, and by virtue of the relationship established between these bodies and non-human elements. They are also examples taken from everyday life, and, as we saw in Chapter 1, the everyday life of organizations is marked by artefacts which, like the chair or the riddle, are only apparently of minor or negligible importance. Moreover, as I have just pointed out regarding the roof-strippers, organizations often benefit from the putting-to-use of skills of this kind.

Polanyi's principal interest was scientific knowledge and its relationship with the freedom of the scientist (1946, 1974). Thomas Kuhn (1962: 44) notes that Polanyi developed 'a very similar theme' to his own argument that 'the existence of a paradigm need not even imply that any full set of rules exists'. Polanyi, in fact, was just as critical of neopositivism as Kuhn, and in waging his polemic against it he joined Feyerabend, Lakatos, Popper and Toulmin. He conducted his attack, as observes Arcangelo Rossi (1988: 9–10), on the level of the personal manner in which scientific knowledge is acquired, validated and developed. Science, writes Polanyi (1962: 49), 'is operated by the skill of the scientist and it is through the exercise of his skill that he shapes his scientific knowledge'. His criticism was therefore directed against logical positivism's claim that it justified the genesis of scientific knowledge on the neutral basis of experience and by employing an impersonal process of induction. In other words, Polanyi strove to create space for personal variability and difference in the formulation of judgements relative to knowledge, in polemic with the neopositivist account that justified these judgements on the basis of neutral experiences and impersonal universal norms. This is evidenced by one of Polanyi's examples, that of keeping one's balance on a bicycle (1962: 49–50).

In his investigation of how physicists, engineers and bicycle constructors address the question of how cyclists keep their balance, Polanyi came to the conclusion that the principle which makes this possible is unknown. Nevertheless, cyclists observe a rule: when they realize that they are about to fall to the right, they turn the handlebars to the right; if they are about to fall to the left, they turn the handlebars to the left. These corrections are constantly made, and they produce a centrifugal force which pushes the cyclist in the opposite direction to the one in which s/he is falling. This centrifugal force counteracts the force of gravity, which would otherwise pull the cyclist to the ground.

These corrective adjustments involve a manoeuvre whereby, if the cyclist is toppling to the right, s/he makes an action which unbalances him/her to the left. S/he reacts to this imbalance by moving the handlebars so that s/he is unbalanced to the right. The cyclist thus makes curves with the bicycle, and his/her balance depends on his/her ability to make appropriate curves. One can calculate that for a given angle of tilt, there is a particular curvature to trace with the bicycle, because this deviation must be inversely proportional to the square of the cyclist's velocity. But are we sure that this tells us how to keep our balance while riding a bicycle?

Polanyi's question is an important one. An analytical description of how to keep one's balance on a bicycle may suffice as instruction to someone wanting to learn how to ride a bicycle. Thus the traditional form of on-the-job learning based on the pupil/teacher relationship will disappear. The figure of the teacher has a close bearing on my examination of the relation between aesthetics and tacit knowledge. It dispels the aura of sacredness that surrounds the relationship between the pupil and a master of rare sensitivity and ability. However, Polanyi's reply is that 'no', this description does not tell us how to ride a bicycle.

> You obviously cannot adjust the curvature of your bicycle's path in proportion to the ratio of your unbalance over the square of your speed; and if you could you would fall off the machine, for there are a number of other factors to be taken into account in practice which are left out in the formulation of this rule. Rules of art can be useful, but they do not determine the practice of an art; they are maxims, which can serve as a guide to an art only if they can be integrated into the practical knowledge of the art. They cannot replace this knowledge. (1962: 50)

If the rules of intellectual and rational knowledge must be integrated into practical knowledge, and if they are unable to determine the practice of a skill, how reliable is the understanding of the meaningful action of organizational subjects which derives from rules of this kind? The practice of skills is the key feature of organizational courses of action, and knowing how to do what must be done is an essential aspect of both an organization's *raison d'être* and its operating principles. The shortcomings of an explicit description of the skills in practice require us to re-examine the heuristic contribution made by the intellectual and rational knowledge of organizational life, of its quotidian construction, of the intentional action that goes on within it. More than outright theories, involved here are rules which depict certain particulars of organizational life but which are unable to describe how such life unfolds, and are useless for its management. Explicit description of the practice of skills can indeed bring out some underlying features, and it can provide some guidelines for action, yet it is unable to tell us what an actor is doing or to teach him/her to do it.

A first reason for this, Polanyi observes (1961a: 458–9), is that it is impossible to provide an adequate explanation of skills in terms of their particulars. It is usually possible to identify a certain number of the particulars of a 'comprehensive entity' – as was done when discussing bicycle riding. But gestalt psychology stresses the limitations of knowledge about a social phenomenon in terms of its particulars, because identification of the particular in some way alters the phenomenon's appearance. Thus limits are set on the specifiability of a meaningful action by two factors.

First, the process of specification, precisely because it is a process which isolates the particular from a comprehensive entity, turns the latter into something else and modifies its original meaning. Polanyi illustrates this phenomenon by referring to colour, pointing out that since 'the colour of any patch of a surface varies with the context in which it is placed, coloured patterns are not specifiable in terms of their isolated particulars' (1961a: 459). It is by being practised, therefore, that the skills of organizational actors acquire their true 'colour'. If they are considered distinctly and separately from their being-in-use, knowledge is acquired of their isolated and modified particulars alone. The practice of skills is the metaphorical locus in which they can be seen. If the three roofers had been down in the yard preparing the materials to fix the roof, instead of being up on the roof and doing their work, I would not have seen their skills in use.

Second, there is always something that is left unspecified, there is always something that evades explicit knowledge. And this something is by no means of secondary importance. Indeed, we are obliged to acknowledge its supremacy in the crucial dimension of the meaningful action constituted by the putting-into-use of skills, by the practice of intentional action. Polanyi calls this something 'tacit knowledge', and sets this form of knowledge in relation to our bodies, given that a 'peculiar combination of skilful doing and knowing is present in the working of our sense organs' (1961a: 461).

Rational knowledge is unable to comprehend what is being done at the moment when it is done, and how it is done. It is only able to grasp a set of particulars of intentional action, but these particulars are denatured by this cognitive act. Knowledge about what is being done is acquired not intellectually but tacitly. It is thus knowledge which is unsayable, which does not respond to objective and universal criteria, and which each of us possesses in an entirely personal way. Yet it is knowledge that we know that we have. However much the three workmen may have been unable to say how they kept their balance on the roof, they knew that they were able to do it, just as a cyclist knows how to ride a bicycle without being able to explain how s/he keeps his/her balance. In order to convey what he means by 'tacit knowledge' in the practice of skills, Polanyi (1962: 55) draws a distinction between two types of awareness: focal awareness and subsidiary awareness:

> When we use a hammer to drive in a nail, we attend to both nail and hammer, *but in a different way*. We *watch* the effect of our strokes on the nail and try to wield the hammer so as to hit the nail most effectively. When we bring down the hammer we do not feel that its handle has struck our palm but that its head has struck the nail.

The two kinds of awareness concern (a) the impact of the hammer on the palm and the fingers, and (b) the driving of the nail into the wood on the other. The sensations in our palm and fingers as they grip the shaft of the hammer enable us to wield it more effectively. We pay close attention to these feelings not because they are the object of our attention, but because they are the instruments of our attention.

They are not watched in themselves; we watch something else while keeping intensely aware of them. I have a *subsidiary awareness* of the feeling in the palm of my hand which is merged into my *focal awareness* of my driving in the nail.

The impact of the hammer on the hand is unspecifiable, just as 'the muscular acts composing a skilful performance are unspecifiable', writes Polanyi (1961a: 462). These are muscular acts, therefore, like those of the three workmen on the roof; acts, that is, of which one is aware in terms of instruments which produce internal stimuli that are then merged together to form perceptions. The body is used as if it were an instrument in all transactions with the surrounding environment, and we have only subsidiary awareness of the elements that we integrate into our bodies; subsidiary awareness of what the body touches, feels and sees externally, of the fact that we assimilate the instruments that we use, like the hammer. Indeed, the better we are able to use a particular instrument, the more distant and suffused are the sensations that it arouses in our bodies. Hence we do not notice the instrument that we are using, just as we do not notice the hands with which we are using it, or the eyes with which we watch where the hammer strikes, or the ears that hear the tapping of the hammer, or our nostrils that smell the metal and the paint. When all this happens, then we may say that we have true mastery of our bodies and of the non-human elements with which we complete it; such mastery that we are aware neither of our bodies nor of non-human elements distinct from us.

The conclusion is that, in general, we do not have focal awareness of the instruments over which we have achieved mastery. We instead experience them in subsidiary manner, as we do our own bodies, and in this sense subsidiary elements are internal to the bodies in which we live. In other words, we come to identify ourselves with everything that we experience in a subsidiary manner (Polanyi, 1969: 183). The instrument returns to our focal attention when it is looked for, prepared or adjusted; that is to say, when it is not-in-use, just as our bodies attract our focal attention when we hurt ourselves, when we are irritated by a noise, when we are tired or when we are hungry, in short in all those situations where we are not in command of our skills. This should make it clear that focal and subsidiary awareness 'are definitely *not two degrees* of attention but *two kinds* of attention given to the *same* particulars' (1961a: 463). It should likewise show that 'recognized processes for acquiring knowledge, whether by experience or deduction, apply only to the knowledge of things we are attending to', and that they do not apply to those that we know 'by relying on our awareness of them in the process of attending to something else' (1961b; reprinted 1974: 123). And it should be equally evident that the act of sensory perception is 'the most fundamental manifestation of intelligence' (1961b; reprinted 1974: 122), and that the process of knowledge-acquisition is both personal and social at the same time. Behaviourism, by establishing an 'I–it' relation in the knowledge of other persons, forgoes social 'I–thou' knowledge. It relies on observations of particulars and tries to relate these particulars to each other by a process of explicit inference. But since most of these particulars in question cannot be observed in themselves at all and, in any case, their relation cannot be explicitly stated, the enterprise ends up by replacing its original subject matter with a grotesque simulacrum of it in which the mind itself is missing. The kind of knowledge which I am vindicating here, and which I call *personal knowledge*, casts aside these absurdities of the current scientific approach and reconciles the process of knowing with the acts of addressing another person. (1961b; reprinted 1974: 127)

Polanyi (1969: 55–7) acknowledges his indebtedness to Dilthey for the thesis that knowledge is acquired by self-identification. He states that his view of science as determined at its every stage by unspecifiable powers of thought and his theory of non-explicit thought can be called both the 'informal logic' of science and of knowledge, with reference to Ryle's analytic philosophy, and the phenomenology of science and knowledge, with reference to the thought of Husserl and Merleau-Ponty. Polanyi's extension of empathic understanding beyond the confines of cultural sciences analysed by Dilthey is, as he himself declares, contrary to these philosophies. In other words, he goes beyond the boundary that, as we saw in Chapter 2, empathy draws between the social and natural sciences. But by doing so he depicts an understanding of intentional action which is of particular significance for the aesthetic approach to the study of organizations. Indeed, in his analysis of matters pertaining to the natural sciences, Polanyi argues in a manner directly contrary to Jean-Pierre Changeux (1994), whose theories were criticized at the beginning of Chapter 2. It will be remembered that Changeux propounds an evolutionary and biological–social view of meaningful action in terms of the 'cerebralization' of feeling, so that aesthetic pleasure, for example, is explained in terms of interactions among different areas of the brain. Polanyi, by contrast, 'improperly' extends the process of empathic knowledge-gathering to the realm of the natural sciences, and immerses himself in the non-human elements that are experienced in subsidiary manner.

Thus Polanyi formulates his opposition to objective, universal and impersonal explanations starting from examination of what happens in the natural sciences, in particular of how skills are transmitted therein:

Scientists and technologists are accordingly always striving to depersonalize knowledge as far as possible by representing it in terms of measured quantities, and wherever we see them still rely on connoisseurship, we may assume that it has not been possible to replace it by measurement. The large part of their time spent by students of chemistry, biology, and medicine in acquiring connoisseurship by attending practical courses therefore shows directly how greatly these sciences rely on personal knowledge that is not specifiable. (1954; reprinted 1974: 88)

Polanyi also discusses these limitations on intellectual knowledge with reference to the endeavour by scientists to explain artistic talent. Various attempts have been made to explain the skill of a painter or a musician, amongst other things in order to reproduce their work mechanically. The results have undoubtedly been interesting: one thinks, for example, of the robot-musicians able to play Beethoven's Ninth Symphony which were constructed at the end of the 1970s. However, Polanyi stresses, this is not enough to yield explicit knowledge of a musician's talent. He cites the decades-long controversy surrounding attempts to explain the 'touch' of a pianist, where analysts have tried to show that it can be learnt from accurate study of its particulars, and to argue that, in terms of knowledge, there is no difference between that of a great pianist and that of a beginner. The controversy is pointless, Polanyi writes (1961a: 460), because it is universal experience that this difference exists. The only conclusion to be drawn is that 'no skill can be acquired by learning its constituent motions separately'. This is even more evident in cases in which the performance of routines, reliance on reversible work processes, and obedience to formal procedures are set aside for what Polanyi (1962: 105–6) calls 'heuristic acts'. These courses of action – which are based on the fact that we can reduce explicit knowledge to its underlying premises whenever we wish to do so – are abandoned to make way for new premises which are not accessible 'by any strict argument from those previously held. It is a decision, originating in our own personal judgement' which modifies both the premises of our judgement and our existence as subjects which simultaneously know and act. Learning to do something new, or assigning a different meaning to something that we already know how to do, 'is a tacit, irreversible, heuristic feat' which profoundly changes our personal knowledge:

> For the capacity for making discoveries is not a kind of gambler's luck. It depends on natural ability, fostered by training and guided by intellectual effort. It is akin to *artistic achievement and like it is unspecifiable*, but far from accidental or arbitrary. (1962: 106; emphasis added)

This view, which relates art and aesthetics to discoveries in general, and to discoveries in the natural sciences in particular, is very different from that propounded by logical positivists like Van Evra (1971) and examined in the previous chapter. It does not claim to explain the scientificity of a discovery on the basis of its beauty. Instead it leaves the discovery phenomenon surrounded by its opacity, complexity and capacity to arouse aesthetic sentiment. It leaves it with its essence constituted by knowledge which evades explicit description or is inevitably denatured by such description. A scientific theory, writes Polanyi (1962: 133), may direct attention to its beauty, it may rely on its beauty to assert its heuristic capacity, it may even resemble mystic contemplation – 'a kinship shown historically in the Pythagorean origins of theoretical science' – it may display a passion which evokes particular forms of emotion. It does so, however, not because these aspects demonstrate its scientific validity, but because it, too, as a scientific theory seeking to teach 'its own kinds of formal excellence', is one of the 'constituents of culture' and should accordingly be treated in the same way as art, law, morality or religion. It should always be borne in mind, Polanyi continues (1962: 135), that only a very small proportion 'of all knowable facts are of interest to scientists'. We should always remember that scientific passion also guides the scientist in his/her definition of what is of particular interest and of what instead is not. This decision is based on appreciation that 'depends ultimately on a sense of intellectual beauty', because:

> Scientific research, in short, is an art; it is the art of making certain kinds of discoveries. The scientific profession as a whole has the function of cultivating that art by transmitting and developing the tradition of its practice. The value which we attribute to science – whether its progress be considered good, bad, or indifferent from a chosen point of view – does not matter here. Whatever that value may be it still remains true that the tradition of science as an art can be handed on only by those practicing the art. (1945; reprinted 1974: 23)

This is also apparent if we examine the reverse phenomenon to the heuristic act: namely the act of remaining within the ambit of a theoretical paradigm or a tradition of study rather than seeking to change it. A case in point is the 'internal enjoyment of astronomy which makes the astronomer interested in the stars' (1962: 195) or the joy aroused by adhering to a given theory, whether it be scientific or artistic, whether the framework of a mathematical discovery or that of a symphony. The 'joy of grasping mathematics' (1962: 321), for example, leads to an ever more profound understanding of mathematics itself, and to personal preoccupation with its problems. This highlights both the fact that the 'personal participation of the knower in the knowledge he believes himself to possess takes place within a flow of passion' and the decisive importance of sensing the beauty inherent in the knowledge that one possesses. The aesthetic sentiment has nothing to do with the inner logical coherence of a theory, nor with its capacity to depict objective reality. It instead functions 'as a guide to discovery and as a mark of truth' (1962: 300) for scientific inquiry.

These observations pose significant questions for the analysis and management of organizational life. On the basis of what scientific criteria can we objectively and universally quantify the pianist's sublime touch, the surgeon's perfect stroke with the scalpel, the radiologist's skilful adjustment of the dial, the mechanic's accurate turn of the spanner, the teacher's impassioned speech? The sense of organization based on universally valid rational principles is radically undermined by the awareness that these rules are only guidelines, or only maxims. This prompts the following three general considerations concerning the relationship between aesthetics, tacit knowledge and the practice of skills in organizations.

First, if the practice of skills in organizations evades the organization's explicit knowledge, and if aesthetic understanding and tacit knowledge are fused together in such practice, this strengthens the definition that I have given to aesthetics in organizational life, which should be regarded *imprimis* as the personal patrimony of individuals and not of the organization.

Second, skills are ephemeral. Or if preferred, they are not immortal. They are negotiated both internally to organizations and in the relations between organizations and the rest of society, so that one witnesses the appearance of certain skills, like the electronic impagination of books or newspapers, and the simultaneous disappearance of others, like manual typesetting. The negotiation of the practice of skills means that on some occasions they are sought after, on others they are even celebrated, but on others they are marginalized or eliminated. But – and this is the point – it is absolutely not the case that when they are eliminated, skills come to be re-created or in some way made to reappear. No memory remains of them, because no adequately detailed description of them is possible, and because their handing-down from master to apprentice has ceased. 'There are hundreds of examples of this to which the process of mechanization is continuously adding new ones,' writes Polanyi (1962: 53), and generally the loss is 'irretrievable. It is pathetic to watch the endless efforts – equipped with microscopy and chemistry, with mathematics and electronics – to reproduce a single violin of the kind the half-literate Stradivarius turned out as a matter of routine more than 200 years ago.'

The third consideration turns on whether the practice of skills is an organizational artefact – whether, that is, we can employ in this case a concept whose usefulness emerged when analysing aesthetics with reference to the riddle-based lesson and the chair in Chapter 1. By 'organizational artefact' is meant any characteristic of an organization which is able to 'tell' us something about that organization. If we reconsider what has been said so far about skills in organizations, we find that an organization:

(a)   does not know how skills are put to use because its understanding of them is based solely on explicit, intellectual and rational description;
(b)   does not possess knowledge about the skills practised within it or on its behalf, and therefore cannot render it into some form of organizational knowledge to be made available to its members or traded with other organizations;
(c)   negotiates the existence and duration of the skills that arise from aesthetic understanding and tacit knowledge, thereby gaining control over them, although it is still unable to master them.

Now, is the practice of skills an organizational artefact in the sense that it 'tells' us something about an organization? Indeed it is. If we observe skills as and when they are used by individuals in organizations, we note that although they remain the patrimony of the individual, they 'tell' us something about those organizations. The ability to work on a roof, for example, was personally possessed by those particular workmen, but it told us something important about their roofing organization because, as said earlier, it highlighted a feature of its excellence. That the practice of skills is an organizational artefact is made plain by linguistic expressions. If we use for a moment a manner of writing widespread in the organizational literature – and precisely the style which I have already criticized for its improper extension of people's goals to an organization and which I shall criticize again for its improper extension of aesthetic understanding from people to organization – we may write that not only did the three workmen know how to keep themselves 'fixed' to the roof but 'That organization is able to work on roofs as if it were fixed to them'. Hence, as well as the people concerned, intellectual abstraction enables us to 'see' the organization itself in action. It is a linguistic artefact which should easily evoke other widely used expressions such as 'That department is dreadful at doing its job' or 'That firm is incapable of doing its work'. This is a process whereby the characteristics of individuals are reified into characteristics of organizations; and thus reified, too, is the practice of skills. Indeed, it is also by means of this process that the character of the organizational artefact is celebrated. To continue the train of argument, one notes that when praising the gifts of a surgeon one may also think that 'He or she won't be staying much longer with this clinic', or in complimenting the prowess of a skilled worker one may say 'You're wasted here.' Here, however, there emerges an aspect which is the opposite of the one discussed above, because the putting-to-use of skills by an individual is contrasted with the organization in which or for which s/he does so. Thus, instead of grasping organizational excellence through the prowess of the individual, the emphasis is placed on the organization's limited ability to negotiate command over such prowess. In proof of this, consider how difficult it is to argue that an organization possesses skills which its members do not; one can hardly say 'That firm is excellent, given that its workers are all bumbling incompetents', only perhaps that 'It would be a good organization if its employees were a bit more competent.'

To conclude, the practice of skills foregrounds people in the study of organization. By doing so it is a highly particular instrument with which to explore and understand the pragmatic dynamics of organizations (Strati, 1985: 87). The practising of skills highlights that they constitute a link between knowledge of the sensible and construction of organizational life, between feelings and the production of organizational reality, between tacit knowledge and the mastering of crucial elements of the organization. But if the practice of skills gives a distinctive identity to each individual, it extends characteristics peculiar to the individual to the organization, to the point that the linguistic artefacts constructed in this regard celebrate the reification in the organization of that practice of skills. In this sense, as they are put-into-use in the organization, aesthetic understanding as well as tacit knowledge and one's personal stock of knowledge are also 'organizational artefacts' in that they 'tell' us something about that organization. They are not created or produced by organizations, because the activation of the sensory faculties, like the putting-into-practice of tacit knowledge, falls outside the organizational domain and remain characteristic of the person, although its existence is negotiated and its refinement is either facilitated or obstructed. It is as if there were a constant one-way flow from persons to the organization; a flow which emphasizes the impossibility of localizing and circumscribing aesthetics in some particular aspect of organizational life, and which evidences the elusiveness of organizational aesthetics.

Aesthetics as a dialogue for non-causal knowledge

As I have repeatedly stressed, aesthetics does not only pertain to the organization that is beautiful, to the activity that fascinates, to the work that pleases, to the service provided with elegance, to the brilliant outcome of organizational action. Aesthetics also concerns the smelling of unpleasant odours in the workplace, and those given off by colleagues, or the lack of concentration due to the noise made by those who share organizational spaces with us. That is to say, it also pertains to the unpleasant occurrences of everyday life in organizations, to distasteful undercurrents, to annoying details – in short, to the sensory perceptions that we would prefer not to receive, or be subjected to, even less those to which we must give organizational or more general meaning. Ugliness, unpleasantness or tragedy are as much part of the aesthetic knowledge of organizations as beauty, pleasure or enjoyment, and they similarly highlight the physical and sensory nature of work and of the organizational contexts in which it is carried out.

Declaring that an organization is beautiful or ugly, that the work performed within it is beautiful or otherwise, that its members are beautiful or otherwise, is to pass judgement on the organizational life constructed and reconstructed from day to day. This is an aesthetic judgement. It is worth emphasizing the importance of this type of judgement with regard to the social and collective construction of organizational life by briefly resuming the discussion on the chair conducted in Chapter 1. The aesthetics of this artefact are negotiated by organizational actors – from those who design and make it to those who commission it and use it in their organizations. Negotiation based on aesthetic judgements, therefore, yields a quantity of organizational artefacts which differ in terms of shape, material and use.

The process of social construction of these organizational artefacts displays the simultaneous presence in an organization of a plurality of organizational aesthetics which preclude the assertion of one single organizational aesthetic, namely the one desired by the dominant power group in the organization. The aesthetic judgements of those who own, direct, or at any rate claim the right to use organizational resources to maintain and increase their power – for example, the heads of departments or divisions, or those who affirm a male view of organization – are negotiated, translated, overturned or negated by the other persons involved in that particular course of organizational life. In other words, whether or not a particular chair is beautiful is not given once and for all, since its beauty is not objective. Nor is it sanctioned by some explicit organizational norm, because its beauty cannot be imposed by those who formally hold positions of command in the organization. The aesthetic judgement 'Look how beautiful that chair is' passed by the chairperson of the organization is immediately gainsaid by the statements 'I wouldn't know', 'I don't think so', or 'I really don't like it at all'. If the chair is then purchased by the organization, this does not entail any change in sceptical or negative judgements in its regard, nor the cessation of the disputes that may arise between 'Now are you convinced how beautiful it is?' and 'Now do you realize how ugly it is?!' To sum up:

1 However little power is available to them in their relations with others, all participants in organizational life are able to pass aesthetic judgement, and they are all equally entitled to make aesthetic evaluations.
2 Aesthetic judgement does not exert its influence on organizational life by virtue of its objective truth, but by virtue of the negotiative dynamics conducted so that it takes one form rather than another, so that the organization's products respond to some canons rather than others; in short, so that some aesthetics affirm themselves as 'dominant' with respect to a given organizational artefact, while others are marginalized or even eliminated.

I have so far stressed the importance of aesthetic judgement in organizational life. I have pointed out that organizational aesthetics is constantly negotiated in a process whose outcome is by no means certain, given the different sensibilities of the actors belonging to organizations. We must now examine what is meant by 'aesthetic judgement' and how the concept helps to characterize organizational aesthetics as an elusive phenomenon. The fact that people express aesthetic judgements concerning the organization in which they work raises a number of problems for the organization scholar.

For example, the foreman of the roofing workers declared that his work aroused a sense of beauty which could only be felt by being 'up there'. 'There's fresh air up there' and 'you can see everything down below', he said, leaving it to me to intuit what he meant. For my part, I realized that there was pleasure to be had from working on the roof, from getting the job done, from dropping the debris with a crash, from being 'up there'. And when the foreman gave me his aesthetic judgement on working for that organization and in that setting, the other two workers apparently agreed with him; they seemed satisfied with their work and indeed proud of it. I have already pointed out the ambiguity of the situation, in the sense it was not clear to me whether the workers' evident pleasure was due to the fact that the foreman's aesthetic judgement was shared by the group, whether it was a judgement common to all roofing firms, or whether the judgement itself was immaterial and what mattered was purely the act of saying something 'highbrow', and which gave dignity to their work, to someone who was not only an outsider but apparently well educated. There was also ambiguity in my observation that 'they must get some pleasure from what they are doing', because this was an immediate and one-off impression. Equivocal, too, were the foreman's aesthetic judgements that 'There's fresh air up there' and 'you can see everything down below', taken both jointly and separately. All these features signal the presence of at least two sources of imprecision in aesthetic judgements:

1 *The ambiguity inherent to the formulation of the aesthetic judgement.* Both in my aesthetic judgement and that of the foreman, it was clear

what was being referred to, and it was also clear that it was the same object, namely working on the roof. But it was not clear what the judgement meant. The ambiguity of the aesthetic judgement resides in the act of signifying with what one is saying; because what is said does not, obviously, only denote something, which in this case was the pleasure taken by the workers from working on the roof, or from the fresh air 'up there', or from seeing everything 'down below'. Of course, denoting, witnessing or attesting these things had their own importance inasmuch as the various aspects of working on the roof were noted rather than being taken for granted. The ambiguity consists in expressing a judgement, in the suspension created, in the evocative process that it is intended to trigger, creating the implicature that something else is being referred to.

2   *The ambiguity relative to participation in a judgement.* Ambiguous in this case was the referent of the two workers when they expressed their approval of what the foreman told me, and therefore what was being endorsed by their non-verbal language.

These two sources of ambiguity highlight the elusiveness of organizational aesthetics. Statements of the type:

> Working in that organization is ugly. Buildings are ugly, people are ugly, everything's ugly, and we grow more and more ugly as the days pass,

crop up during empirical research in organizations. And they are sentiments sometimes endorsed by other members of the organization, but with nods of the head rather than words. What are the implications of these qualitative data from in-the-field research for the aesthetic understanding of organizations? In order to explore this definitional and methodological problem, I shall draw on Valeriano Bozal's discussion (1996: 31–4) of the aesthetic judgement 'grandiose', which he analyses as regards mountains but which I shall relate to organizations.

Five senses plus one

The issue addressed by Bozal, if transposed to the context of the organization, can be stated as follows: suppose that it is said that a specific organizational action 'is' or 'has been grandiose'. What is being stated about this act as a part of organizational life? The organizational action concerned may be a strategic choice, like the planning of a new department or its organizational structuring. It may also be an action on a more modest scale, like repairing a product flaw, starting up a machine which has inexplicably broken down, correctly re-running a computer program after the computer has crashed. It may be an official ceremony like the opening of a new plant, the official speech made at a meeting, or an act of defiance by someone at the meeting hostile to its symbolism. One might be prompted to call these actions 'grandiose', 'grand', 'magnificent'.

Bozal observes that aesthetic judgements are immediate, but they claim to be universally true. The knowing subject perceives the grandiosity of the act of organizational planning or of the organizational course of action that solved the 'glitch' in the computer program. S/he states that it 'is' or 'has been' in order to emphasize its universal truth. Even if s/he says 'It seems to me that . . .', s/he is seeking confirmation or denial of his/her statement through the processes of organizational negotiation that I have already discussed. Appreciation, however, is the outcome of a perception, not of a train of argument whose validity can be assessed. Consequently, to say 'That organizational project is grandiose' does not indicate the grounds for making the judgement, as instead happens when it is claimed that 'It's a really well-designed organizational project'.

The Latin origin of the term 'judgement' (*judicium*) locates aesthetic judgement among the essential capabilities of the mind, but does not make it amenable to logical proof. In fact, aesthetic judgement lacks a principle which guides its application, and it must be exercised case by case. It is therefore something that cannot be learnt, observes Hans-Georg Gadamer (1960; It. trans. 1990: 55), because it lacks proof based on concepts that guide the application of valid rules case by case. Consequently, owing to the fact that the judgemental faculty (*Urteilskraft*) is effected with regard to the particular, in the aesthetic and *a fortiori* moral sphere, it does not obey reason.

On the other hand, nor is aesthetic judgement the arbitrary projection of the organizational actor's subjectivity onto events and actions. Rather, it is the knowing subject's appreciation of the quality of organizational action. This aspect of the aesthetic understanding was stressed when I discussed Dilthey's, Lipps's and Husserl's notion of empathic knowledge, Polanyi's notion of subsidiary awareness, Pareyson's of the endless process of interpreting, and Derrida's of the irreducibility of difference.

I must clarify what is meant by the statement that aesthetic judgement is not the arbitrary projection of the knowing subject's subjectivity. Imagine that you are standing on the highest balcony of a large organization. Below you lie the workshops, the office building, the goods yard, the car park, the service vehicles, the people on the pathways, the colour of the buildings, the lights reflected by them, the smoke from the chimneys. And then imagine that you are in the presence of something that warrants the description 'grandiose'. This specific aesthetic judgement demonstrates the existence of a relation between this organizational and the knowing subject who expresses the judgement. But what is this relation?

It is certainly not a scientific one. 'Grandiose' does not express the surface area covered by the organization, or the volume of its buildings, or the size of its machinery. Grandiosity, therefore, is not a measurement, nor does it correspond to some method of measurement, although it is applied to a large organization. The fact that 'grandiose' is used to indicate that the organization is large is a first step towards saying something about the organization.

Although the evaluation expressed by the adjective 'large' is not a measurement, it denotes a property which, though imprecise, inheres in the organization and therefore relates to one of the terms in the relation between organization and knowing subject. But 'grandiose' does not mean 'large' exactly, and it is an aesthetic not a factual judgement. This type of judgement reveals not a property of the organization, but a property of what the organization represents to the knowing subject. That is to say, it reveals how the latter represents the organization to him/herself.

We may now summarize the discussion of the aesthetic judgement on the organization when viewed from the balcony:

1   The grandiosity of the organization is not a property of the organization independently of the specific context created by its being-in-relation to the knowing subject. This judgement demonstrates the relation between organization and a subject who states that it is 'grandiose' in this case but who might in others declare that 'It's ugly' or 'There's something beautiful' about working on the roof.

2   This judgement arises from the sensations provoked by what can be seen from the balcony, but also from other reactions which have nothing to do with reason.

3   This is an assertion which is at once untrue and true: it certainly does not have the truth value of the statement that the organization is large, which can be proved by measuring the surface area or the height of the buildings. And yet it is not entirely untrue, because it states something truthful about the organization and about the experience of the knowing subject, and about the relation between them. Hence, the simultaneous truth and untruth of the statement makes it ambiguous, indefinite and imprecise, but at the same time neither false nor arbitrary.

4   It is asserted by the knowing subject as if it were a demonstrable truth.

This places us in a dilemma in many respects similar to the antithesis between empathic knowledge and rational explanation of the meaningful action of organizational actors discussed in Chapter 2. The 'grandiosity' of the organization seen from the balcony cannot be explained, nor can it be argued; and it can be neither taught nor learnt. 'Grandiose' is instead a judgement expressed deliberately in those specific circumstances and at that specific moment, when the intention was to grasp the nature of the organization from the bird's-eye-view of the balcony. The judgement tells us how the knowing subject represents the organization to him/herself; it does not tell us what the organization actually 'is'. As *judicium* it is a form of knowledge very distinct from intellectual knowledge. In this case the knower is the sensible-individual, and his/her faculty of judgement is a faculty analogous to those which govern the sensory perceptions of the five senses.

Gadamer (1960; It. trans. 1990: 54–6) points out that eighteenth-century German philosophy did not place the judgemental faculty among the higher capabilities of the mind, but located it among the inferior faculties. Under this definition, the act of judgement is not applied to a concept that exists previously to the thing known. The latter is instead grasped in and of itself, and the confluence of the multiple into its internal unity and coherence is revealed. The foreman's 'There's something beautiful' about working on a rooftop, or the statement 'We grow more and more ugly as the days pass', are judgements which reveal an inner unity to organizational life, which is judged in its particular, individual and, in Kantian terms, 'immanent' being.

What, therefore, does the aesthetic judgement concern? For both Baumgarten and Kant, continues Gadamer, the aesthetic judgement applies to the perfection or imperfection of the particular thing. As sensible judgement (*judicium sensitivum*) it does not yield concepts but assesses the perfection or imperfection of the thing perceived and has the nature of sentiment or taste: it is the *gustus* or the taste judgement.

As regards the sensible judgement, Alexander Gottlieb Baumgarten, who coined the term 'aesthetics', argued in several works – *Meditationes philosophicae de nonnullis ad poema pertinentibus* (1735), *Metaphysica* (1739) and *Aesthetica* (1750–8) – that it involved the faculty of judging feelings (*sensorum*), phantasms (*phantasmatum*), fictions (*fictionum*) and other things which the intellectual judgement is unable to comprehend.

Let us take the beauty as it exists, writes Baumgarten (1750–8: 7), and let us try to embrace and understand it as a whole or the beautiful alone, or the ugliness alone. Let us do so not like the observer of refined taste (*saporis eruditi spectator*), that is, through intuition, when he is able, but through intellectual knowledge. What should we do? We should try to transform beauty or ugliness into a series of distinctions which differ by virtue of their specific character and extent. We should, that is to say, seek to know beauty or ugliness on the basis of distinct, complete and adequate representations, divided numerically, and which are as profound as possible. But beauty or ugliness are confused phenomena, and it is thus that they affect our sensory perception, so that it is on the judgement of the senses that we must rely.

The judgement of the senses (*iudicium sensuum*) is the confused judgement of the perfection of sensations (*de perfectione sensorum*) which is ascribed to the sense organ impressed by the sensation (1735; It. trans. 1985: 76–8). Hence, the negative judgement of the auditory organs is that provoked by a confused representation which generates displeasure, and the greater the displeasure to the hearing, the less auditory attention the hearer will pay, with the consequence that very few or no representations will be communicated. The negative judgement of the hearing therefore gives rise to aesthetic insensitivity in the listener, while the opposite happens when confused representations arouse the positive judgement of the hearing; and the more they provoke pleasure, the greater will be the attention aroused by the representations in the listener. It is therefore the ability to arouse pleasure to the hearing that constitutes poetry (*summam voluptatem auribus creare poeticum*).

By 'aesthetics', therefore, Baumgarten means whatever affects our senses and belongs to our sensory experience, which is non-mental. Every non-distinct representation is sensory, and sensory knowledge is the complex of representations which avoid distinction. The confused representations that determine the aesthetic judgement constitute knowledge that is wholly different from knowledge created by drawing analytical distinctions among representations so that they can be divided into the species and measures that the intellectual judgement needs. Baumgarten's definition of aesthetics – which is one of the foundations of the aesthetic approach to organizations – emphasizes the close connection between aesthetics and the tacit knowledge of subjects in organizations that was discussed in the previous section. One notes close similarities between Baumgarten's distinction between sensory knowledge and rational knowledge and Polanyi's distinction between tacit knowledge and explicit description. By virtue of the sensitivity of their sense organs, humans have knowledge of the world which is analogous to that furnished by the reason and which is symmetrical to intellectual knowledge: this is the challenge that Baumgarten raises with his philosophical aesthetics.

There is no philosopher, writes Baumgarten (1735; It. trans. 1985: 28), who is not to some extent beset by confused knowledge. Hence it follows that there is no scientific and intellectual knowledge which does not reveal a nexus with sensory knowledge. However, the confused judgement should not be extended beyond the ambit of the sensations; nor should aesthetic knowledge be made ancillary to the knowledge of the intellect. Aesthetics is part of philosophy as lower-order gnoseology (*gnoseologia inferior*), Baumgarten states (1750–8: 1). It acknowledges the primacy of intellectual knowledge, but it does not allow itself to be subjugated by it. This is because aesthetics does not yield an understanding of the sensible world which the reason and intellect can process, refine and improve. The sensible representations are not knowable, in fact, by means of the analytical procedure of rational distinction on which the intellect is based; they are knowable through the lower-order gnoseology of aesthetics which works through the perceptive faculties and the sensible judgement. Intellectual knowledge and sensible knowledge, therefore, are entirely different matters, and aesthetics *qua* the science of sensible knowledge (*scientia cognitionis sensitivae*) should be viewed as both the art of beautiful thought (*ars pulcre cogitandi*) and the art of the analogy of reason (*ars analogi rationis*), whose goal is the perfection of sensible knowledge as such (*aesthetices finis est perfectio cognitionis sensitivae, qua talis*).

Baumgarten thus attributes especial importance to the sensibility of aesthetic knowledge. Kant, by contrast, focuses on its subjectivity. He adopts a perspective which differs from the phenomenological, existentialist, hermeneutic and deconstructivist account which underpins the aesthetic approach to organizations. But Kant, too, emphasizes the elusiveness of organizational aesthetics. In *Kritik der Urteilskraft* (1790), he examines the relationship between scientific knowledge and moral judgement, and does so on the basis of the concept of reflective judgement. This is manifest in two distinct transcendental forms, that of the aesthetic judgement, which expresses our feelings of pleasure or displeasure aroused by nature, and that of the teleological judgement, which is the faculty to gauge the final purposes of nature on the basis of reason.

Assigned to the aesthetic judgement is 'task of deciding the conformity of this product (in its form) to our cognitive faculties as a question of taste (a matter which the aesthetic judgement decides, not by any harmony with concepts, but by feeling)' (1790; Eng. trans. 1952: 35). When we set out to decide whether something is beautiful or not, we do not refer to its understanding on the basis of a cognitive and logical judgement; instead, we use our imagination. 'I must present the object immediately to my feeling of pleasure or displeasure,' observes Kant (1790; Eng. trans. 1952: 35), so that the feeling of pleasure in this aesthetic judgement is 'dependent doubtless on an empirical representation, and cannot be united *a priori* to any concept (one cannot determine *a priori* what object will be in accordance with taste or not – one must find out the object that is so)' (1790; Eng. trans. 1952: 32).

In this way, the representation is related to 'the Subject and its feeling of pleasure or displeasure' (1790; Eng. trans. 1952: 41), and it is a subjective representation which bears no relation to the object, but which manifests a sentiment of the subject and the manner in which its subjective sensibility is affected by the representation. If the green colour of an object is part of its perception through the sensory faculties, and constitutes a sensation which we may consider objective, writes Kant (1790; Eng. trans. 1952: 45–9), its agreeableness is part of a sensation that should be considered subjective, in that it is a sensation which involves not cognition of the object but the feeling through which the green colour of that object is seen. The agreeable, the beautiful and the good stand in different relations with the faculty of feeling pleasure or displeasure: the first is what gratifies the human person; the second is what pleases him/her; the third is what is esteemed by being approved.

> Of all these three kinds of delight, that of taste in the beautiful may be said to be the one and only disinterested and *free* delight. (1790; Eng. trans. 1952: 49)

The aesthetic judgement, that is to say, is the judgement which is disinterested, which expresses purposiveness without purpose. And it is precisely in the interplay of purposiveness without purpose that David White (1996: 205–6) discerns the most significant elements with which to grasp the elusiveness of organizational aesthetics. Consider, for example, suggests White, the case in which the purpose of an organization is clearly established, and that it consists in producing a beautiful car: can this question the validity of Kant's account of the knowledge of beauty, given that beauty is already posited as the purpose of the object? No, because, as we have just seen, Kant treats sensible knowledge in a highly complex manner where representations stand in diversified relations with the faculty of feeling pleasure and displeasure. The car can be not only beautiful but also useful, for example, or safe and economical, so that the fact that the beauty of the car depends on this being its declared purpose belongs within a system of more complex relations. Moreover, the connection between the beauty of the car and its purpose should be 'purely felt and impossible to translate into discourse' because, White points out (1996: 206), 'an appropriate Kantian formulation would be to appeal to the automobile's purposiveness'. In other words, White continues, the car is beautiful because this purpose is achieved through 'an interplay of elements that realizes this purpose by the appearance of the automobile and the manner in which this appearance is felt by the observer'. And it is here that Kant's interplay of purposiveness and purpose demonstrates to us the elusiveness of aesthetics in organizations. As White observes:

> It is true that Kant's position does imply an irreducible and essential element of incompleteness in the articulation of this experience. In a sense, then, the manager must *cultivate* this aura of elusiveness when attempting to evoke the beauty in the organization's product. (1996: 206)

In other words, beauty cannot be established a priori; nor can it be analytically divided into measures and distinctions which are then dutifully summed; nor can it be sharply separated from organizational processes and dynamics. It is not possible to define how much of the beauty of a car is due to the labour of one worker rather than another. This would require that intellectual understanding which impedes knowledge of the beauty of the car, because such knowledge stems from a confused feeling that someone looking at the car can only judge aesthetically, even though s/he has contributed his/her labour to creating its beauty. This is the position of Bozal and Baumgarten, and also of Kant, although, as already mentioned, Kantian aesthetics cannot act as a theoretical referent for the aesthetic understanding of organizations, unlike phenomenological and hermeneutic aesthetics.

A challenge against the 'moralization' of organizational life

In discussing the relationship between aesthetics and tacit knowledge in the practice of organizational life, I have sought to restore to organizations something that has been deprived of them, judging from the bulk of the organizational literature. I restored to them the factuality and the physicality of everyday situations and actions: the air that we breathe, the air that shifts with people's movements; the air that announces that something is about to happen; or the noises that interfere with the sounds we want to hear, the noises that accompany and signal people's movements, the noises made by the non-human objects used in organizations; or again, people's faces, the smiling and cheerful ones, the sullen ones, those that bear the marks of fatigue, of tension, or of excessively heavy make-up.

I have examined meaningful action as embodied in its subjects, and I have stressed that an organizational actor is a hybrid entity made up of non-human elements inseparable from the human person and from his/her corporeality. I have therefore emphasized those characteristics of organizations which, in many cases, are not all beautiful or attractive for the people that work in them, but are instead felt to be ugly, tragic, grotesque or in execrable taste.

In fact, it is not the decorations and embellishments of organizational life that constitute the privileged domain of the aesthetic approach to organizations, but those that tie – closely but not equally intelligibly – people to organizations and their work within them. Shifting the focus of attention to an elusive research 'object' excludes the theoretical assumption that there are places, physical or imaginary, set aside for aesthetics in organizations. Thus, in contrast with the 'museification' of art in contemporary societies, organizational aesthetics is not separate from the daily lives of people in organizations. In other words, organizational aesthetics is not synonymous with the design office responsible for the artefacts produced by an organization, nor with the press office responsible for publicizing its products. Instead, it relates to everything realized by the design or press office, and also by, for example, the firm subcontracted to clean the organization's premises.

This definition of the aesthetics of organization life rests on a set of theoretical assumptions that we have already seen – namely, the *pathos* of the sensible, the finiteness of organizational knowledge, the irreducibility of difference in aesthetic understanding, the latter's link with tacit knowledge, the indefiniteness of the aesthetic judgement. These various basic principles of the aesthetic understanding highlight two features: (a) the influence of aesthetics in the methodological discussions of the social sciences; (b) the overinterpretations and oversimplifications produced by the rational descriptions of organizational action which still dominate a large part of organization research and theory. On several occasions in this book, but especially in the second chapter when I discussed the theoretical and methodological question of empathic understanding, I have emphasized that strongly rationalistic interpretations underestimate or exclude some of the most important motivations for the intentional action of organizational actors.

My intention has been to debunk the knowledge-gathering process predominant in organization theory, which seeks to 'cleanse the *pathos* from the sensible' in the intentional action of people in organizations. Minimizing or excluding knowledge of the 'sensible' has purged organizational life of the *eros*, the sensuousness, the pleasure, the enchantment of (and also the irreducible differences among) the subjects who collectively construct the quotidian reality of organizations. Organization theory and management studies have thus made a major contribution to the 'moralization' of the intentional action of organizational actors. In organizations, action can be regarded 'meaningful' only if it corresponds to the organization's goals, to organizational rationality, and to the norms of organizational ethics.

The main thrust of my argument has been the contention that, instead, people possess personal knowledge about organizational life constituted by tacit knowledge and *pathos* of the sensible. They acquire this knowledge by activating the perceptive faculties and formulating of aesthetic judgements, and by deploying non-mental and non-intellectual abilities and knowledge which are not empirically describable. Accordingly, the intention of this chapter, and of its discussion of the aesthetic approach to organizations, has been to emphasize the following:

1   Everyone who belongs to an organization, even if temporarily, possesses aesthetic knowledge about it and about the work performed within it or on its behalf. Indeed, all knowing subjects without exception are able to activate their perceptive faculties and formulate aesthetic judgements; there are no barriers raised by education or by knowledge of art and its history.

2   This is not to imply that aesthetics should be confused with the equality of subjects in an organization, so that nobody is excluded from aesthetic knowledge. Not everybody is able to work on a roof, not everybody is able to appreciate the beauty of being 'up there'. Aesthetics highlights the ineradicable differences among abilities to know the 'sensible' that distinguish among individuals. These differences in turn constitute power resources in organizational life, and even more so in settings like that of working on the roof, where distinctive value is attributed to the activation of the sensory faculties.

3   One should not conclude, therefore, that aesthetic understanding in organizations is an innate, immediate and instinctive form of knowledge; on the contrary, it is 'refined' or 'cultivated'. The worker who can move agilely across the roof has cultivated his knowledge of the 'sensible'; he has refined it and made it more subtle and sophisticated. He has also defined the risk and security present in that organization, because the safer his work, the more he has used his capacity to know the 'sensible' in order to master his work environment. Aesthetic understanding in organizations is also the ability to 'read' the aesthetic understanding of others, as when a newcomer's ability to work on the roof was evaluated.

4   Learning how to work and behave in an organization is based on the putting-to-use of the sensory faculties. This means that organizational actors deem newcomers able to acquire aesthetic knowledge, and they employ this form of knowledge to train them and to develop their skills. But it also means that subjects interact in organizations by virtue of their ability to know the intentional action of others by empathetic and not solely rational means; they seek to 'put themselves in the shoes' of newcomers aesthetically, and not purely on the cognitive or emotional plane.

5   The constantly ongoing process of negotiation in everyday organizational life often involves assertions that are not objective, universal and

verifiable, but are instead utterly personal, ones which convey something otherwise unsayable. This 'something' is represented by their aesthetic judgements, which have little to do with the explicit description of organizational phenomena.

This chapter has discussed the theoretical principles that give greater sophistication to the conceptual apparatus of the aesthetic understanding of organizations, and it has concentrated in particular on the elusiveness of organizational aesthetics. It has examined what it means to formulate an aesthetic judgement, the relationship between the subject who knows an organization aesthetically and the aesthetic dimension of the organization itself, and the relationship between the aesthetics and tacit knowledge of organizational actors, exploring their polemical implications for dominant theories of organization, with their insistence on intellectual knowledge and the rational explanation of meaningful action in organizations.

The intention has been to illustrate the particular definition of aesthetics which informs the aesthetic approach to organizations; a definition formulated in terms of a conception of organizational aesthetics as an elusive phenomenon comprehensible in the light of its everyday experiencing by organizational actors. This elusiveness was emphasized in the first two chapters, when I explored the dynamics whereby the dominant aesthetics of organizational artefacts are socially and collectively constructed, and investigated the motives for meaningful action by organizational actors. However, it is a conception which, when set out in previous works of mine (1992, 1996a), aroused the criticisms of Brian Rusted (1999) and the cautions of James Kuhn (1996).

Rusted criticizes the aesthetic approach because elusiveness and connoisseurship render aesthetics in organizations into something that is mysterious, hard to grasp or difficult to pin down. The cautions instead concern the fact that, as Kuhn (1996: 222–3) points out, emphasis on organizational aesthetics as 'a fleeting phenomenon', although persuasive, may induce one to overlook the stability of organizational life and neglect the fact that

[i]n dealing with their own and others' wisdom and follies, managers as well as governors – those in authority – must help their followers, adherents and backers *sustain* a point of view, *despite the flux of events*, bolster an image of who they are, and maintain a vision of what their world (that complex network of interrelations) is and what it can become.

In other words, Kuhn points out that if overemphasis is placed on the elusiveness of organizational aesthetics, there is a risk, as stressed by Edward Ottensmeyer (1996a: 193), that one will 'assume that aesthetic processes in organizations are necessarily transitory'. I, too, share this preoccupation, in the sense that there is nothing to rule out that a heuristic process which demonstrates the elusiveness of organizational aesthetics will not be collectively and socially translated into the metaphysical assertion of the transitoriness of organizational aesthetics. And my preoccupation is increased by the fact that, on the contrary, the definition of aesthetics set out in this and other chapters, as well as in previous works, does not comprise any ontological paradigm that could be construed as asserting that organizational aesthetics *are* this or that characteristic of organization.

In emphasizing the elusiveness of organizational aesthetics I have argued that aesthetics, for the aesthetic approach, is a dialogic form of understanding of organizational life; a dialogue which constitutes, as Elio Franzini and Maddalena Mazzocut-Mis (1996: 386–9) write, 'the methodological arena comprising the philosophical possibilities of investigating the non-causal meaning of forms, of qualities, of events and of corporeal acts, receptive and poietic, of subjects and historical communities'. The theoretical ground for my emphasis on organizational aesthetics is a conception of aesthetics as a dialogic form of organizational knowledge which is not causal nor, as has frequently been pointed out, normative. Knowledge as dialogue has been stressed by Polanyi and the other philosophers on whose theories I have based my arguments. Derrida above all has taken particular pains to warn us that dialogue should not be confused with harmony, nor with the disappearance of violence from the process of knowing. Which is what I have sought to show by emphasizing the negotiative processes underlying the collective and social construction of organizational aesthetics.

Having examined the definition of aesthetics adopted by the aesthetic approach to organizations, in the next chapters I shall discuss the categories of the aesthetics used by the approach and their influence on the organizational research that has used it.

4   The Beautiful in Organizational Life

In previous chapters we have seen what is meant by 'aesthetics' with reference to the aesthetic approach to the study of organizational life. I emphasized the *pathos* of the sensible in knowledge about the meaningful action of the persons who construct and reconstruct organizational life, and I pointed out the importance of their sensory faculties and of their aesthetic judgement – judgement which I described in terms of a sixth sense additional to those of sight, hearing, smell, touch and taste. In this and the next chapter I shall examine the aesthetic categories that prove useful for the aesthetic understanding of organizational life, and discuss their employment, also independently of the aesthetic approach, in studies of organizational aesthetics.

The aesthetic categories are those of the ugly, the sublime, the gracious, the tragic, the picturesque, the comic, the holy; they are also the so-called 'agogic' categories which concern rhythm. And then, obviously, there is the category of the beautiful, on which I shall concentrate in this chapter, reiterating some of the themes treated in previous ones – especially that of aesthetic judgement – and illustrating the understanding of everyday organizational life that it yields to the researcher who uses the aesthetic approach to organizations.

I shall conduct quite detailed discussion of the category of the beautiful – rather than immediately delineating the opportunities offered to the researcher by the various aesthetic categories as a whole – because this is an appropriate moment at which to provide examples drawn from empirical research in organizations which have used an aesthetic category.

The aesthetic category that I have myself most frequently used in empirical research on organizational aesthetics is beauty. It was, in fact, while investigating the sense of the beautiful felt by people who construct and reconstruct organizational life that I began my studies on organizational aesthetics and my reflections on aesthetic understanding of organizational life (1990, 1992). I am therefore most closely acquainted with the use of this particular aesthetic category in the study of organizations. However, this is by no means to imply that the other categories (discussed mainly in Chapter 5) furnish less information on the quotidian experience of organizations. The fact that I shall dwell on a single category merely reflects the methodological foundations of the aesthetic approach. These foundations – as I have frequently pointed out – emphasize the proximity of the researcher to the organizational situation examined, and studies the details and nuances distinctive of a 'fragment' of organizational life, in order to shed light on the intentional action of organizational actors. Accordingly, the aesthetic approach concentrates the researcher's attention on the specificity of each aesthetic category, and likewise on each organizational situation and on the meaningful action of every individual who belongs to an organization or acts on its behalf.

It should be pointed out, however, that each aesthetic category on its own does not exhaust all the knowledge forthcoming from a particular organizational context. That is to say, none of them individually yields complete understanding of the organization investigated. Rather, each of them invites the use of other aesthetic categories. Consider, for example, the following description that I collected during recent empirical research. The person concerned had been forced to close his print and copy shop after many years of business. He had gone to look for work at a larger copy shop which had previously been his competitor. I asked the man to tell me everything that he remembered of his interview with the owner of the firm, who in fact gave him a job. I told him to imagine that he was using a camcorder to record everything that he felt and everything that passed through his mind. At the end of his story, he said:

> So he told me I could go and work for him when I wanted. In fact, he made me feel that he could easily find work for me . . . especially because he needed someone downstairs who would watch the machines and the work, someone who knew the job but could see what was needed, what there was to do, and so on. A little bit of everything, right? Not a boss, but someone who knew the business . . . That was beautiful, because he treated me well, he hinted that there'd be a bit more money for me than the others, and so on. So it was great . . . because he didn't make me feel like a failure. So, everything was fine, everything was going well. But then I had a flash, right? He was talking to me and I saw myself down there from morning to night with the same machines, the ones I'd had to sell, doing the same work for the rest of my life, and perhaps with the same customers . . . and under him, right? But I don't even know if it was that . . . It's that, I don't know . . . it was all, suddenly, a flash, it was all completely crazy. It made me feel bad, it was a bad feeling . . . 'The thought's enough to kill you,' I said to myself. The fact is, I'm here . . . even though I always have that feeling. I'm stuck with it, I don't know . . . but on the other hand, what can I do? Yeah, if I found something else . . . The fact is, I'm here from morning to night and I work and work, because if I lose this as well . . . I'll lose my self-respect, right? Better not think about it, otherwise it's tragic . . .

There is sentiment in this passage, there is *pathos* marked by the statements 'that was beautiful' and 'otherwise it's tragic'. These are expressions in common usage, and not only in that particular copy shop. They are adjectives which embellish or emphasize the problematic of a work choice; they are components, that is, of the ordinary language used by people to describe their everyday lives in an organization. But they are also categories of aesthetics which are sometimes used in parallel, sometimes independently, and sometimes jointly.

In the extract from the interview one notes not only the beauty of the moment when the ex-businessman realizes that he is to be given a job by the organization – and therefore not only the category of the beautiful in organizational life – but also the tragedy that he feels regarding his future, with the rest of his days in the organization spent 'downstairs' in the basement. Even more so because, despite everything, he pledges himself to working as hard as possible to keep his job, at least while looking around for something better. Which makes the situation both grotesque and comic at the same time. The ex-businessman's conversation with the owner of the copy shop was beautiful, but the vision of his future was grotesque and ugly, and his flash of 'insight' into his circumstances was tragic. There was the irony of fate lucidly apparent in his imagined participation in the setting comprised of the machinery, the premises, the customers, the temporal constraint, and when he projected all this into the infinite time-horizon of the 'rest of my life'.

The man had already seen the copy shop's premises and machinery while he was running his own business. He therefore had knowledge of them. But this was not precise and detailed knowledge gathered from within the organization, the knowledge of those who put these premises and machinery to use. It was knowledge gathered from outside, however familiar the man may have been with the copy shop. The same applies to the organizational life glimpsed in the extract, and to the absurdity of the man's future working life. But not only did he imaginatively participate in the organizational life of the copy shop before he was hired, he could still vividly re-create it in the account of his experience and action given much later.

If we seek to understand the man's intentional action from the point of view of the aesthetic approach, then we can make the following observations:

1 'Beautiful', 'ugly', 'grotesque' and 'tragic' are expressions that belong to the ordinary language used by people to describe their everyday lives in organizations. They are adjectives employed with meanings learnt outside and inside the organization, and as they have been shaped and redefined by organizational action both within and without the organization. Calling a momentary experience in an organization 'beautiful' or 'ugly' is to give it concise definition. It is to provide a rapid and graphic statement which makes the speaker's presence felt. It embellishes his/her speech under the pretence of talking about the organizational experience while avoiding any categorical assertion about it. It serves to protect the opacity of the speaker's feelings while being evocative. But it also consists of an assertion comprising an outright judgement which puts an aesthetic category to use in organizational life. To employ these adjectives in ordinary language, therefore, is to state a variety of different things and to assert them in an analytically indistinct form. In the meantime, the 'beautiful' or the 'ugly' come to constitute the essential component of the qualitatively rich datum acquired by talking to people about the organizational contexts in which empirical organizational research is conducted.

2   'Beautiful', 'tragic', 'grotesque' and 'ugly' are, as we have seen, expressions used in ordinary language to evaluate both the presentness of the interview with the owner of the copy shop and the ex-businessman's future working life. They were interpretations of the lived present and of the imagined future, as if they were co-present in the man's aesthetic understanding of that particular organizational life. Added to his interpretations were others, which again took the form of an aesthetic judgement. These interpretations were formulated by the researcher, who evaluated as comic, grotesque and ironic not the account provided by the man, nor the aesthetics of his narrative, but the moment in which he envisioned working in the copy shop. Thus added to and overlapping with the ordinary aesthetic language used by a member of the organization was the aesthetic language of the researcher, who thus interpreted the situation itself and not the interpretation of it provided by the ex-businessman.

3   'There is sentiment' and 'there is *pathos*': these are instead expressions in the aesthetic language used by the researcher to evaluate the ex-businessman's account in and of itself. It is the aesthetic of this extract from the interview that 'grips' the researcher. It heightens his/her sensitivity, focuses his/her attention, and solicits his/her *pietas*, as sympathetic understanding of the beauty, ugliness or tragedy of the moment and of the experience. But the text that elicits all this from the researcher is not the written text. It is the spoken text that was listened to at the time, and then listened to again during the transcription and the inevitable editing process that adds the commas, dashes, semi-colons and full stops, and a name to identify and emphasize the organization being described and its describer, or the dots in square brackets which protect its anonymity. It is also the text reproduced here for the reader, who will appreciate its aesthetic – hopefully – translated into English and therefore subjected to further interpretation in addition to that effected by the first translation, namely from spoken to written language.

4   Not only are 'comic', 'beautiful', 'tragic', 'ugly' and 'grotesque' expressions used in the ordinary aesthetic language of organizations and of empirical research, they are also aesthetic categories. Like the 'sublime' or the 'gracious', they are categories that have driven the development of European aesthetic philosophy since the eighteenth century; a philosophy which, together with theories of art, has produced a dense web of interpretations of these categories, and which today constitutes an important and controversial tradition of study. The aesthetic approach draws on this web of interpretations when it explores the aesthetic category of the beautiful, tragic or ugly as it emerges in the course of empirical research into organizations, and it brings its own difference to it. In fact, these categories from aesthetic philosophy and the theory of art are not merely applied to organizational life as if the researcher were employing a conceptual apparatus extraneous to it and which instead belongs to his/her exclusive stock of knowledge. On the contrary, they

inhere in the organizational life from which they emerge. In other words, they are part of the ordinary language of organizational actors and of the researcher.

I shall dwell for a moment on the multicategoriality of aesthetics, because it is one of the essential components of the aesthetic understanding of organizational life. The aesthetic categories arose and consolidated themselves in aesthetic philosophy and theories of art after what was described in the last chapter as one of the greatest upheavals in the paradigm that defines humankind: the aesthetics of the eighteenth century. The history of beauty has followed a different course, however, because for more than two millennia beauty, aesthetics and art have been regarded largely as different ways to refer to the same phenomenon. Indeed, it was as a result of the crisis of the category of beauty – a category which originated in the pre-Socratic philosophy of Magna Graecia with Pythagoras, and in ancient Greece with Aristotle and Plato – that the aesthetic categories developed independently of each other, so that although the close connections among them still persisted, they grew distinct and different.

As Elio Franzini and Maddalena Mazzocut-Mis inform us (1996: 261–2), it was Friedrich Schlegel, at the end of the eighteenth century, who first drew the distinction between beauty, in the restricted sense of the term and therefore as a modern aesthetic category, and beautifulness, in the broad sense as synonymous with 'aesthetic value' and as a concept which embraces, besides beautiful in the strict sense, also the gracious or the sublime, again in the strict sense. Subsequently, in the mid-nineteenth century, Karl Rosenkranz analysed the ugly and disharmonious, the vulgar and the repugnant, the asymmetrical and the clumsy, and thus prompted re-examination of the aesthetic value represented by beauty. It should also be noted that the affirmation of the 'multicategoriality' of aesthetics was flanked by the growth of expressive forms and narrative devices – the tragic, the grotesque, the pathetic, the grandiose, the monstrous, the comic, the melodramatic, and other aesthetic categories besides – which in the same period were given separate treatment.

The multicategoriality of aesthetics stems largely from reflection on individual categories, like the analyses of ugliness by Schlegel and Rosenkranz, who sought both to separate off the ugly from the beautiful and to challenge the supremacy of the latter. However, it was only at the beginning of this century that a multicategorial account of aesthetics was elaborated by Charles Lalo (1927), Étienne Souriau (1929) and Raymond Bayer (1934), provoking a wide-ranging debate on the multicategorial nature of aesthetics in which was proposed, on the one hand, the excessive expansion of the aesthetic categories and, on the other, their drastic restriction. This serves to remind us that the multicategoriality of aesthetics is not a configuration defined and established by contemporary inquiry, but a problem 'broad, variegated and difficult to circumscribe' (Franzini and Mazzocut-Mis, 1996:

268) tied both to the crisis of beauty and to the emergence of the multiple aesthetic values that separated aesthetics and art from beauty.

However, although the multicategoriality of aesthetics means that one can pass from a large number of aesthetic categories to only a few, it is a fundamental theoretical assumption of the aesthetic approach. As we shall see in the next chapter, only very few aesthetic categories are considered in the analysis of organizational life, and precisely because only a limited number of aesthetic categories have been explored with regard to organizations. And yet the diverse interpretations to which the categories of aesthetics have been subjected provide valuable knowledge for those who adopt the aesthetic approach to organizations; always bearing in mind, however, that it is the qualitatively rich datum gathered during empirical inquiry in organizational contexts which constitutes the approach's focus of reference. Bearing in mind, that is to say, that some or other category emerges as the category-in-use in an organization, whether the organizational actors refer to it spontaneously, or whether they do so on the promptings of the researcher.

The essential focus of empirical aesthetic research, therefore, is constituted by statements such as 'There's something beautiful about being up there' proffered by the worker for the roof-stripping firm discussed in the previous chapter, who thus made an assertion about his everyday work based on a category envisaged not by organization theory or management studies but by philosophical aesthetics and the theory of art. The worker employed an aesthetic category and formulated a judgement, this also aesthetic; a judgement, as we saw at the end of the previous chapter, very different from both an evaluation measurable in terms of rational explanation and an opinion as a statement of fact.

When the members of an organization say that it is 'beautiful', although the statement may be of relevance to the aesthetic approach, it does not signify that the organization is objectively and universally beautiful. Nor does it signify that, although the organization is by no means beautiful, it is considered so by the speaker because s/he arbitrarily projects onto it his/her emotional and mental state or his/her cognitions of beauty and aesthetic education. The aesthetic judgement, as I pointed out following Bozal (1996) in the previous chapter, informs us how the person expressing the judgement represents the organization to him/herself. Its importance for the aesthetic approach to organizations resides precisely in the 'representation' that the aesthetic judgement conveys to the researcher; a judgement which expresses the relation that ties the knowing subject to the organization in question at level of aesthetic understanding and therefore of the *pathos* of the sensible.

The aesthetic judgement has a particular feature that should once again be stressed: it 'represents' to the researcher a relation in which both the judging subject and the judged organization are ever-present. And to do so it employs an aesthetic category. Those who wish to grasp the sense of the aesthetic categories in the study of organizations must take account of this interweaving among 'organizational life', the 'faculty of judgement as the subject's sixth sense', and 'aesthetic categories'. It is by virtue of this relation, in fact, that the categories of aesthetics are also the categories of the aesthetic understanding of organizational life. The interpretations of the beautiful and the ugly furnished by philosophical aesthetics and theories of art are supplemented by those provided, along with their differences, by the organizational analysis which employs them to investigate the manner in which a participant in organizational life represents the latter to him/herself. The aesthetic approach focuses on organizational life, therefore, and for this purpose uses an aesthetic category, although the information yielded by it about organizational life is also information about the category itself. The latter, as already pointed out, is not a predefined category that happens to be applied to organizational life; it is one that emerges in the course of the inquiry, and which is indeed a category of aesthetics but also a category-in-use of that specific organizational life and, consequently, an interpretation which imparts specificity and difference.

The categories of aesthetics are thus categories employed by the aesthetic approach to organizations. They suggest, indeed they mark out, specific paths for the analysis of organizational life; paths, though, which depend not on philosophical aesthetics and theories of art but on a blend between the aesthetic and the organizative in the understanding of organizational life. This is a hybridization, therefore, which merges philosophical interpretations with whatever differs from them in the interpretation yielded by the knowledge of the 'sensible' of each knowing subject in the organization being studied – whether this knowing subject is an organizational actor or the researcher. Organizational research which employs the aesthetic approach is thus 'impure', because it draws no distinction between what is organizative and what is aesthetic, but fuses the two together. Consequently, when one listens to others remarking on the beauty of an organization or of an activity performed within it or on its behalf – or even when one remarks thus oneself – due account must be taken of the fact that reference is being made to a category that:

(a) has a tradition of interpretations which constitute a stock of ordinary language employed by the members of an organization – this language is subjected to negotiative processes and dynamics which make one meaning prevail over others, one idiom over others, one aesthetic category over others;

(b) is not studied by the members of the organization, but is instead the knowledge that they use to indicate, interpret and 'state' some characteristic of everyday organizational life;

(c) has, however, been widely studied, with diverse outcomes, by the philosophies and religions that have developed in Europe and elsewhere.

On the one hand, therefore, ordinary language in organizations extends the meanings of the categories of aesthetics, enriching them with further and unusual properties which have nothing to do with either philosophical reflection or works of art. On the other, the boundaries between one aesthetic category and another are often blurred, and the definition of each category has a history behind it of subtle distinctions drawn by philosophical theories at polemical odds with each other and accompanied or stimulated by constant changes in the techniques and languages of art. All this, I would stress, concerns European philosophical aesthetics, because it is to these that I shall refer when illustrating the use of the aesthetic categories in the study of organizations. It is European philosophy, therefore, and the theories of art developed in European culture, that engendered the process of 'hybridization' which informs the aesthetic understanding of organizational life yielded by empirical research which employs the category of beautiful. It is in fact the origins of this category in the pre-Socratic thought of ancient Greece and of Magna Graecia, in the polemics waged against Pythagoras, Plato and Aristotle by the sophists and sceptics, and in the transformation of beauty from the equivalent of aesthetics into one of the numerous categories of aesthetics in late eighteenth- and early nineteenth-century European philosophy, that constitute both the mainstream and the cultural *humus* in which the contemporary aesthetic approach to organizations has developed.

The beauty of the organization

In the course of empirical research conducted in organizational contexts, when informants express aesthetic judgements using the category of beauty, they apply them to their work, to their colleagues, or to their working environment: 'I've got a great job!', 'I love what I'm doing here', 'I did something beautiful that time', 'I work in lovely surroundings', 'I've got a lovely job', 'I work with nice people', 'I listened to a great speech, beautifully delivered', 'I saw something which was beautifully made, something really beautiful.' Only seldom do they pass aesthetic judgement on their organization as a whole, saying, for example, 'I work for a fine organization', 'for a beautiful organization', 'for an organization which makes beautiful things', or something like 'Ours is a beautiful organization', 'The organization where I was before, that was a beautiful organization', 'We want this to be a beautiful organization for all those who visit it and also for those who work in it', 'I really like the organization where I work.' Appreciations of this kind are rarer than appreciations of work or of a specific course of action, unless the researcher has overtly solicited them.

In this section I shall illustrate the specific features of the aesthetic category of the beautiful with reference to the organization considered as a whole. I shall analyse two interviews which I recorded and transcribed during research conducted some years ago, and which proved especially fruitful in my early studies of organizational aesthetics. Their merit was that each interviewee thought that his organization was aesthetically beautiful as regards the physicality of its spaces, its working atmosphere and its vitality. I shall first discuss the texts in their entirety, so that the reader can gain an overall impression, as well as the elements necessary for personal study of them if s/he should so wish. I shall subsequently break the excerpts down into parts, picking out words and phrases to illustrate the interpretations of organizational life suggested by the interviewees, and to indicate insights provided by the philosophical tradition of the category of the beautiful.

The extracts are taken from interviews conducted with two businessmen operating in different sectors: computer services and the culture industry. The main activity of the first businessman's organization was hardware and software assistance; that of the second was the mounting of photography exhibitions and the promotion of photography as an art form. Both organizations were Italian. The first was located on the outskirts of a small to medium-sized town, the second in a large city.

The first interviewee had opened his business some years previously and still had vivid memories of getting started. He told me that his was a small firm with a modest turnover compared with the multinationals operating in the sector. But, perhaps precisely because it was small, it was well integrated into its environment, with the infrastructures and communication networks vital for its business. The building in which the firm had its offices was almost entirely new, and he himself had painstakingly drawn up the plans and organized the construction work.

Look, I think that mine's a beautiful business, that is . . . we do clean work which doesn't pollute, and in a place with a beauty that for me, this may strike you as ridiculous, this firm in this place, for me it's a little jewel. Perhaps saying it's a little jewel is not the correct expression, and perhaps you could find the right words, better than mine, to express what I want to say. But with this I want to say that for the moment it has its beauty which I hope that time and Italy's economic problems won't spoil for me, won't spoil it. You see, for me, and for lots of other businessmen in our sector, but customers as well, and some of our suppliers too, when they come here, they say – according to me because they know it gives me pleasure and so perhaps I'll give them a good price – there's already a certain atmosphere when you come in here; there's something that makes you feel good, that lets you breathe. I don't know about you, perhaps you wouldn't say so, but every day when I come up that little avenue with the trees, you see I've had some more planted and we'll see how they grow, but already the entrance harmonizes with the environment. And then, I don't know if you noticed when you arrived, its a big building and then there's that interplay between the mirror windows and the fountain in front of the main entrance, which I wanted because it reflects something inside the gates from the landscape outside, which, you see, is really beautiful, and we were so lucky to get this place. So, for you perhaps it's nothing, but leave the main road and after a few hundred metres, perhaps not even that, and you're in another world. You leave the traffic and the stress behind and you find, I reckon, an air of peace and quiet which, if you go into other firms like mine, you won't find, and instead of tree-lined avenues and light-filled offices you'll find basements cluttered with outdated equipment and little cubbyholes to work in. Here it's beautiful because there's no mess, but there's nothing oppressive either, because everything's been kept as simple as possible, like a little jewel in the chaos of the computer business . . .

Some thirty years before I interviewed him, the second businessman had opened the first gallery entirely devoted to photography in Europe. His profits were not as high as those earned by the first interviewee, since his main source of income was the numerous sponsors of the cultural events that he organized. I had known him for some time. I asked:

Q: But for you is the gallery a beautiful thing or a means to make beautiful things?

A: For me it's something beautiful, nothing more or less. It enthuses me, otherwise I wouldn't spend all this money [on the gallery] instead of getting a yacht, or travelling more, taking time off, buying a car which I wouldn't use just for transport but to appear . . . I don't know, it's a woman that isn't beautiful straight away, she's a beautiful woman who should be dressed well, be decked out with nice jewels, be well perfumed. Above all she should be cherished. Actually, for me the word is loyalty, even if it's said in different ways there's a loyalty, there's joy, that's all, and there's not much you can do about it. For me the gallery is exactly joy, otherwise I wouldn't put up with all the sacrifices, all the scrimping and scraping.

The first feature shared by the two interviewees is that they had both created their own organizations. People who set up their own businesses occupy a distinctive position in that they always view the organization as their own personal creation. In other words, they have an overview of the organization which they are able to take in at a glance, because in many respects it is the product of their labours, of their emotional investment, taste and talent. The fact that each of the businessmen had created his own organization prompted him to believe that he had created something beautiful, while he simultaneously referred to it as a whole.

The second feature is this: the more closely we examine the accounts of the two businessmen, the more differences we find in the categories of beauty that they employ. This is the most interesting finding to emerge from the two interview extracts, and it is for this reason that I reproduce them here. They highlight the plurality of the meanings of the category of the beautiful to be borne in mind when conducting empirical research on organizational aesthetics.

The relevance of philosophical aesthetics

The two businessmen referred to different features when they described the beauty of their organizations. The two organizations in their turn differed by sector of activity, turnover and age. And, although both of them were small, the gallery had less than half the personnel of the computer firm. These, however, were not the organizational features that the two businessmen mentioned when they talked about the beauty of their organizations; neither did they refer to organizational goals or objectives. Which signifies that it is not these aspects of an organization that make it beautiful; there are other aspects that do so. If we examine these 'other' aspects, what understanding of organizational life do we gain?

The first businessman emphasized the harmony of his organization with its natural surroundings, and the architectural linearity and simplicity of its buildings. He stressed the ecological care taken when the organization was first created. His organization did not spoil the landscape in which it was embedded like, as he put it, a jewel in a crown or a necklace. It was as if aesthetic proportionality had been deliberately established between the organization and its surroundings.

The beauty of the first businessman's organization has its roots in the school of Pythagoras founded in 530 BC at Croton in Magna Graecia. It is in fact the Pythagorean concept of harmony that transpires from the beauty of the organization as a jewel; harmony created by the proportion among the relations established in that organization's particular setting, without their being forced or distorted. This proportion is symmetry and peacefulness, two key concepts for Pythagoras and his followers. Pythagoras developed the first theory of beauty as constituted by the 'consonances' manifest in visible symmetry or musical intervals. This, however, was a rational conception of beauty which, by emphasizing commensurability – that is to say, proportionality among the parts of a whole without residues left over – sought to find logic even in the irrational. I illustrate this point by referring to Pythagoras' well-known theorem of the proportion between the hypotenuse and one of the sides of an isosceles right-angle triangle. By squaring them one obtains a 2:1 ratio, which reveals that there are proportion relations which, although not apparent at first, can in fact be demonstrated. Consequently the incommensurable can be converted into the commensurable; a fact which adds beauty to the elegance of the proof, in that it underscores Pythagoras' genius and the aura of magic and esotericism that surrounds his name. The Pythagorean category of the beautiful thus bears out Remo Bodei's point (1995: 23) concerning Pythagoras' theorem, when he describes 'the "magic" of a rationality that paradoxically springs from the multiplication of the irrational by itself'.

Another feature to be noted – again with reference to the description provided by the first interviewee – is that he uses a category of the beautiful which privileges the perceptive faculty of vision. This, too, originates in the philosophy of Pythagoras, and more generally in that of ancient Greece, where priority was given to the senses of sight and hearing. These were the 'public' senses, while the others – smell, taste and touch – were not: first, because they yielded perceptions to which the principle of commensurability could not be applied, unlike in the cases of sight and hearing; second, because they were much more 'personal' senses, or indeed 'intimate' ones, like taste, for example, which yields sensory perceptions internally to the body.

I said earlier that the aesthetic category of the beautiful employed by the aesthetic approach has its origins in the European philosophical tradition. I now provide an example of what this means, given that the interview with the first businessman neatly illustrates the point. Whereas, in fact, the first businessman bases his description of the beauty of his organization on the scent of the trees or the rooms, and thus gives priority to smell, his category of beauty is not necessarily that of pre-Socratic rational philosophy. It can also be related to the Jewish or Muslim religions, or to the oriental philosophies and religions whose prohibition on images of beauty is associated with the value set on the beauty of fragrances and tastes. Or again it may have originated in European aesthetic philosophy, but in its eighteenth-century version which, as we have seen, broke the domination of the pre-Socratic notion of beauty as harmony, symmetry, proportion and the public.

The emphasis on the public and on the commensurable in the beauty of the organization described by the first businessman is evident in his constant reference to others, be these the researcher, the customer, the supplier or another businessman. His 'jewel' gives something to all of them: it gives them a feeling of well-being as they enter the building, relief from the stress symbolized by the traffic on the main road, the clean and soothing air that they breathe. The offices are filled with light, the avenue is adorned with trees, in a symmetrical interplay which transposes the beauty of the external landscape into the internal landscape of the organization. This cleanliness, space and brightness are contrasted with the basements, disorder, obsolescence and useless clutter of other firms in the sector, in application of the commensurability principle.

The simplicity mentioned by the first businessman to illustrate the beauty of his organization is another feature of the category of beauty which relates to Greek philosophy. The simplicity of beauty was expounded by the neoplatonist philosopher Plotinus, who, in the second century AD, studied in Egypt and then taught in Rome. Plotinus saw beauty as residing in the individual part as such, and not in the proportions among the parts. He described absolute beauty, that of a colour *per se*, not the beauty arising from its proportionate relation with the other colours. Hence the colour of a flower was beautiful just as it was, in absolute, not insofar as it harmonized with the colours of the other flowers in a bunch. 'Plotinus exalted sensible beauty, its "appearance" in a world of the most diverse forms,' comment Stefano Zecchi and Elio Franzini (1995: 91), and his conception of beauty was that of a ' "visible" beauty, on the basis of which we may ascend towards the intelligible world, towards the metaphysical purity of the One'. Thus, the beauty of the businessman's organization in some way detaches itself from harmony and symmetry to display, with its simplicity, an aesthetic tension towards the purity of sensible forms.

Again Pythagorean is the relation between the beauty of the organization and the ethic that it embodies. The beautiful and the good are set in relation by the antithesis that contrasts 'something that makes you feel good' and the 'light-filled offices' with the 'traffic and the stress', the 'basements cluttered with outdated equipment', the 'cubbyholes' for people to work in, and the 'chaos of the computer business'. There are no clearcut distinctions in the Pythagorean trinity of the beautiful, the good and the true. 'In a broad sense,' writes Remo Bodei (1995: 24), 'any moral attitude based on the principle of proportion is beautiful, and this applies to the whole of classical civilization, which bequeathed the notion to all subsequent epochs almost up to the present day.' However, the beauty of the organization described by the businessman does not display that total identification of the beautiful with the good that Plato propounded when he took the Pythagorean interpretation of the beautiful and applied it to the problem of the good (Zecchi and Franzini, 1995: 35–7). The businessman does not point to rightness and goodness as essentially characterizing the beauty of his organization. Instead he treats beauty separately from the good, and relates only some of its aspects to the quality of the working environment in his organization, which he deems better than that of many other firms in the sector.

The beauty of the organization described by the first businessman also highlights an aspect of its creator, namely the businessman himself. He uses the analogy of the jewel to emphasize that his organization is the result of good craftsmanship rather than being a work of art. He talks of the beauty of his organization as the distinctive beauty of a small object, although this only brings out the vagueness of the boundary that he draws between craftsmanship and art. However, he makes no artistic claims, in the sense that he never declares that his organization is as beautiful as a work of art. Nor does he resort to similes of the type 'It's as beautiful as a fourteenth-century miniature' or 'It's as beautiful as Man Ray's iron'. These, too, are small objects, but they belong to art not to craftsmanship, no matter how refined it may be, and even though what is art and what prevents craftsmanship from being art are controversial issues in art theory, in artists' manifestos, and also in philosophical aesthetics. Whatever the case may be, one discerns a relation which locates the beauty of the organization, and the unpretentious and practical talent of its owner–founder, in a paradigm of commonplace beauty embodied in the practicality of the organization and not in any rare genius displayed by its creator. In other words, the organization–jewel manifests the taste, and if not the talent at least the skill, of the businessman. He had employed this skill not only in setting up his business but also in assuming the guise of an architect and ecologist, and also that of a progressive industrial executive, thereby converting himself from a manager into a refined and welcoming host.

The organization is a jewel that the businessman hopes will not be 'spoilt' by economic difficulties and the passage of time. The beauty of the organization is definite: it is a 'thing', to put it à la Husserl, or 'already formed matter', à la Pareyson. 'Jewel' is the term that makes the beauty of his organization 'sayable' for the businessman, and it evidences what the sophists stressed in the fifth century BC: namely that beauty is discourse, rhetoric, artful speech (sofizesthai). The organization–jewel is an analogy in many respects similar to that of the organization as 'beautiful as a picture', for example, and in many respects dissimilar to that of the organization 'as beautiful as a symphony'. A jewel, in fact, more closely resembles a painting than it does great music. It is already made, rather than being in fieri, and it is the knowing subject who scrutinizes its surfaces and workmanship.

Listening to a symphony is a cumulative process because the music is not given once and for all, like a jewel, but develops note by note and phrasing by phrasing as it impinges on the hearing. In other words, the beauty of the organization–jewel 'is present' in its entirety, and in this definitive form 'it presents' itself to the knowing subject, engendering a cognitive shift where it is the horizon to which the subject is oriented. The opposite movement can be observed in the organization–symphony, where it is the music that moves towards the subject, making itself progressively heard and thus known little by little in its dynamic and processual becoming, as in the businessman's description of the beauty of his organization.

Whilst the first businessman used the analogy of the jewel, the second one also used an analogy, but in order to emphasize how to make an organization beautiful. An organization is not beautiful like a beautiful woman, he says. It must instead be dressed, bejewelled, perfumed and cherished like a woman. Compared with the beauty described by the first businessman, that of the second is highly imprecise and it must constantly be constructed.

This concept of beauty sheds the measurability and calculability distinctive of the harmony and proportion of the relations among the elements which constituted the category of the beautiful applied by the first entrepreneur to his organization. In fact, we might have agreed or disagreed with the first businessman that his offices were well lit because there was an objective criterion to apply. But the category of beauty employed by the second businessman was not amenable to confirmation or denial. The beauty of his organization was based on the immediacy of his personal feelings, and the philosophical roots of the category of the beautiful that he employed did not lie in the paradigm of objectivity and calculability which, prior to the eighteenth century, had only ever been questioned by the sceptics in the Greece of the fifth century BC, and by the sceptics between the fourth century BC and the second century AD. Nor was it based exclusively on the senses of sight and hearing whose public and precise nature I have described, or on the exactness and the well-formedness of an object delimited in visible space, like the organization as a jewel set in a splendid Italian landscape described by the first businessman.

What the second businessman's description instead highlights is that imponderable quality which makes his organization beautiful, so that his gallery is 'exactly joy' for him, because 'there's joy, that's all, and there's not much you can do about it'. This imponderable quality, which appeared with the aesthetic philosophy of the Renaissance and, some centuries later, with the first generation of the German romantics – and with them more generally in European romanticism – shows that rather than the perceptive faculty of vision, at work here is the imagination, which lies beyond the barrier of the senses and creates bridges among them.

The beauty of the organization was not sayable for the second business-man using the analogy of the beautiful woman *tout court*. The beauty of his organization was sayable by virtue of what Pareyson called 'forming as *doing* by inventing the mode of doing' (1954: 59), given that the gallery was 'a beautiful woman who should be dressed well, be decked out with nice jewels, be well perfumed. Above all she should be cherished.' The second businessman underscored his emphasis by employing 'is' rather than 'is like', so that the beauty of his organization resided in its being 'dressed well', in being 'decked out with jewels', in being 'well perfumed', in being 'cherished'. The beauty of the gallery, in other words, lay in its being made beautiful and not in its being made 'as if' it were being made such, using the sensory faculties of sight, smell as well as the other senses, but above all by working at the level where aesthetics are commingled with ethics – the level, that is, where there is no beauty of an organization that is not morally right as well.

The beauty defined by formal criteria that we observed as regards the first organization is thus flanked by the vague beauty of the second organization, a beauty which manifests the second businessman's effort after an imponderable and indefinite quality constituted by his organization itself. This 'presents itself' as self-sufficient: the female figure to which he refers is mysterious and fickle, given that she is neither depicted in her completeness nor portrayed as a solid and stable stature, nor as a static artefact like the jewel described by the first entrepreneur.

This is further emphasized by the following consideration. While the first businessman is still more closely involved in the start-up of his firm than he cares to admit, the founder of the gallery almost disappears as the creator of his organization. He can only ensure that his organization–woman *in fieri* is beautiful to the sight and to olfaction – in short to the senses – but this beauty is not exclusively of his own doing. Rather, beauty resides in the gallery in and of itself and consists in its giving 'joy' to its curator.

Plurality of organizational beauty

If we compare the two interview extracts, they display shared characteristics of the beauty of an organization and characteristics which instead differ markedly. The features in common are, first, the consideration of the organization as a whole in terms of the aesthetic category of the beautiful, and by small businessmen who had partly or wholly created their own organizations. Another shared feature is that neither businessmen treated the beauty of his organization as serving some other purpose, as functional to some other end, as instrumental to achievement of the organization's goals. Note that the second interviewee was explicitly asked about this aspect, but he dismissed it out of hand. A further shared feature is that in both extracts the principles of the beautiful and the good are intertwined. Good is deemed to be what is ethical, not what is practical: it is whatever is morally right and not, for example, whatever is utilitarian. A final shared feature is that the category of the beautiful is flanked in each case by a second aesthetic category: that of the picturesque in the first extract, where it is used to refer to an artefact bearing some relation to a work of art; that of the tragic in the second, evidenced by 'otherwise I wouldn't put up with all the sacrifices, all the scrimping and scraping', and of the sublime which involves both the joy that fills the soul and the mysterious pleasure of the tragic.

What distinguishes the two extracts is the aesthetic category of beauty used to refer to the organization as a whole. As I have already pointed out, in the first extract classical beauty is commensurable with the rationalism that, from Magna Graecia onwards, dominated European aesthetic philosophy for more than two millennia. In the second, beauty relates to feeling, to the imponderable and the inexhaustible, and it is endlessly reinvented (*poieîn*). Both interviewees employ analogy to illustrate the beauty of their organization, and they do so with reference to conceits that theories of art have consecrated – female beauty and the beauty of jewels – and which the institutionalization of museums in recent centuries, with the advent of modernity, has conserved and disseminated. But they do so in very different ways, because if the organization–jewel can be viewed as a work of art, the organization-as-'non-beautiful woman *tout court*' simply cannot be seen at all. Therefore, while the idea of the beauty of the computer firm is defined once and for all, at least at the time of the interview some years ago, that of the photography gallery is not even momentarily defined. Instead, it is given by default, by analogy with something that it is not, and its beauty is endlessly created.

I have also said that these are aesthetic judgements and not factual ones. They tell us how the two businessmen represent their organizations to themselves. But they do not tell us how the two organizations effectively appear in respect of their beauty, nor how the two businessmen conceived beauty externally to their organizations. It is their appreciation of the organization that we understand through their judgements of beauty. But this is an appreciation and not the arbitrary projection of their aesthetic culture or of their subjective feeling.

In both cases, we have gained knowledge of the businessman's managerial philosophy, of his relationship with his organization, of the tasks he performs and the initiatives that he undertakes, and of the aesthetic enjoyment that he derives from his work. We have seen how the first businessman views his organization as belonging to a network of activities involving other firms in the sector, and other computer businessmen, how he defines the quality of his working life, and how he envisages his organization as hospitable or as endowed with autonomous life. We have also seen that the main difference between the two businessmen is that the second finds immediate aesthetic (and also heroic) rapture in his organization, and this demonstrates the power of the beautiful in organizational life.

In fact, whereas the first businessman manifests a certain cool detachment from his organization, the relationship of the second with his organization is turbulent. But this turbulence is due to the imponderable nature of the organization that he has created and not to the economic difficulties cited by the first businessman as the possible cause of organizational breakdown, so that if any turbulence arises, it stems from the external organizational environment. The rapture felt by the second businessman is the joy that 'is exactly' the organization for him; the 'non-familiar' emotion so distinctive of beauty and which demonstrates the power of the beautiful. We are never able to subdue this power, Stefano Zecchi (1995: 3–4) writes, just as we are never able to suppress the power of beautiful surroundings which divert our attention from our work, or of an especially beautiful person who distracts us. We can only handle the power of beauty by eliminating its presence. We may, writes Zecchi, change the position of our desk or dismiss the secretary whose beauty distracts her colleagues from their work. These are actions that can be undertaken with regard to our everyday work and to organizational life, and they are commonplace. I think, for example, of the many lecture halls devoid of natural light and of a view on the outside world that I have seen; or more generally of the frequent occasions on which both women and men are ordered by their organizations to cover up their beauty, so that it is in keeping with the lack of *eros* that imbues organizational life with morality, as discussed in Chapter 3. There are numerous cases, therefore, in which organizations endeavour explicitly or implicitly to inhibit beauty, thereby living up to the ideal of the rational control of even the exotic. However, this does not mean that individuals always comply, or that beauty has been erased from organizational life. This is evidenced by the words of the two businessmen, in particular those of the second when he states that there is a 'loyalty to a situation' which is joy and causes joy, no matter what costs and sacrifices it may entail.

The symbolism of the 'representation' of organizational beauty

The two businessmen furnished different representations of the beauty of their organizations as regards both the organizational features emphasized and the aesthetic category of the beautiful employed to describe it. In the previous section I offered some interpretations of these representations, deconstructing and reconstructing the topics touched on or merely hinted at and the rapture and sensibility with which they were recounted. In other words, I used these representations of the beauty of the organizations to reconstruct a knowledge that is aesthetic, not a knowledge that is analytic. I shall now examine the concepts involved in this reconstruction and the method that was employed.

Representation versus representativeness

Let us assume for the sake of argument that we wish to validate scientifically my foregoing analysis of the beauty of the organization. We thus view what was found out as being merely the first phase of the empirical inquiry, the exploratory one, which furnished 'discoveries' that must now be verified scientifically. The representations of the two businessmen comprise concepts that can be operationalized and themes that can be further explored to discover more about what was learnt. We may therefore continue with analysis of the beauty of the organization by asking other members of the organization whether or not they agree with the businessmen's statements, focusing, for example, more closely on shared meanings than on manifest differences. We may do so by means of in-depth individual interviews or by setting up *ad hoc* work groups, perhaps administering a questionnaire and using qualitative techniques of organizational analysis and case study.

If instead we are interested in how only entrepreneurs in the computer business view the beauty of their organizations, structured interviews can be conducted, or a questionnaire administered, in order to establish whether, for example, the beauty of the organization's setting explains the sense of beauty experienced by the businessman more than does the beauty of the buildings or the brightness of the offices. Or if it is preferred to compare among different sectors of activity, again restricting the inquiry to business-men alone, the concepts of the two representations can be operationalized and a sufficient number of items constructed to determine whether there are sufficiently significant statistical correlations to conclude, for example, that in one particular geographical area small businessmen view the beauty of their organizations in a manner akin to that of the second businessman and that, instead, only when small firms are closely linked with a larger company does a sense of beauty of the type described by the first businessman predominate. In short, both qualitative and quantitative analysis can be used to identify the causes of the attribution of beauty to the organization and to specify the circumstances in which these causes exert their influence.

The aesthetic understanding of the beauty of organizations based on the aesthetic judgements of the two businessmen was not acquired in this manner, as we have seen, because the theoretical foundations of the method used were at odds with the rational and causal explanation of the meaningful action of people in organizations. The understanding gained was aesthetic, not logico-analytical, and it had a theoretical basis which has been discussed in previous chapters and which now, with regard to aesthetic judgement, will be examined more closely using a further example.

Let us assume that we are admiring the beauty of Caravaggio's work *The Death of the Virgin*, commissioned in 1601, painted before May 1606 and now hanging in the Louvre. This is a dramatic and violent painting whose strong contrasts of light and shade give an immediate sense of the brutality of the reality depicted. The woman portrayed as the Madonna seems real: she strikes the observer as truly a dead woman, with her corporeality, weight and sensuality. She may have been a drowned prostitute, or she may indeed have been Caravaggio's mistress (Bologna, 1992: 44–5 and 375–6), although he did not paint her in the ethereal manner customarily used by artists at the time to depict their beloved. But whether she was a prostitute or a lover, it is not she that is the original of the painting, however much realism Caravaggio may have given to the dead Madonna. The Madonna is a woman, to be sure, both in this and other pictures that Caravaggio painted in the same period, but it is not a particular woman who is portrayed. If we 'recognize' in the picture only the figure of the lover or of the dead prostitute because she has been painted realistically, we have failed to understand the painting aesthetically: beauty is symbolic, and it is precisely as a symbol, argues Zecchi (1990: xi), that it is able to change form and acquire new meanings, 'raise doubts' and be the 'enigma and problem of reason'.

The example of Caravaggio's painting is particularly apt because it highlights the meaning of knowledge that is aesthetic rather than analytic and rational. Caravaggio was a painter of reality, writes Arnold Hauser (1955; It. trans. 1956, vol. I: 468–9), and his bold and harsh realism earned him the disapproval of his contemporaries and the repeated rejection of his works by his ecclesiastical patrons. The 'realist' artist does not posit 'reality' at the origin of his/her discourse, Roland Barthes writes (1970: 173, 27–8), but a real that has already been written, however far back one wishes to go, and a perspective code alongside which one can only see an '*enfilade*' of other codes which interweave and hide the traces of their origin, as in a 'texture of voices'. The aesthetic understanding required by Caravaggio's painting is not based on the scientific evaluation of the veridicality of the portrait of the prostitute or the lover. Nor is it rational analysis that determines whether the sentiment of beauty aroused by the painting is due mainly to the factor 'prostitute as model of the Virgin' and much less to the 'fleshy colour' of the hands and feet which frame the red of the dead prostitute's dress. Aesthetic understanding is based on entirely different factors, because it grasps and sustains the truth of the beauty of the painting in the symbolism whereby, for example, Caravaggio restores worldliness to the exceptionality of the Madonna and earthly corporeality to her sacred depiction.

My purpose in referring to art has not been to argue its equivalence with the representation furnished to our sensibility as organization scholars. I have instead sought to highlight the equivalence that may exist in the process itself of knowledge-gathering – that is, in the approach to organizational life based on aesthetic judgements. We should therefore examine the representation of the organization in the aesthetic judgement, bearing principally in mind that it is not the veridicality of the brightness of the offices or of the tree-lined avenue that is represented by the aesthetic judgement, but rather their symbolizing of beauty for the businessman who talks about it, and for us as we listen to him. However realistic the representation may seem, it is not the elements of which it is composed or the aspects most emphasized that yield understanding of organizational beauty. This is because the representation of the organization should not be confused with a photographic or audiovisual depiction of it. Consequently, it is not by isolating the act of cherishing the organization by dressing it and perfuming it, or the act of installing mirror windows, and by viewing the beauty of the organization as the outcome of this action, that we aesthetically understand that particular organizational life on the basis of the category of the beautiful.

In truth, beauty cannot be explained, writes Roland Barthes (1970: 40–1); we can only 'say' it in the terms in which it is what it is, given that its possible predicates are a tautology, as when one states that a face is beautiful because it is a perfect oval, or a comparison involving an infinity of codes, as when one says that a face is like that of an angel. Furthermore, when conducting rational analysis, we find ourselves using an approach which is exactly the reverse of the one employed so far: the approach, that is, of detachment and distance which asserts the separation between the researcher and the organizational actor, rather than the difference between their interpretations. In this case, also qualitatively rich data, and not merely the quantitative data gathered, describe a beauty of the organization devoid of enchantment and of poetry; a beauty shorn of the *pathos* of the sensible, therefore, and thus of the quality most appropriate to it and most wholly distinctive of it. Stefano Zecchi (1990: 14) writes that the rationalism which arose with modern thought imposed 'the logic of *validity*' – with its procedures of verification and proof – instead of the 'meaning of *truth* in judgements' based on symbolic production, which becomes 'the means to comprehend and narrate the world'.

The representation produced by the aesthetic judgement, therefore, should be neither confused with the representativeness of the concepts and themes that it yields, nor transformed into it. This representation should instead be understood in its symbolic being. By so doing, in fact, we valorize the fact that the sense of beauty of an organization is never objectifiable, instead of reifying it into an organizational artefact or into a course of organizational action. The symbolism is highlighted by the 'representation' itself because it is constitutive of it. As Hans-Georg Gadamer writes:

> The symbolic does not simply point toward a meaning, but rather allows that meaning to present itself. The symbolic represents meaning. In connection with this concept of representing one should think of the concept of representation in secular and canon law. Here 'representation' does not imply that something merely stands in for something else as if it were a replacement or substitute that enjoyed a less authentic, more indirect kind of existence. On the contrary, what is represented is itself present in the only way available to it. (1977; Eng. trans. 1986: 34–5)

The representation of the organization as a whole yielded by the subject's aesthetic judgement therefore does not stand for something else. It is not a proxy, but exactly the way in which the organization is beauty for the businessman. Once again, it is by reference to art that one gains a clearer idea of what this means for the aesthetic understanding of organizational life, and of the extent to which the aesthetic approach is antithetical to the analytic and rational knowledge of organizational aesthetics. In art, observes Gadamer (1977; Eng. trans. 1986: 35), one finds something 'of this representative existence', because in the presence of a work of art 'we are not simply concerned with a memorial token of, reference to, or substitute for the real existence of something'. Consider the portrait of a famous person, continues Gadamer: this person is representatively displayed in the portrait, and the portrait itself, once exhibited in public, is itself present and representativeness, beyond any idolatry or any cult of image. A work of art, therefore, is a heightening of being and not a reference or allusion to being. It is irreplaceable, which becomes even more evident if one thinks of the reproducibility that characterizes photographs or audiovisual recordings. Reproduction is not art, in fact, although like art it involves imitation and representation. It is not art because it correlates with an original of which it is always possible to obtain a better reproduction, one more precise and clearcut. The *mimesis* of art, by contrast, is not the reproduction of something or someone, but the production of the representation (*Darstellung*) of something or someone; a representation which is symbolic and does not stand in a dependence relation with the something or someone that it represents.

It is not another reality, therefore, which is reproduced and represented in the aesthetic judgement. Instead a representation is produced which is itself truth, because the beauty of an organization is a symbol and not the concrete result of objective and measurable causes. The aesthetic approach therefore considers beauty to be a non-copy of organizational truth, just as there is no copy from the truth in a work of art, nor is there an allegorical device that states one thing and invites us to think of another. The aesthetic approach considers beauty exclusively in and of itself, because what it brings to light by representing the experience of the beautiful in organizational life is something symbolic. What are the implications of this for theories of organization and management studies?

New organizational awareness and the construction of a symbolic community

Hans-Georg Gadamer writes that the 'significance of the symbol and the symbolic lay in this paradoxical kind of reference that embodies and even vouchsafes its meaning' (1977; Eng. trans. 1986: 37). It is only in this form – in the form, that is, which resists pure comprehension through conceptualization – that art brings itself to bear. Consider great art and its impact on us. Such art comes as a shock because we are unprepared for it, and when confronted by a convincing work of art we find ourselves to be defenceless. Therefore, the essence of the symbolic and of what can become symbolic, Gadamer writes, 'lies precisely in the fact that it is not related to an ultimate meaning that could be recuperated in intellectual terms. The symbol preserves its meaning within itself' (1977; Eng. trans. 1986: 37). It is this keeping-within-itself of its meaning that constitutes the essence of the symbolic. However, as I have frequently pointed out, the symbolic, and what may become symbolic, require the performance of an initial operation of deconstruction and reconstruction on the part of the knowing subject. If the beauty of an organization is valorized as being symbolic, it can only be understood as 'experience of the simultaneity of absence and fullness' (Zecchi, 1990: 178), thus reinstating the original philosophical meaning of symbol as the expression of a half and simultaneously of a lack, and therefore as necessitating the reconstruction of its sense. It is this that constitutes the process of understanding the beauty of an organization on the basis of the representations of the beautiful produced by the subjects who talk about it. But these subjects do not render these representations into a copy of some authentic organizational truth. Instead they socialize themselves to the truth of these representations and at the same time produce differences among them by interpreting them.

It is at this point that the cleavage arises between aesthetic understanding and analytical knowledge of organizational aesthetics. In order to capture this difference, it is again to the knowledge acquired from experience of a work of art that we must turn, because there is no other experience that so well conveys, through direct experience, the meaning of aesthetic knowledge as familiarization, socialization and acquisition of awareness both new but also ambiguous and opaque. The purpose of every artistic creation, Gadamer points out (1977; Eng. trans. 1986: 39), is to 'open us up' to the language spoken in that work of art, and by so doing make it our own. It does not matter if this happens because a shared view of the world prepares and also sustains the formation and configuration of the work of art. Nor does it matter if, instead, it results from the 'spelling out' of the form that confronts and challenges us, so that we study it and learn its alphabet and language. Whatever the case may be, the fact still remains, Gadamer writes, that 'a shared or potentially shared achievement is at issue', and that this presupposes the work of a community which supersedes previous ones:

> The artist no longer speaks for the community, but forms his own community insofar as he expresses himself. Nevertheless, he does create a community, and in principle, this truly universal community (*oikumene*) extends to the whole world. In fact, all artistic creation challenges each of us to listen to the language in which the work of art speaks and to make it our own. (1977; Eng. trans. 1986: 39)

Similarly, when the businessman described the beauty of his organization, he formed a community that was distinct from his previous one and which potentially encompassed the whole world. This is not to say – and this warrants repeating – that the aesthetic judgement is a work of art, only that the aesthetic judgement produces a 'representation of the thing' which we should treat as we do an artistic representation, and not, therefore, process it as if it were an opinion and a statement of fact. It is meaningless, writes Carlo Sini (1992: 111), to seek to 'translate' a symbol into pseudo-explanations, or into 'other sign systems' entirely heterogeneous to it. It is equally meaningless to attribute 'revelatory, veritative or salvationary powers' to a symbol, absolutizing it by means of a pagan and superstitious cultural practice. If anything, the symbolism of beauty should be correlated to its 'segnic practice', and therefore, in our case, to its representation expressed through formulation of the aesthetic judgement. It is precisely in segnic practice, Sini continues, that one comprehends the 'locus of the emergence' and the 'definite sensate horizon' of the symbol. It tells us that every human practice is profoundly symbolic, so that 'every practice is a meaning-event which is also a world-event, an opening-up of meaning and its expression'.

The practice of the researcher also is symbolic, as Michael Owen Jones stresses when he points out that during empirical research in organizational settings

> field-workers present themselves symbolically to their subjects and are viewed as symbols, the techniques they employ to gather data are not just instruments but symbolic forms that produce different kinds of symbolism and meaning making, and their reports stand as symbols that also incorporate various symbolic devices affecting readers' responses. (1996: 61)

Full emphasis should be given to the fact that organization theory and management studies are symbolic forms – 'inasmuch as the researcher or consultant is a symbol' (Jones, 1996: 62) – when we deconstruct the judgements collected and reconstruct the organizational beauty of which they speak, socializing ourselves to it and acquiring new and specific awareness of organizational dynamics and processes from lived aesthetic experience. This experience, writes Hans Robert Jauss (1982; It. trans. 1987, vol. I: 87–9), is not restricted to 'seeing that yields knowledge' (*aisthesis*) or to 'recognizing mediated by seeing' (*anamnesis*), in that the spectator – the researcher and reader in our case – may be 'gripped' by what is represented. S/he may allow him/herself to be overwhelmed by the sensation aroused by the representation, until s/he feels a sense of relief when the passions provoked by the representation are released, so that s/he feels a pleasure akin to that of healing (*katharsis*).

This is the aesthetic enjoyment whereby the participation, acquisition and pleasure derived from something, for example a spoken or written text, enter into a single relationship, given that the knowledge and the enjoyment still have not been separated so that the former becomes a theoretical attitude and the latter an aesthetic attitude. *Katharsis* is therefore emotional pleasure that may be aroused as much by a poem as by a speech, whether these are audible words or a visible text, as long as they are able to procure a change in the person's aesthetic state – that is, in his/her perceptive and sensory condition – which is also a transformation in his/her convictions, or in other words, new awareness of the organizational life being studied.

In the fundamental aesthetic experience of communication, writes Jauss (1982; It. trans. 1987, vol. I: 105–6), *katharsis* corresponds both to the practical utilization of art as the mediation, inauguration and justification of rules of behaviour, and to the distancing of the knowing subject from the practical interests and concerns of his/her everyday life and his/her placement in 'the aesthetic freedom of his/her judgement' through self-enjoyment (*Selbtsgenuß*) in the enjoyment that the Other is experiencing and that is presented by the latter. This is an important feature of the aesthetic approach which I have discussed on several occasions: the representation of organizational beauty thus proposed is a representation 'put together' jointly by the organizational actor and the researcher, and not solely proffered by those *identify* who belong to the organization and gathered by whoever is studying the organizational phenomena distinctive of that particular context.

The aesthetic judgement of the beautiful generates this knowledge-producing aesthetic process, and it poses, as we saw with Gadamer, the question of the creation of a community which coincides neither with the organizational actor's nor with the researcher's professional and occupational community. This is a symbolic community which arises on the basis of the sentiment of the beautiful in organizational life, and through reconstruction of the symbolism of this organizational beauty. This is precisely what happens in the formation of communities, given that, as Anthony Cohen (1985: 118) points out, people 'construct community symbolically, making it a resource and repository of meaning, and a referent of their identity'. It does not matter if the initial distinction between those who take part in the construction and reconstruction of organizational life, on the one hand, and those who enter into only temporary contact with it while they conduct their research, on the other, remains unchanged with respect to membership organizations and the reference professional and occupational community (Van Maanen and Barley, 1984). This is because

> [c]ommunity exists in the minds of its members, and should not be confused with geographic or sociographic assertions of 'fact'. By extension, the distinctiveness of communities and, thus, the reality of their boundaries, similarly lies in the mind, in the meanings which people attach to them, not in their structural forms. As we have seen, this reality of community is expressed and embellished symbolically. (Cohen, 1985: 98)

The crucial issue as regards the aesthetic approach, therefore, is that new and aesthetically acquired awareness of the organizational phenomenology is bound up with the creation of a new community, and that aesthetic, as opposed to analytic, organizational knowledge is closely connected with the process that Jauss (1982; It. trans. 1987, vol. I: 195) cites as distinctive of aesthetic identification. This is also awareness, therefore, of the fact that:

(a) the aesthetic knowledge of organizational life possessed by both the organizational actor and the researcher involves a 'to-ing and fro-ing' between the 'aesthetically liberated' knowing subject and its 'unreal object';

(b) when acquiring aesthetic knowledge about organizational life, the subject of aesthetic enjoyment may be startled, amazed, moved, surprised; s/he may cry, laugh, reflect, succumb to mere inquisitiveness, grovel or imitate. What s/he cannot do is remain neutral and detach him/herself from what s/he discovers about that particular organizational life.

Again one notes the importance for the aesthetic understanding of organizational life of seventeenth-century aesthetics, with its definition of aesthetic knowledge as the person's experience that 'exhibits itself', and does so, as Elio Franzini (1995: 178) points out, 'amid the cognitive possibilities that Leibniz called *symbolic* and *intuitive*', thereby emphasizing 'the intuitive character of new knowledge and its objects'.

Logica poetica and organizational life

In my foregoing discussion I have transformed the question of what type of knowledge about organizational life is yielded by use of the aesthetic category of the beautiful into the question of the awareness of organizational beauty acquired by empirical research in organizations. What we are able to do, I have argued, without transforming the 'representation' into 'represent-ativeness', is grasp and reconstruct the symbolism of the organization's beauty in the aesthetic judgement, familiarizing ourselves with it, socializing ourselves to it, and thus acquiring specific awareness of the organizational life with which that symbolism is associated. I developed this theme by examining two very different aesthetic judgements furnished by people belonging to different organizations. But how does one acquire awareness of organizational life by gathering several aesthetic judgements, all based on the category of the beautiful, about the *same* organization?

The answers to this question are inevitably specific, circumstantiated and diverse if the knowledge being sought by empirical means is aesthetic understanding of knowledge life. In this section I shall examine aesthetic judgements with regard to an organization operating in the culture industry, and specifically the oldest photography company in the world still in business. This is a prestigious Italian company which, although it now has considerably fewer employees and lower turnover than in the past, has been able to shift its main activity from photography to the promotion of its photographic heritage.

This organization therefore operates in a context that one could call 'aesthetic', if not indeed 'artistic', albeit in the broadest sense of the two terms whereby entertainment can be called art. The organization does not sell entertainment, however, but has built its reputation on photographs which are now part of Italy's artistic heritage, both because of the intrinsic value of the art, architecture and persons that they portray, and because of their photographic language, to which the company has remained faithful for more than one and a half centuries. When Italian schoolbooks illustrate the beauty of a Renaissance *palazzo* or of a railway station inspired by Italian futurism, or the nobility of a member of the English royal family, they frequently use photographs produced by this firm, and they cite it by name. The same applies to non-school books, to specialized photography magazines, and to exhibitions of photographs, mainly Italian, depicting landscapes that no longer exist, or the offices and workers of nineteenth-century industrial organizations, or those documenting the contents of Italian museums.

The interview extracts that I shall now examine are only some of those recorded a number of years ago with members of this organization while I was researching art photography in Europe (1995). In particular, they consist of answers to two questions asked at a certain stage of the interview, when I had established a certain familiarity with the informant: 'Do you do beautiful things?', which usually preceded, but sometimes followed, the question: 'What is beautiful about the Photographic Company as a company?'

The two questions were not always put in exactly this form, either in the Photographic Company or during other empirical research conducted in other organization settings. Their formulation depended on the relational dynamics that arose between myself and the organizational actor. Nor were these questions asked of all the interviewees, since they depended on how the interview unfolded, on the themes that seemed of greatest interest to the interviewee, and on my impression of his/her understanding of the purpose of my research as explained at the beginning of the interview: namely, the relationship between aesthetics and everyday organizational life. But when the questions were asked, the interviewee could answer by giving free rein to his/her perceptions and cognitions of the beautiful, perhaps reflecting on them for the first time, or seeking to impress me with some learned reference, watching my face to see from my reaction whether s/he had answered properly.

On almost all occasions, reference to the 'beautiful' in the question prompted a request for clarification of the term's meaning. This was a request with which I could not comply, because it was precisely what the informant meant by 'beautiful' that constituted the theme of that particular part of the interview: the category of beautiful that s/he used, and the features of organizational life to which s/he applied it. In other words, the question obliged the interviewee to use an unspecified category so that elements not defined a priori came to light, and this also had to happen amid the uncertainty that these 'elements' would in fact emerge. Although this was in keeping with the concept of elusiveness current in organizational aesthetics, it was unsettling for the interviewees, who had no category to apply and were invited to construct the 'objects' of the conversation on their own, and subordinately, or even implicitly, to come up with some definition of beauty. Reassurance for the interviewee, therefore, could only come from elsewhere: from the relational dynamic with the researcher, from soothing expressions like 'Everything that comes into your mind', 'Everything that strikes you as beautiful', 'Anything you want'.

A further feature emerged. Although the interviewee did not know what was meant by 'beautiful', the reference to work was clear, in the sense that the interviewee was fully able to reflect on his/her work while describing his/her routine life in the organization. Nevertheless, on numerous occasions during this and other research, no reference was made to the organization. 'What do you mean by "beautiful about the organization"?' was frequently the first reaction to my question. To which my rejoinder was 'Yes, precisely as an organization', a repetition and emphasis that usually had a positive effect which cannot be rationally explained in terms of how the question was specified. I usually emphasized the term 'organization' by once again repeating it. Only infrequently did I add 'overall' or 'as a whole', but in any case the interviewee was given a second or two to familiarize him/herself with the question and formulate an answer. As well as reinforcing 'organization' with 'organization', I frequently used the name of the firm, so that the interviewee could visualize the organization on hearing its name mentioned in phrases like 'Yes, the Photographic Company as an organization'.

The following extract is taken from the transcription of the interview with a young researcher working in the Photographic Company, who handled the requests for photographs sent in by publishing houses.

Q: Do you do beautiful things?
A: Eh, working here, yes.
Q: For example?
A: Sometimes I make really interesting iconographic choices.
Q: What difference do you draw between interesting iconographic research and beautiful research?
A: Between?
Q: I said 'beautiful', and you called it interesting research. Can you give a more precise definition of the concept of beautiful in relation to what you do?
A: About what I do? Oh, all right, in the pleasant sense, pleasant like, basically, at the same time, beautiful products, you know, things beautiful to look at, and to . . . pleasurable, in short, which can have, besides . . . how can I put it, besides an intellectual flavour also an aesthetic one of beauty. So it's the pleasure of being able to do something like this, a job which can give pleasure to others. If it was only a pleasure for me, it would be stupid . . . it would be an end in itself. In fact, in this field, photographs are only pictures, and you speak through pictures, there's a language, and therefore this is very important. I did the history of miniatures at university, which is the language for images typical of the Middle Ages, and so the reference to photography is always rather close. Photography served to illustrate books, and so on, so the shift was there.

The category of the beautiful applied to work is closely connected with the organization to which the interviewee belonged. With that 'Eh, working here yes', she attributed to the organization itself the feature of doing 'beautiful things' in its day-to-day work. It should be pointed out that this close relationship between organization and the beauty of one's work is facilitated by the fact that I emphasized earlier: that this firm operated in the culture and art market. It should also be noted that it is not always like this; indeed, on several occasions during my researches it was pointed out to me that the work performed was 'work like any other', in the sense that a job could not be considered beautiful just because it brought a person into contact with beautiful working materials or with artists, or just because it involves mounting an exhibition or putting on a show.

This also happened with the people who worked in the Photographic Company. Some of them – very few to tell the truth – did not talk to me about the beauty of their work. Indeed, one of them did not even give me a chance to ask my question about the category of the beautiful. On the other hand, the beautiful is not the only category that one can employ to gain aesthetic understanding of organizational life. As stressed at the beginning of this chapter and repeatedly in previous ones, the aesthetic in organizational life does not arise from the aesthetic judgement alone. It instead relates to the network of sensory faculties that a subject is able to activate intentionally in the organizational context. It is therefore important to take due account of the fact that we seek to gain understanding of organizational life by means of *one* of the aesthetic faculties, namely the aesthetic judgement, and that the aesthetic judgement is in turn employed using only one of the categories of aesthetics, however important it may be, namely the category of beauty. There are members of organizations who express this judgement with regard to their work and their organization. But there are others who do not, because this is not the way in which they view their everyday work in the organization or on its behalf. Which shows that a judgement is involved, and not a pact sustaining the relationship between individual and organization like, for example, a work contract.

The link between the beauty of the work and that of the organization to which one belongs is further emphasized by the young researcher in the following extract. The passage starts with the reference she made to her university studies, and her emphasis on the close match between her university training and her work: she had studied the history of miniatures, which constituted 'the language for images typical of the Middle Ages', and consequently 'the reference to photography is always rather close'.

> *Q:* And does this give you a particular feeling? The fact that you work for this organization?
>
> *A:* Well, how can I put it, I can say that it's an interesting job, since the Photographic Company is very old and rather prestigious, and therefore has lots of things in its archives, inside itself, let's say. Obviously, it's always a pleasure to work for a prestigious company, or at any rate for something beautiful, in general.
>
> *Q:* For something beautiful. And what's that?
>
> *A:* Something beautiful, which produces beautiful things that can improve the quality of people's lives.
>
> *Q:* That produces beautiful things? What are these beautiful things?
>
> *A:* They're the photographs, or exhibitions, or books, which help people to pass the time in the best way possible.

It is therefore the beauty of the 'very old and rather prestigious' Photographic Company which shapes the beauty of the work that goes on within it. The organization is 'a beautiful thing'; it is beautiful because it 'produces beautiful things' which are such, note, because they 'can improve the quality of people's lives'. We find here the close connection between the principle of the good and the category of the beautiful that I pointed out in the previous section when discussing the judgement of organizational beauty furnished by the first businessman. Here the reference is more explicit, and it concerns not only the members of the organization but also society at large. The beauty of the Photographic Company, in fact, consists not in what is good and right for the organization itself and the people who work for it, but in the improvement that it brings to the lives of the people who use its products. In this case, therefore, unlike the beauty of the organization which the first businessman tied to the 'ecological' environment in which it operated, the beautiful and the good are interconnected, but 'outside' the organization and not 'within' it. It is the relationship between the Photographic Company and external society, therefore, that highlights the category of the beautiful as it applies to this organization. It is the improvement in the quality of life in society externally to the organizational routine that is thrown into relief and related to whatever it is that makes this organization 'a beautiful thing'. It 'produces beautiful things' through which 'one speaks, there's a language'. And this 'is always very important', declares the interviewee, referring to her work in the first extract.

Moreover, the first extract also demonstrates the importance of the relationship between the organization, the beauty of the things that it produces, and Others, namely society as a whole and not the firm's customers or the other organizations to which it supplies its products. It is this aesthetic dimension that is emphasized, and it comprises a close connection between the aesthetic category and the principle of the good inherent both in the work and in the organization. 'If it was only a pleasure for me, it would be stupid . . . it would be an end in itself', the interviewee says about the things that she does. The 'pleasure in being able to do' 'things beautiful to look at', 'pleasurable' things, things that 'besides an intellectual flavour also [have] an aesthetic one of beauty', is not stupid and not an end in itself, in fact, only if things are made which can give 'pleasure to others'. Which reveals the ethical nature of the beauty of her work.

The category of the beautiful used in the young researcher's representation of the Photographic Company brought out the character of an organization that had 'lots of things in its archives, inside itself, let's say', which is 'something beautiful, in general'. This latter was projected externally to society as 'beautiful products' which were both beautiful and morally right because they 'can improve the quality of people's lives'. Working for this organization gave pleasure; it was beautiful because the organization was beautiful, because it made beautiful products which aroused pleasure in others, and because the organization enjoyed prestige in society at large. It was an organization whose inner beauty extended outwards. The work that went on within its walls was intended to arouse pleasure in external society, a pleasure that combined an 'intellectual flavour' with the flavour of beauty.

As I have frequently pointed out, this is an aesthetic judgement whereby the truth of the beauty of the organization and of its work resides in the symbolism of its presentation. Therefore, the question of whether an organization is really as it is described, or whether it is not, is wholly irrelevant to the aesthetic judgement and to the aesthetic understanding of the organization. This is because the representation does not 'represent' the organization: it does not possess representativeness, and is therefore not commensurable with the representations of the organization produced by any of its other members. Gathering a quantity of aesthetic judgements of the beauty of the Photographic Company is pointless when one uses the aesthetic approach, because it is impossible to add up the sum of the organization's beauties or to piece together a mosaic of these representations to produce an overall picture of its beauty. And yet each of these representations 'tells' us something distinctive, specific and important about the artefact 'organization'. I shall now show what emerges from analysis of the replies provided by other participants in the organizational life of the Photographic Company. I begin with the head of new photographic production, an American photographer who had been working for the firm for many years:

> The most beautiful thing is that I come into contact with early photography, something that I didn't know very much about. We put on historical exhibitions, so I'm learning a lot about the history of photography besides organizing beautiful exhibitions, meeting important people in the world of photography, people who belong to the board of the Photographic Company. They are the biggest names in the world, starting with [. . .], and so on. So they're people who it's an obvious pleasure to meet and spend hours talking to. The beautiful thing has been this incredible challenge of carrying on a tradition, because the Photographic Company has a name that opens people's eyes, it opens doors to people who are otherwise very reserved and reluctant to talk to you. You only have to say the name of the Photographic Company and people smile at you with pleasure. There's an almost magical air about it, and therefore the idea of being part of this magic, of this aura of the past, gives me great pleasure. Though I realize that what I have to do is an extremely difficult job: managing to keep up a good qualitative and technical standard at this moment in our frenetic lives. It's also beautiful to work in old surroundings, seeing the old machines that they used in the past, talking to the archivist who's been here for thirty years, seeing how they took photos in churches using mirrors. There are fascinating things in the history of these photographs from the past, they are all very beautiful things.

The representation of organizational life provided by this interviewee uses the category of the beautiful as the link between his work and the organization. In other words, this category is used in analogous fashion to describe both work and the organization, and it has marked significances in both cases. I pointed out something similar regarding the category of the beautiful used by the young researcher in the previous extract. What emerges from the aesthetic judgements of both interviewees is the manifold nature of the organizational beauty of the Photographic Company.

The beauty described by the researcher moves from 'within' the organization towards external society along a trajectory stretching from the aesthetic category to the principle of the good. The beauty described by the head of new photographic production – a department responsible for enriching the company's photographic heritage, not for innovating its style – conjugates work and organization with the representation of the 'incredible challenge' of carrying on a tradition, because the Photographic Company 'has a name': it focuses on the organization and remains circumscribed by aesthetics. In the previous extract, the researcher's representation emphasized the continuity constituted by the language of images used by the miniatures in medieval books, university, and the archive photographs used to illustrate contemporary texts. She was not 'challenged' to carry forward a corporate tradition and a corporate image through her choice of archive photographs. By contrast, the head of photography did indeed have to meet such a challenge, and he consequently highlighted the organizational task of producing new photographs and the glory that surrounded the corporate tradition not as a continuity but as a hiatus, and as a difference which threw the Photographic Company into further relief.

There is a beauty in this relief, however, that appeals to the head of photography. In his representation the corporate name acts as a *passe-partout*: it opens people's eyes, it opens people's doors, and gives access to 'the big names' of photography. It is a *passe-partout*, however, of which he is an integral part. And this is pleasurable to him not for instrumental reasons, nor because it brings him personal advantage or career advancement. It is pleasurable to him because he can continue to be part of it and 'part of this magic'.

Organizational as festival

The representation of organizational beauty and of work to be found in the words of the head of photography therefore differs greatly from the one provided by the researcher. Whereas in the latter's representation we observed the inward–outward tension of the organization, in the former's we discern a different tension, one which ties the individual to the organization. The category of the beautiful that emerges from the head of photography's representation, in fact, emphasizes the pleasure that he feels by virtue of belonging to that particular organization. This pleasure is illustrated by his statement that 'the most beautiful thing' is coming into 'contact with early photography'. It is emphasized by his daily struggle to produce photographs that will carry forward the organization's glorious tradition. And it is expressed in his sense of belonging to 'this aura of the past' which is the 'magic' of the Photographic Company.

The improvement of the quality of life enjoyed by others through the beauty of one's work and organization is not a part of the head of photography's representation, which instead emphasizes participation in the 'festival' created by the beautiful. It is this particular category of the beautiful – which the head of photography relates as much to work as to the organization – that renders what 'opens people's eyes' and what makes 'people smile at you with pleasure' with 'an almost magical air' part of the organization's magic. Hans-Georg Gadamer writes (1977; Eng. trans. 1986: 39–40) that the experience of 'festival' precludes isolation of one element from another, and of one person from the others. In other words, a festival celebrates a communal experience, and it does so in the most complete form, because the 'celebration of a festival is, in technical terms, an intentional activity'. A festival does not consist in the fact that all of us are gathered together in the same place, but in the fact that there is 'an intention that unites us and prevents us as individuals from falling into private conversations and private, subjective experiences'.

The beautiful resides in the challenge of handing on the organization's tradition. But it also resides in taking part in the festival of back-slapping and smiles where it is possible to meet clever and famous people, and during which something can be learnt about 'the history of photography' while working in 'old surroundings'. It is at this festival that one learns 'how they took photos in churches using mirrors', and other 'fascinating things about these photographs from the past', and at which one has the pleasure of talking to 'the archivist who's been here for thirty years' – a veteran, therefore, of the festival. But does the sense of participating in a festival emerge from other aesthetic judgements of the Photographic Company. And if it does, is the emphasis on the same things and on the same features of the organization?

Once again the answer is 'No, this does not happen'. For example, the head of the press office stressed the beauty of everyday routine in the organization, and not its magic:

> Well . . . I don't know . . . I reckon . . . I think there's beauty in the Photographic Company, but it's that in all workplaces there's beauty . . . also in this everyday routine, you know, finding yourself every day, for good or ill, with the same people, though they're people . . . So, let's take it in order. With the same people because you inevitably form a human relationship, with likes and dislikes, the arguments, all that microcosm in here . . . I mean, the Photographic Company as a microcosm, as a workplace like an all-embracing microcosm. Which creates a continuity, that is, it creates a . . . also an affective dimension, if you want. And I like that very much, even though, obviously, it only comes out sometimes. More often there are problems, rows, you're in a hurry, right, to do things, so that there's no time to talk, and so on. But every so often there are these intervals when you joke, chat, tell each other things, and I find that's really nice. Beautiful I believe is . . . for me at least, the fact that there's a constant flux of people who come in because they collaborate with the company, or they've been called in, or because they've got a proposal to make. So there's constant networking, right? A constant forming of relationships which perhaps stop when the thing's finished, but they may start again with the next job or the next thing to do. Something else beautiful, well, I wouldn't know. But perhaps I'd also say the work in and of itself, frankly, because it's much better to argue every day when staging exhibitions than to row every day over 'You go and get that file', 'No, I'll go', and so on. So that's what I think. There's also a disadvantage, because thinking, I don't know, about finding, looking for another job, because by force of circumstances you have to go in this direction, which isn't easy.

Here the sense of participating in a festival is emphasized by the fact that both the company and the workplace are viewed as 'a microcosm', as an 'all-embracing microcosm' which 'creates continuity'; one, that is, which creates an 'affective dimension' which the head of the press office 'likes very much'. However, we do not find the same emphasis, nor even the same overtones, evident in the representation provided by the head of photography. Abstruse terms like 'aura' are not used, nor are esoteric and mythical ones like 'magic'. This interviewee does not talk about faces and doors that open. Compared with the head of photography or, especially, the researcher, he concentrates much more closely on the inner life of the Photographic Company. This is important if one bears in mind that work to promote the company's activities may lead to particular value being assigned to its beauty on the outside, instead of emphasis being placed on the enjoyability of its inner life and its everyday routine, the enjoyability of 'all workplaces'; a beauty, therefore, distinctive of organizations that are beautiful organizations.

It is consequently the fact that there 'is a constant flux of people', a 'constant networking', a 'constant forming of relationships' which constitutes the quotidian nature of an 'all-embracing microcosm' in which people 'joke, chat, tell each other things'. The flow of people is constant, and the Photographic Company is an arena in which human relationships are created among persons who actively participate in the construction and reconstruction of the beauty of its everyday routine. They come into the building because they 'work with the company, or they've been called in, or because they've got a proposal to make'. The microcosm is vital, therefore, because the people who belong to it are select, and they make proposals and collaborate.

The press officer posits the beauty of his organization as residing in its vitality. His description thus makes its beauty more specific and particular than he is willing to admit, in view of his qualification 'but it's [the beauty in] all workplaces'. Relationships are established with special people so that their constant flow becomes 'all that microcosm in here', rather than the fleeting, awkward and stressful relationships of a vortex. Moreover, in this case too, the beauty of the organization is closely bound up with the beauty of the work that goes on within its walls. 'Something else beautiful' about the company, in fact, is 'the work in and of itself'. Here, therefore, the press officer further accentuates the specificity of the organization in which he works, and he does so by citing what we have already seen to be a fundamental characteristic of beauty: namely that it is 'non-familiar'. The beauty of the work 'in and of itself' is dangerous; it is something to protect oneself against because it may beguile one away from what must be done, given that were one to be 'looking for another job', it would have to be just as beautiful, and this would lead one in a direction that 'isn't easy'.

There is marked emphasis in the press officer's words on participation in a specific festival, and not in any festival whatever. This is expressed by his remark that 'it's much better to argue every day when staging exhibitions', especially if one bears in mind that the press officer's involvement in 'staging exhibitions' comes at a later stage, when the exhibition has been decided and planned and it is his task to promote it. Consequently, this is not strictly speaking participation in the staging of the exhibition. There is instead a sense of shared purposiveness which transpires from his comment on the daily struggle to create the corporate product, because this signifies something beautiful. There is also a reference here to organizational activities which, however much they may be performed separately, create a basic distinction in terms of competences, at least as far as the team responsible for 'staging exhibitions' is concerned. The Photographic Company is therefore beautiful: certainly because beautiful things are made in it, as the researcher also pointed out, but above all because it is a 'flux' and a 'microcosm' which reduces the sense of the parcelling-out of activities and the division of tasks, while it instead underscores the sense of creating a vital quotidian work environment.

This does not only apply to the aesthetic judgement of the head of the press office, because flux, movement and purposiveness are elements characteristic of the beauty of the organization for other people who work for the Photographic Company. Some of them show this by drawing comparisons with the company's recent past, as one notes from the following extract from the interview with a member of the exhibition department:

> *Q:* So you see [the organization] as something beautiful?
> *A:* Yes, really beautiful. Very beautiful and especially now. Until a few years ago, let's say ... the Photographic Company was only considered an archive, something old, at a standstill, motionless. But now, since the museum opened, and because of the new acquisitions, the fact that we've started to take photographs again, for me it's taken on a new dimension, what should really be the dimension of the Photographic Company.

The organization is beautiful in this new dimension because it has made acquisitions and started to take photographs again. This beauty is contrasted with when the company was at a 'standstill', 'something' that was 'motionless' and 'old'. In short, it is the organization's refound vitality that has restored its beauty. This was also stressed by a photographic print-maker working for the company, although he specified that it was more evident from outside the organization:

> *A:* Less inside, more outside. When you meet friends, they say 'You work for the Photographic Company', they say, 'Really! Ah, beautiful! I've heard this, and I've seen that . . .'.
> *Q:* They immediately say 'beautiful'?
> *A:* Yes! 'Beautiful', 'Really beautiful', 'It's marvellous'. Even recently someone came in who I . . . the schools often have something to do . . .
> *Q:* But according to you, why do they say 'beautiful'?
> *A:* They say 'beautiful' because it's partly history and it's partly a projection, a reproduction of something that you feel, let's say, they see an image that was out of their perspective. I remember in '77 when they put on the first big exhibition which, let's say, revived the Photographic Company, because presenting the exhibition to [. . .], I don't know if you were able to . . .
> *Q:* Yes, I heard about it.
> *A:* Part of the organization was very beautiful, very complex, with celebrities who came to the opening. But it was off-set by a rather pedantic search for a

reconstructed setting . . . a style was re-created, Liberty, as it was, with those soft furnishings, and then a chronological survey of all the parts divided into sections . . . There were art historians here, I remember [. . .], and so there were all these people that I pampered a bit, really pampered them. In fact I was praised for it, because they congratulated me more than once. So it was a really beautiful moment, very beautiful, which reawakened the Photographic Company's heritage in people's minds.

The festival in this case is one whose beauty is truth, as evidenced by the fact that it is felt by people external to the organization and who therefore do not have interests in common with it. This is disinterested or Kantian beauty, and it proves that the beauty of the organization exists, given that it is felt even by those who have nothing to do with it. Once again, the festival is different from those examined previously, because it celebrates 'the really beautiful moment' which 'reawakened the Photographic Company's heritage in people's minds'. This festival is not faces that smile and doors that open before you as if by magic, therefore; nor is it a microcosm of the quotidian, nor is it the life-quality of people external to the organization. Rather, it is a festival of reawakening and of admiration whose participants are struck by the beauty of the organization's heritage; just as happens, one might say, when one is in the presence of a great work of art.

This festival first arose in contrast to organizational memories of a tragic period in the past, of organizational events which proved critical for the persons concerned, and which they brought to light by default, using the category of the ugly to imply the opposite. The head of the photographic archive described the crisis period as follows:

I remember I was on the bus going off to lunch, I was on the rear platform and there were two people talking about [the town of . . .]. One said 'They're closing that shop,' the other said 'But how come, that's not possible,' 'But you know, they're also closing the Photographic Company,' he says, 'Ah, that shop in [Via . . .], that beautiful old one,' he says, 'It was in the paper that they're going to close it,' he says, 'No. It's not possible!' And because he was next to me, I said 'Yes, unfortunately it's true, I work for the Photographic Company, I don't know whether it's an institution, because . . . it's been there for so long, but it's going to close anyway.'

The tragic fate of the organization outweighed the informant's personal tragedy: he makes no mention of economic loss or of the loss of his job. He pushes his personal tragedy into the background, while it is the heroic demise of the organization that he foregrounds. It is in this tragedy that he must now participate if he wishes to be part of something heroic and grandiose, and demonstrate his 'greatness' to others as well as himself. One notes the high-flown and romantic overtones of 'I don't know whether it's an institution, because . . . it's been there for so long, but it's going to close anyway'; a statement which highlights the sentiment as well as the sentimentality that overtakes the archivist when he relives that period and those events. The head of exhibitions, who had worked for the company for many years and had risen from the rank-and-file, also remembered the time in her interview. She had been hired by competitive examination, and she had won, she was subsequently told, because of her beautiful handwriting:

> What I have noted in all these years . . . that is, the elements . . . beautiful things and ugly things follow one another. But a really ugly, ugly thing . . . The only thing, the danger, that moment of danger when it seemed that the Photographic Company would probably close. That sensation of . . . that it could happen! But not because it was the Photographic Company in itself, because according to me, since this is a company . . . that it, I'm a very traditional person, but not because I'm a traditionalist, because I'm modern, I like things . . . But according to me, because for me, culture is something that gradually comes about, it's formed inside . . . But culture for me doesn't mean an intelligent person who has studied, oh no! Culture is lived experience, it is how . . . So the fact itself that this company might close, meeting the same fate as so many other beautiful Italian things, that was really a difficult moment. Not so much, not insofar as I'd lose my job, because I'll tell you sincerely, perhaps also it was different in those days . . . But I was never scared that the company would close, saying 'Oh God, I won't find a job,' no. It was also because . . . perhaps today it would frighten me, perhaps today. Because for good or ill I believed that I had given something to the company, so I wanted it to continue, because for good or ill I'd lived here, apart from working eight hours a day. That is, I could never have worked for a company in which I did a job I didn't like. So, perhaps because I liked it, I felt that I had also given it something of myself. And that's absolutely not to be presumptuous.

Unlike the archivist, the exhibition organizer does not place herself in the shadow of the event, although this is paradoxically a way to demonstrate one's participation in its unfolding and give – as Ernst Gombrich (1995) argues regarding the 'cast shadow' in myth and legend – certification of the substantiality of what it is that casts the shadow, which in this case is the beauty of the organization. Instead, she states very clearly that her greatest concern was not losing her job but losing the company – that is, losing the artefact in whose construction and reconstruction she had directly partici-pated – because 'for good or ill' she believed that she 'had given' something to it. She had done so because she liked what the organization did, and could claim the right to feel that she 'had also given it something' which was not generic but intimate and personal, because it was part of herself.

The organization was the fruit not only of her involvement but also of its segnic practice, because she had 'lived' in the company and not just worked there. Consequently, her organizational culture was the 'lived experience' of the tragedy that 'this company might close, meeting the same fate as so many other beautiful Italian things'. Participation in the dramatic festival celebrating the danger of the company's closure comprises both an aesthetic dimension constituted from within the organization (the pleasure deriving from working in it, the feeling that it is the locus of one's life and the fruit of one's labours) and an aesthetic dimension constituted from without (the organization as one of many beautiful Italian things, and its cultural importance). Flanking both dimensions is the exhibition organizer's feeling about the Photographic Company, which he encapsulated in 'I wanted it to continue'.

We may now conclude discussion of aesthetic judgements on the beauty of work and organizations, for they already suffice to pose a question of considerable importance for the aesthetic understanding of organizational life: is it not mythical thought that emerges with such clarity from these representations of organizational life by the subjects involved in its construction and reconstruction?

Mythical thinking and aesthetics

A myth, writes Roland Barthes (1957; Eng. trans. 1973: 107), 'cannot possibly be an object, a concept, or an idea; it is a mode of signification, a form'. The organizational myth of the Photographic Company which transpires from representations of its beauty and of the work that goes on within its walls comprises, as we have seen, the following: the company's renewed vitality; the improved quality of people's lives in society externally to the organization; the company as a 'beautiful Italian thing'; its ability to open doors and make people smile; its status as a precious part of the Italian cultural heritage; its nature as a 'microcosm' of beautiful interpersonal relations; a beauty that would disappear if the company closed down.

We thus have a plurality of modes of signification of organizational life, all of them related to one particular organization. A myth is particularly rich in symbolic virtualities, observes Dan Sperber (1982: 108). It suggests diverse and not necessarily compatible interpretations which demonstrate, first, that it is not necessary to attribute a single structural pattern to them, and, second, that these virtualities give rise to as many outcomes as there are individuals, including the scholar. The significance of myth, writes Gillo Dorfles (1967: 77), is always 'transrational' and 'transconceptual', and it is characteristic of myth that it is always subjected to some sort of interpretation or hermeneutic scrutiny.

It is precisely this that emerged from the foregoing analysis of the representations provided by the employees of the Photographic Company: not a single and well-defined organizational myth but the differences among each subject's mythological description of the relationship between him/herself and the organization. None of the representations discussed above, however different they may have been, describes this relationship in terms of rational action taken in pursuit of a cognitive-rational goal. On the contrary, all of them evidence the 'being-in-situation' of these people, who were 'thrown' into the situation, one might say *à la* Husserl, and who gave part of themselves to it, whether the context was the 'challenge' recounted by the photographer or the 'microcosm' of which the chief press officer felt himself part, or the vague awareness felt by the exhibition organizer that she had given something of herself to the company and 'lived' in it. All these representations also reveal the *pathos* of the sensible of these mythic interpretations of organizational life. They display the intensity of these people's feelings and their 'transport' with regard to the everyday organizational reality that they construct and reconstruct with their active participation.

These are the reasons adduced by the interviewees to account for their meaningful action in the organization, and they are reasons that can be grasped on the basis of the aesthetic understanding of organizational life. I shall examine this theme in the rest of this chapter, seeking to show how the close connection between the aesthetic understanding of organizational life and the mythical thought of the organizational actors in the Photographic Company has a theoretical grounding in the philosophy of one of the founders of aesthetics: the Neapolitan philosopher Giambattista Vico (1725) and his *logica poetica*.

The 'discovery' of aesthetics is a matter of dispute and polemic among philosophers and art historians. Franco Restaino (1991: 13–14) notes that although modern aesthetics originated in the thought of Vico, Baumgarten and Kant, if we wish to be more precise, also of considerable importance was Joseph Addison's *The Pleasure of the Imagination*, published in eleven instalments between June and July 1712 in the London periodical *The Spectator*, for which Addison wrote his finest essays. Indeed, in certain respects, if one considers the 555 issues of this cultural periodical, which sold 3000 copies a day, as well as the fact that it was published in volumes 'which reached even the most isolated villages of the provinces' (Restaino, 1991: 33), one realizes that Addison's aesthetic reflections on taste, wit, novelty, the sublime and the beautiful must certainly have had more influence and reached a wider audience than Vico's *Principi di una scienza nuova*.

But the manner in which the Neapolitan conceived his *logica poetica* was so radical and so distinctive that it is to him that we owe – according to both the Italian philosopher Benedetto Croce (1902: 277) and the German philosopher Ernst Cassirer (1923–9; It. trans. 1961, vol. I: 108) – the 'discovery' of aesthetics. This, too, however, is disputed by scholars, not all of whom are convinced by Vico's radical anti-Cartesianism or, more generally, by eighteenth-century aesthetics. Maurizio Ferraris (1996: 104, 112–13), for example, reminds us of Descartes's early interest in the imagination and of the eccentricities and millenarian fantasies of scholars of aesthetics. Although these unresolved issues counsel caution, the conception of aesthetics used in this book is decidedly anti-Cartesian and entirely opposed to any subjection of aesthetic knowledge to rational explanation. Accordingly, as I have also argued elsewhere (1999), Vico's aesthetic philosophy is of fundamental importance for the aesthetic approach, but in the reading of it provided, amongst many others, by Croce and Cassirer. Indeed, it is precisely Vico's radical anti-Cartesianism that enables us to gain full understanding of the findings yielded by the research at the Photographic Company. Vico was firmly opposed to Cartesian rational explanation. He instead emphasized mythical poetry, the *mythos*, the mytho-logical imagination, reasoning by metaphors, in short the mythical thought of individuals and the close and direct connection between their thought and their feelings based on the sensory faculties of their bodies.

Vico's thesis in proposing *Principles of a New Science concerning the Nature of the Nations by which are Found the Principles of Another System of the Natural Law of the Gentes* – as the complete title of his *La scienza nuova* (1725; Eng. trans. 1968: xix) runs – is that human behaviour does not obey the abstract principles of Cartesian logic. Nor do feelings obey them, not even thought, he maintains, if one considers historical phenomena and if one wishes to uncover the foundations of human communication with the world. Those who seek to discover how individuals actually construct their social world must examine their mythical thought. This they must do for various reasons: because no exact reasoning exists, only the metaphors, the images and the gestures with which individuals express themselves and communicate; because sacred and secret hieroglyphics constitute a large part of the language used by people to think, as well as to feel, and enable them to construct the civil world; because non-reasoned connections, writes Vico (1725; Eng. trans. 1968: 116), based on 'robust sense and vigorous imagination', yield wisdom, and this form of knowledge is not rational but poetic (*sapienza poetica*). The outcome is poetry rooted in sensible knowledge of our surroundings, knowledge which we fully comprehend because it was the original knowledge of humankind (*sapienza della gentilità*). It is metaphysics, but 'felt and imagined' metaphysics not the 'reasoned and abstracted' kind of the learned.

Vico's mythical poetry is born from dismissal of the reason; it is the poetry that astounds us with the wonder of all things; the poetry based on the senses and the imagination. It is the fantasy able to create false but enormous images of a mind; a mind, however, which is not abstract and 'too withdrawn from the senses' but instead entirely immersed in the senses and the passions. Wholly 'buried in the body', writes Vico (1725: 118), is the mythical mentality on which humanity is founded. *Logica poetica*, therefore, is the logic best suited to understand this mentality, because it is 'imaginative metaphysics' (1725: 130) which – although it does not rationally explain either mankind's mind or surroundings – is able to show how humans make 'the things out of' themselves and become them 'by transforming' themselves.

The mythical thought described by Vico, therefore, is fantasy, metaphor and image. It is a way of seeing and knowing the world that has nothing to do with analysis, explanation or reason. Instead, it involves the construction of civil society through the 'translation' of people into it, and through its adequate understanding 'from within'. Vico's theory concerns 'society as such', observes Alberto Izzo (1994: 31), and works on the basis of an empirical science that is neither exact nor true; a science of humankind *qua* a science of society irreducible to the world of nature. We thus meet again the crucial issue in the debate on the method of the social sciences examined in Chapter 2: the distinction between the social sciences and the natural sciences, where society – *mondo civile*, in Vico's terms – is knowable from within but the world of nature resists human understanding because it is not constructed by humans. Vico envisages an empathic rather than rational understanding of civil society by arguing that humans identify 'with the world and with things', writes Gillo Dorfles (1967: 19), 'precisely because they are unable to comprehend it cognitively' but 'affirm it imaginatively, which is a sort of *Einfühlung ante litteram*'.

The 'logic' described by Vico is not a science of the judgement, states Elio Franzini (1995: 145–6). It instead revives the original meaning of the term whereby *logos* was synonymous with *mythos* and related to both the word and the original creativity of humankind. Consequently, the senses and passions underlying mythical language convey a communicative reality which is part of the historical and anthropological genesis of society. Thus Vico, 'with his construction of a "poetic" logic, the first "logical" exegesis of principles already expounded by Leonardo and Bacon', observes Franzini (1987: 15–16), poses the question of language as an 'aesthetic problem' and hence as the 'original dimension of intersubjective communication' rather than as a 'logico-discursive, psychological or ontological theme'.

With his *logica poetica*, therefore, Vico legitimates the fabulist and mythological thought of humans and the mythical representation of their participation in the construction of society. Insofar as this civil world is certainly made up of people, Vico writes (1725: 96–9), then it is in their mythical thought and sentiments that one must seek the principles of the society that they have constructed. It is exactly this that constitutes the importance of Vico's *logica poetica* for the aesthetic understanding of organizational life; a new methodological ideal, as Ernst Cassirer (1941–2) put it, a new *Discours de la méthode*. Applied to history, after almost a century of Cartesian logicism and mathematicism, Vico's philosophy of society anticipated both the rise of sociology and the spirit itself of romanticism. In the hieroglyph, which is not a mysterious and mystic sign but the communicative reality of a social context and a civil society, in the metaphysical elaboration which yields fantasticated interpretation of relationships with society as well as with nature, in gestural language, and in the myth whereby humans transform themselves into the world that surrounds them and into what they do, there is nothing that is false, as Cartesian rationality would have us believe. On the contrary, hieroglyph and myth, the sensory faculties and the imagination, inasmuch as they precede rational thought in the comprehension of nature and society, 'generate narratives' which, Franzini (1995: 146) declares, 'are *true*, they comprise the truth itself of history'.

Myths, fables and rituals are forms of self-expression and communication based on the awareness of feeling, on the human capacity to create, and on the productivity of the imagination. It is the visual thinking or 'thought by images', writes Dorfles (1967: 15), that was rediscovered and revalued in the mid-twentieth century, most notably by Herbert Read (1955), who analysed the precedence of imaging thought over conceptual thought. And it is this imaging thought, Dorfles again notes (1967: 6–7), that Susanne Langer (1942) finds in the 'presentational symbol' or in the fact that the symbol of our sentiment 'must allow us to conceive the idea that it *presents*' regardless 'of any more or less conceptualized meaning' and of any discursive 'truth'.

It is the synthetic capacity of the imagination that ties people to society and to nature, therefore. And it is the image itself that is true, for it is the translation of thought into the sensible. As Vico declares (1725: 336), it is 'a poetic or creative nature' that ascribes 'to physical things the being of substances animated by gods'. In Vico's aesthetics, observes Dorfles (1967: 21), myth is the 'means of transrational communication' which tells us 'the *truth of the image*' that 'in like manner to *artistic truth*' 'is often more reliable than *historical* truth'. This productivity of the imagination is the 'poetic or creative nature' which 'is most robust in the weakest at reasoning', writes Vico (1725: 336), thereby stating a theme which, according to Franzini (1995: 148), constitutes 'the crux of the scientific foundation of aesthetics' and 'runs as a leitmotif throughout eighteenth-century culture', marking out 'the boundaries of anti-Cartesianism'.

5   Artefacts, Form and Aesthetic Categories

Research studies on organizational aesthetics do not generally make explicit reference to the aesthetic categories, apart from the category of the beautiful. The latter, however, has been considered not so much as a specific category of aesthetics as one synonymous with aesthetics, style and art in organizations. It is not therefore the organizational literature on aesthetics that has emphasized the importance of the multicategoriality of aesthetics for aesthetics' understanding of organizational life, with the exception of my notes on the subject in previous writings (1992, 1999). To illustrate this distinctive feature of the aesthetic approach, in this chapter I shall refer to two essays published in manuals of organization studies and which can be considered as general introductions to the theme of organizational aesthetics and as the first systematizations of research and study on the subject. Publication of works examining this strand of organization studies signals that, happily, this area of organizational research is no longer in its infancy. This, it will be remembered, was stressed in the introduction to this book, where I provided a brief outline of its origins and some of its main debates, and emphasized:

(a)   the dissatisfaction voiced by some scholars: Jeoffrey Pfeffer (1982: 260) for instance, with the 'little systematic work on linking the physical aspects of organizations into organization theory more generally', the reference being to the first analyses of the physical settings of organizations conducted by, for example, Fred Steele (1973) and Franklin Becker (1981); Russell Ackoff (1981: 39–40), with his concern that the lack of progress in the domain of aesthetics and management 'is responsible for one of our most critical social problems: *a decreasing quality of life*', and 'of work life in particular';

(b)   discussion within the organizational symbolism approach (Benghozi, 1987; Gagliardi, 1990b; Jones et al., 1988; Linstead and Hopfl, 1999; Turner, 1990) and the dramaturgical approach to the study of organizations (Mangham and Overington, 1987), as well as the analyses scattered in collective works inspired by sometimes highly disparate approaches and paradigms (Clegg et al., 1996; Cooper and Jackson, 1997; Costa and Nacamulli, 1997; De Masi, 1993; Hassard and Parker, 1993);

(c)   the fact that various journals, besides *Dragon* between 1985 and 1988, have published articles on aesthetics in organizations: for instance, the *Academy of Management Review* in 1992, with a special issue on new intellectual currents in organization and management theory edited by Linda Smircich, Marta Calàs and Gareth Morgan, and in 1993, with an essay by Anat Rafaeli and Michael Pratt; *Organization* with a special issue devoted to aesthetics and edited by Edward Ottensmeyer (1996b); and, since its first issue of 1995, *Studies in Cultures, Organizations and Societies*.

All in all, therefore, this strand of organization studies is much less impoverished in contributions than it was even as recently as the 1980s. Let us see, therefore, how it is presented in the chapter 'Exploring the Aesthetic Side of Organizational Life' by Pasquale Gagliardi (1996) and 'An Aesthetic Perspective on Organizations' by James W. Dean, Rafael Ramirez and Edward Ottensmeyer (1997).

The relevance of artefacts and form

In this section I shall show how two lines of systematic reflection on the aesthetic strand of organization studies flank one another and interweave, but nevertheless emphasize different aspects of organizational aesthetics and their study. The first analysis, that by Gagliardi, belongs to the tradition which concentrates on the physicality of the non-human elements that crowd and 'mark' organizational life. The second, by Dean, Ramirez and Ottensmeyer, instead emphasizes the influence of aesthetics on the processuality of organizational dynamics.

Organizational control through artefacts

In open polemic with Edgar Schein, Pasquale Gagliardi (1990a: 10–11; 1996: 568) writes that artefacts are not the superficial embodiment of deeper-lying cultural phenomena; rather, they are themselves 'primary cultural phenomena'. Schein (1984: 4) posits, in fact, basic invisible, preconscious and taken-for-granted assumptions as the foundations of artefacts which, no matter how visible and audible they may be, are not usually decipherable. Gagliardi argues instead that the scholar's attention should not focus on basic assumptions but on artefacts themselves, and that if we consider artefacts in and of themselves, we find that they

> influence corporate life from two distinct points of view: (a) artefacts make materially possible, help, hinder, or even prescribe organizational *action*; (b) more generally, artefacts influence our *perception* of reality, to the point of subtly shaping beliefs, norms and cultural values. (1996: 568)

An artefact, Gagliardi writes, results from human action but it exists independently of the authors of this action. It is perceived by our senses 'in that it is endowed with its own corporality or physicality' (1990a: 3). Indeed, by means of artefacts organizational cultures exert control over their members and educate their perceptive faculties – that is, their 'sense of taste, of smell, of touch, of hearing, as well as sight' (1996: 573).

An artefact is an intentional product of human action or something that is made (*factum*) with a view to solving some problem or satisfying some need. One should also bear in mind that not all artefacts possess the same amount of 'concreteness', in that they are not all able to affect all our sensory faculties simultaneously. The logo of an organization, for example, may affect our sight, and perhaps also our sense of smell if it is printed on a letter from the organization or on the packaging of one of its products. An architecture may affect, besides our sight and smell, also our sense of touch and even that of hearing. The important point, writes Gagliardi (1996: 565), is that if we employ the concept of organizational artefact, then we can view an organization as a '*tangible* reality', '*a place*', a thing:

> Things – as compared to people and ideas – have the singular property of restituting to the self a feedback that is steadily and immediately perceptible to the senses. Even the feedback from our investment in ideas or people comes to us unquestionably through material signs and things: if, for example, we seek confirmation of our identity as thinkers through the working out of ideas, it is only the 'written page' in front of us – it is only the 'materialized' idea – which reassures us about our capacity to pursue such aims. (1996: 569)

Artefacts are the most faithful depiction of the cultural identity of an organization, of its material culture, of its symbolic landscape, of its forms of control. Artefacts therefore:

(a)   render an organization into the tangible reality crowded with non-human elements (Latour, 1992), with the 'things' that restore identity to the people who belong to an organization, because it is in the items of quotidian organizational life – the chair, the work table, the tools used in their work – that people find their 'sameness', observes Gagliardi (1996: 569), citing a remark by Hannah Arendt (1958: 137);

(b)   render organizational control sensorially perceptible, in that they constitute the 'perceptual premises in determining the effective course of events in corporate life' (Gagliardi, 1996: 575); premises which, by their nature, evade the control of the mind and which derive from 'sensory knowledge and communication' and not from the logic and ideology that distinguish the 'informative premises' of organizational courses of action. Artefacts therefore constitute a further level of organizational control as well as those identified by Charles Perrow (1972) in the directly given order, programmes and procedures, and the ideological premises of organizational action. They do so on the basis of their specific characteristics; those whereby they are experienced holistically and directly, argues Gagliardi, drawing on the philosophical theories of Susanne Langer (1953, 1967). In other words, artefacts constitute a level of organizational control on the basis of the presentational language that enables us to say several things simultaneously, even if they are mutually contradictory. This is the distinctive feature of 'knowledge by acquaintance' (Gagliardi, 1996: 574), which is a form of knowledge quite distinct from that based on description – that is to say, on the discursive language which enables us to say only one thing at a time, and not several contradictory things simultaneously.

Both the artefact and the pleasure that it gives us, or the sentiment of beauty that it arouses in us, are cultural products, and in principle there is no event or object that is not potentially able to evoke these sentiments in us. In order to provide examples taken from the organizational literature with which to illustrate his argument – namely that the aesthetics of artefacts exert organizational control – Gagliardi selects four studies: one on colour, two on the architecture of physical spaces, and one on an organization's main previous activity. It will be noted that this selection of studies on organizational aesthetics pays close attention to the perceptive faculties, as well as to the work routines which condition, at the level of individual sensibility, the people who operate in organizations.

The study on colour is by Joseph Sassoon (1990), who examines it as a code which ties subjects to social movements of marked ideological connotation, showing that the sensory perception of shades of colour grasps immediately, rather than discursively, the changes of meaning so distinctive of organizational artefacts. The first study of the architecture of an organization's physical spaces is by Robert Witkin (1990), who analyses the physical make-up of the boardroom of a large company to show how it induces a two-dimensional understanding of reality and blunts its three-dimensional comprehension. The second study on architecture was carried out by Gagliardi himself and examines the contradictory feelings aroused by the monumentality of a bank's entrance and premises when compared against its staff sensitization campaign which emphasized the organizational value of 'being at the client's service'. The study of routine activity within an organization was also carried out by Gagliardi, and concerned a telecommunications company in which the telegraphic sequentiality of the origins of the work process gave rise to the 'presence of a "decompositional-sequential" archetype' (1996: 575) recognizable in the physical arrangement – one after the other in sequence – of the organization's structures as well as its work processes.

Organizational management through feeling and form

In the second part of their essay on 'An Aesthetic Perspective on Organizations', James W. Dean, Rafael Ramirez and Edward Ottensmeyer (1997) ask what aesthetics can tell us about organizations. In the first part of their essay the three authors introduce the idea of aesthetics, which they discuss in the light of the philosophical theories of Susanne Langer (1942, 1953) and of her master, Ernst Cassirer (1923–9). They develop the concept of 'form', and of the connection between the form of the feeling and the form that the mind experiences and symbolizes, in the sense that if the mind is able to appreciate life through feeling, it does so on the basis of the forms that it (the mind) connects with felt and lived experience. Thus, on the basis of Langer's view that the facts that are experienced aesthetically are those that are symbolized presentationally, Dean et al. propose an interpretation of aesthetics as responsiveness to 'patterns that connect', as also argued by Gregory Bateson (1972, 1979). This is responsiveness whereby, if we can only access reality independent of us experientially, in our action, *qua* our creation and therefore *qua* fact (*factum*), the fact is constructed through different kinds of knowledge forms, among which are the mental activities that fashion lived experience into presentationally symbolized experience.

In the second part of Dean et al.'s essay, the meaning of aesthetics in organizations is grounded in the experience of beauty, an aesthetic concept highlighted in contrast to the opposing experience of ugliness. The authors acknowledge developments in this area of organizational research, and of the fact that it has not yet been systematized into a theory of aesthetics in organizations. Nevertheless, they argue that the aesthetic perspective tells us the following about organizations:

1 People may decide to participate in organizational life on aesthetic grounds, as regards both the work that they intend to do and the organization itself.
2 People's job satisfaction may be influenced by their sensory perceptions of the technologies they use and by the settings in which they work, as well as by the pleasure they feel when they employ those technologies and work in those settings. The close attention that has traditionally been paid by studies of organizations and work to job content and to the everyday environmental conditions of the workplace may, therefore, also be directed to their aesthetic perceptions.
3 The resistance to organizational change raised by the people affected by it may be due to the fact that they experience beauty in the work that they already do in organizations or on behalf of them. Hence, by resisting organizational change they protect and defend their aesthetic experience.
4 Organizational decision-making – precisely because it is not directly connected with the choices that ensue from it – should be viewed as an organizational process able to engender aesthetic experience. Decision-makers may find beauty in the decision process that they have created and, rather than complete the process by making a choice, they may try to delay it. This can give rise to the procrastination of decisions and to a reluctance to reach conclusions, as well as to an uninterrupted flow of choices to make and of information to give and receive.
5 The design of the organization itself, besides that of its products, may respond to aesthetic criteria such as proportion and harmony. Organizational processes in their turn may be influenced by a sense of proportion, of rhythm, of flow, and by the visualization of these properties in flowcharts.

6   The leadership has the capacity to create visions which, by virtue of their aesthetic characteristics, are able to capture the attention of the organization's members and to galvanize their enthusiasm, while at the same time signalling leadership styles likely to succeed.

Dean et al. consider aesthetic experience as the experience of the beautiful that may encourage, or otherwise, the flow of organizational life and the structuring of organizational processes. Beauty, they argue, can explain a person's decision to join an organization, the success of a certain leadership style, the planning of organization and of organizational processes, resistance against organizational change, reluctance to reach decisions, and worker dissatisfaction with a particular technology. These are aspects of organizational life which demonstrate that aesthetics are important in several respects: the physical and material one of technology or the product; the impalpable one of leadership style or satisfaction; aspects closest to the subject like his/her job; ones more distant, like judgement of the organization as a whole; the features most legitimated by organizational ethics like product design; the one least legitimated, like the resistance to change induced by the sentiment of beauty felt with regard with what one is already doing in the organization.

Dean et al. suggest that these organizational themes should be subjected to research based on the organizational aesthetic perspective. Such research should give priority to cultural theories of organizations based on a conception of aesthetics as an embedded characteristic of people in organizations, and it should privilege process theories in organization studies based on the aesthetics of process and the artistry of managing. In both cases, the intent is to employ aesthetic concepts like 'beautiful' and 'ugly' to describe and comprehend contemporary organizations, and not to put aesthetics to work to make the organization's activities more profitable, as transpires from organization theories based on the functionalist paradigm.

This is a perspective akin to that adopted in Gagliardi's essay. Combined with the numerous organizational issues raised by both essays, it highlights the importance of aesthetics for the study of organizations. In the sections that follow I shall examine only some of the themes adumbrated here, those most distinctive of debate on organizational aesthetics since the mid-1980s and relating most closely to methodological issues concerning empirical research.

Aesthetics of the non-human and the artistry of the human

In this section I shall discuss organizational communication based on aesthetics, the relations between organizational space and organizational time, the processes whereby aesthetics are negotiated within and without the organization, the projection of organizational meanings and values through aesthetics, and the influence that art may exert on interpretation of corporate management and on the definition of manager training. These are topics addressed in the organizational literature, and I shall dwell on them in order to emphasize their importance for the study of organizational aesthetics and to highlight how they modulate between what has already been interpreted and new interpretations or ones still required, between what has already been constructed and what is still to be planned and realized, between what has already been formed and what is still to be formed.

The section begins with discussion of aesthetics relative to non-human elements and artefacts. It closes with examination of the artistry of the intentional action of people who work for organizations, and the importance of talent, creativity, passion and aesthetic sentiment in the management of organizational life. These are themes that have been treated on several occasions in previous chapters. Here, however, they are related to writings in the organizational literature which have examined the aesthetic dimension of organizations.

Corporate architectures as organizational communication

Organizational communication has a tradition of study in organization theory which, write Linda Putnam, Nelson Phillips and Pamela Chapman (1996: 376), dates back to the 1920s as regards interest in industrial communication, and to the 1950s as regards human relations: 'Two dominant interests, then, formed the foundation of the field: (1) the skills that made individuals more effective communicators on the job; and (2) the factors that characterized system-wide communication effectiveness.' The radical shift of the 1980s, observe Putnam et al. (1996: 376–7), criticized these interests on the ground that they treated organizational communication as linear transmission, and it redefined the subject of study as the meaning of organizational events, of organizational symbols and cultures, of communication rules, of the exercise of power through the filters imposed on organizational communication. Also organizational aesthetics can be considered an integral part of organizational communication. One need only cite the definition of organizational artefact, which, as Mats Alvesson and Per Olof Berg (1992: 80) write, constitutes that 'physical vestige' of human activities performed in organizational contexts. Organizational culture itself, Alvesson and Berg again point out (1992: 103), can be considered a cultural artefact – that is, a set of cultural expressions like 'rites, rituals, ceremonies, myths, stories, jokes, logos, corporate architecture and other materialized symbols' which all relate to the totality of the organization:

> Meaning and values are created, reinforced, maintained and communicated through the artefacts. Authors who speak of organizations as cultures in this sense generally emphasize that the symbolism in the artefact is specific to the organization.

Every organization is therefore viewed as having specific symbols associated with it, and, when they are more general in nature, the scholar seeks to single out and understand 'the nuances involved in the symbols' in relation to the organization in question. The organizational artefact, that is to say, 'tells us' something about the organization that we are studying, something that is specific to it, as we have repeatedly seen in previous chapters. However, this is not solely linear communication, nor is it the transmission of information, values and meanings, although this, too, is involved. It is communication which takes place at the aesthetic level and which is itself aesthetic and closely bound up with philosophical aesthetics and theories of art.

To illustrate this argument I shall draw on remarks made by Umberto Eco regarding architecture. We have seen that corporate architectures – 'the architectural interior, and architectural designs of corporate buildings and settings' (Berg and Kreiner, 1990: 46) – not only symbolically condition the individuals who participate in organizational life, but are themselves outright forms of organizational communication. Eco (1968; reprinted 1983: 192) writes that if we make a 'phenomenological consideration' of our relationship with the object 'architecture', we find that 'we commonly use architecture as if it were communication, even though we do not exclude its functionality'. When I look at a window in the façade of a building, continues Eco (1968; reprinted 1983: 202), 'I do not think so much of its function as I think of a meaning "window" which is based on its function, but which absorbs its function to such an extent that I may even forget about it and see the window in relation to other windows as elements in an architectonic pattern.' Indeed, 'an architect may even make fake windows whose function does not exist', a function which does not function but is communicated.

These windows function, therefore, not as windows but insofar as they constitute windows in an architectural context where they 'are enjoyed communicatively'. Fake windows thus satisfy an aesthetic need. What does this imply in terms of symbolization? That their form, number and arrangement in the façade relate to a certain conception of inhabiting spaces and of using them. In this way, they 'connote a global ideology', namely the ideology that has presided over the architectural operation, writes Eco (1968; reprinted 1983: 203–4), an operation which rests on codification processes which existed previously to it.

This entails a view of the artefact not only as expressing dynamics internal to organizational life but also as embodying the relations between, for example, corporate functional needs and aesthetic patterns in society. Per Olof Berg (1987: 25) points out that whatever

> is seen as beautiful and appealing is thus as much a matter of fashion as of function. Consequently, changes in design are not only the result of changed materials or functions, they are also the result of a changed world view and belief systems in society at large.

The relation is a complex one, therefore, because it envisages corporate architectures as influencing people's sensory premises by both (a) communicating organizational patterns and (b) communicating a 'global ideology' which rests on pre-existing codes and which also develops externally to organizations. I shall return to this point later. In any event, Per Olof Berg and Kristian Kreiner (1990) argue, if we look at the aesthetics of both buildings and structures, and of the internal architectures of the premises occupied by organizations, it is possible to observe:

(a) the symbolic conditioning effected by corporate architectures on people's organizational action, both through their capacity to evoke individual and collective memories and through their capacity to communicate creativity, standardization, repetitiveness, flexibility, sense of community, hierarchization, vertical mobility, positions of power, expressions of status or good taste, as the principal values embraced by the managerial philosophy;

(b) the packaging of the organization as a whole which, like the packaging of the organization's products or promotional material, symbolizes and communicates the organization's distinctive features;

(c) the institutionalization of the organization through the 'totem' value (the unifying symbol) assumed by the building in which the organization has its premises, providing a 'central organizational reference' for the organizational symbologies and cultures of those who work for the organization.

Finally, corporate architectures perform the basic communicative function, at once elementary and essential, of 'signalling a presence': the organization exists, it belongs to society, and its presence therein has a history behind it which is part of the history of that society.

Physical settings as metaphors of organizational time

The co-presence of the materiality and non-materiality of organizational aesthetics is a further aspect discussed on several occasions in this book. If we continue to reflect on corporate architectures, we find that this co-presence is particularly important. Especially if we realize, as pointed out by Emma Corigliano apropos of private dwellings (1991: 26–35), that inhabited space, besides being a 'phenomenon observable, real, tangible and belonging to the sphere of concrete experiences', is also an abstract and intangible phenomenon, the place with which we are familiar and which we invest with sacredness, the ambit that is ours and which is also our image of the universe. 'If we look around, the first thing that strikes our attention', Corigliano writes (1991: 131, 87), is 'the emotional investment and the interest that people devote to their habitative space', their 'pleasure of inhabiting', and their sensation of being 'able to master and – why not? – "halt" time' in this space that they feel to be inviolable.

Corporate architectures may evoke this sensation of halting time because they symbolize an organization's existence in society and its roots in it, both as traces of the organization's past and history and as projections of it into the future. The architectures of organizations 'represent' what with Burkard Sievers (1990a) we may call the organization's project of immortality, which stands in antithesis to the temporary and the ephemeral, therefore, and which connects the organization's physical space to the conceptions of organizational time (Gherardi and Strati, 1988) that predominate in it. There may be organizational times related to an immortal time-horizon, or to a merely temporal and mundane one; but architecture, writes Sandra Bonfiglioli (1991: 170), 'claims for itself the "ethic of the projectual intent" that inspires it', an intent which is 'rationalization oriented to the future of the reality given at present'. Indeed, it is the image itself of architecture that evokes an 'imaginary array of the temporally multiple' in relation to the present and the actual, writes Bonfiglioli (1990: 332).

Time is once again present in the destruction of corporate architectures: for instance, in the architectural ruins that constitute the traces of the existence of a factory, mine or works which has closed down and which is therefore no longer inhabited and used. Georg Simmel writes (1907; It. trans. 1981; reprinted 1996: 160–1) that architectural ruins engender contrasting symbolizations: those of destruction, which relate to the destructive work of human beings, and those which instead are connoted by fascination with the destruction wrought by time and by the ravages of nature. In the former case, we also recognize the organizational times of shortsighted management, besides the failures due to the success of rival firms. In the latter case, time is not organizational time, and the ruins show that in destruction and disappearance 'other forces and other forms have grown'. These are the forces and forms of nature, writes Simmel. Thus, from whatever still survives in the ruined architecture of its artistic being, and from what within it 'already lives of nature, there springs a new whole, a distinctive unit'. This is an extraordinary phenomenon, Simmel comments, which does not occur in the cases of other types of art, because although the imagination is able to reconstruct these from their fragments, it is always restricted to them and confined to them, and as a consequence is unable to create a new 'distinctive unit'.

Designing corporate meaning

The designing and redesigning of corporate architectures is a process constantly present in organizational life and which highlights a number of organizational issues. This has been analysed by Mary Jo Hatch (1997: 243–54), who distinguishes among:

(a)   the geography or 'location' of the organization, which accentuate the organizational issues of organizational communication and information-sharing, of the recruitment of personnel, and of the local laws which regulate work, of the necessity of transporting goods which are needed or have been produced;

(b)   the layout of the organization, that is, the buildings or structures that it uses, which highlight the issues of organizational interaction, coordination, conflict and control; a layout which brings people working in the organization closer to each other and enables them to interact more intimately (Hatch, 1987), allowing informal relations, brief interruptions and confidences which, with time, strengthen relationships among people, whereas physical barriers, walls and distance interfere with them – individuals, in fact, attribute value and meaning 'to offices within their work environments', and 'office designs might best be analyzed as symbols produced by organizational cultures' (Hatch, 1990: 143);

(c)   the style of the organization's physical spaces, which highlights issues of status, image and organizational identity: 'Façade, landscaping, furnishing, lighting, ceiling and wall treatments, floor coverings, use of color and form, displays of art or technology, and many other details', writes Hatch (1997: 250), 'can range from being ugly to being tolerable, pleasing, beautiful, and inspiring.'

Interorganizational and intraorganizational physical space, like the social, hierarchical space which relates to one's perception of persons, objects and settings, and like symbolic, linguistic–communicative and linguistic–codificatory space, writes Lucio Biggiero (1997: 126–7), all have important consequences on organizational designing and redesigning. Accordingly, account should be taken of the non-linearity and the non-coherence of the impressions that the physical structure of organizations may arouse in regard to the corporate image and organizational identity:

> For example, an exquisite new corporate headquarters building may favorably impress investors ('they must be generating great wealth to afford such a wonderful facility'), customers ('this kind of opulence indicates real staying power'), and community leaders ('what a marvelous aesthetic complement to the community'), while simultaneously being viewed as irresponsible by union leaders ('that money could have gone into better wage packets') and environmentalists ('a little less squandering on executive perks and more environmental projects might have been possible'). (Hatch, 1997: 257)

That is to say, one should bear in mind that although an organization's physical structures are socially constructed and convey values and ideologies which belong to the corporate identity and to the corporate culture, and thus symbolically condition the action of the organization's members, it is always possible that the actual outcome of the design will differ from what was originally intended.

A study by Hatch (1990: 142), which compared the attitudinal and behavioural responses of personnel with private offices against those of personnel assigned non-private offices, in two American large, high-tech companies, found that open-plan offices inhibited, rather than facilitated, communication and the work flow. Which means that although open space symbolizes, in principle, the openness of the organization, in its being-in-use, it symbolizes a privation of organizational openness, thereby breaking the presumed linear continuity and coherence between open space and open organization.

The likelihood of conflicting outcomes is greater, the less attention the designers of architectonic spaces for a social collective pay to the features of its work and organizational culture. This was evidenced in particular (Strati, 1990: 219) by the mathematicians of an Italian university department for whom a modernist and rational building had been designed, but who found it ascetic, alien and incomprehensible because the aesthetic criteria that inspired them as mathematicians were antithetical to those of rational functionalism, being founded instead on their free action as mathematician-artists.

And yet corporate architectures are able to reconstruct the symbolic world that we wish to inhabit. This is true of postmodern architecture, writes Mary Jo Hatch (1997: 260), in that it 're-introduces an awareness of the symbolic potential of built space and the possibility of exploiting it – for good or evil'. We may therefore enquire, as does Dennis Doxtater (1990: 124), whether office design is able to relate 'territoriality' and 'ritual space' so that a 'relatively independent, spatially structured set of thematic meanings' is produced.

Spatial structures are based on concepts like axis, direction, threshold, centre, which are 'heavily laden with powerful symbolic meaning' (Doxtater, 1990: 108). But once the design has been realized, we may instead find that human territorial spaces, such as many work settings are, have been transformed into something else: for example, they may have become 'neutral zones', or no-go areas created by conflicts among groups of office-workers. Organizational space, in fact, is 'mythic space' comprising, for example, the 'thresholds' which, as Bruno Bolognini writes (1986b: 89–90), once we have crossed them make us feel no longer 'at home'. In other words, organizational space expresses both 'actions' and 'human presences'. The latter may stem from both the past and the present, an example being places invested with sacredness because they have been or still are occupied by people who represent mythical figures for the organization (Strati, 1990: 220). The design of corporate meanings, therefore, in its logico-geometric structuring of physical spaces, creates organizational spaces which, as Bolognini points out (1986b: 91), effect a 'mythical signification' which is primary and not derived signification, and acts as 'the prime element of the structuring of the experience' of organizational values that discriminate and divide participants in organizational life, and not only of those values which they may share.

This is a first major problem encountered by designers of corporate meanings. Since it is a problem difficult to foresee, given that it is tied to the putting-to-use of corporate architectures, when a designer plans the transformation of a territory into an office, s/he must interpret the cultural potential both of that particular office and of that particular organization. But the designing of organizational meanings through corporate architectures encounters a further problem, and this concerns the conditions in which the designer must interpret the organization's cultural potential. These conditions are extremely important. As Doxtater stresses (1990: 125–6), it is one thing to work within an organizational and social culture that values participatory design and 'participatory control over our shared environments' together with a 'common set of conceptions about cultural themes and their spatial structure'; it is quite another to work within an organizational and social culture that is indifferent and alien to these concerns.

The negotiation of aesthetics as a pervasive process

The design of corporate architectures highlights the relations between designers and organizations, and the fact that these are relations which involve the negotiation of organizational aesthetics and of the ways in which corporate architectures are invested with the meanings and values of the corporate culture. These are relations of some complexity, and they regard both the organizations that commission design work and the organizations which employ the designers. They emerge with particular clarity if one studies not the organizations that use the work of designers, but the aesthetic philosophies and ethical codes of the latter.

In a study carried out in the mid-1970s of 152 'elite' Manhattan architecture firms, Judith Blau (1984, 1993) shows how negotiations and conflicts proceeded on several levels among the designers studied. Her analysis reveals negotiative processes within the professional community of architects and the fact that these negotiations were matched by negotiations between the architects and the organizations commissioning their work. In other words, conflict internal to the community of architects developed in two directions: on the one hand, it centred on the relationship between the architects and what they regarded to be the users of the constructed space, rather than clients; on the other, it centred on the relationship between the senior partners of the architecture firm and what they regarded to be clients, rather than users.

Blau illustrates the complexity of the organizational cultures of the Manhattan architecture firms and the conflicting ideologies within them centring on the priorities set by the senior partners and the design philosophies of the rank-and-file architects. The architects felt that they belonged to a professional community for various reasons: because of the importance given to architecture in their lives; because they were aware of the work of even the most obscure American architects; because of their recognition of a number of heroic figures, some of them European architects; and because of the fundamental value attributed to theory in their work. The four hundred architects interviewed did not regard themselves as united by any specific design approach or any particular style (1984: 80–1; 1993: 91–2), whether modernist and therefore expressed in aphorisms such as 'form follows function', 'less is more', 'really important is proportion', or postmodern ('every age has its "feeling" and its aspirations'), or structuralist or post-structuralist.

Blau concludes that:

> First, although in the heady days of the early 1970s design debates were prominent in the literature, the vast majority of rank and file architects were far more unified around issues dealing with the social purposes and social uses of buildings. The disagreement or lack of consensus about style must be seen in a context of consensus about responsibility to users. Second, what architecture 'means' nevertheless plays an important role in structuring the lives of working architects. [. . .] Finally, unlike the employees and junior partners, private owners and senior partners of firms are greatly constrained by business priorities and place users' needs below the financial well-being of the office and the artistic merits of projects. (1993: 96)

There thus emerges from Blau's study the complex ongoing negotiation that took place in the architecture firms among the people who worked for them. And there also emerges the fact that, in this negotiating process, the other organizations were always present, in the guise of either users or clients. It was through these complex processes that not only the production of the 'thingliness', so to speak, of the organization, but also the wielding of power over it was managed (Bruce, 1995; Fukasawa, 1995; Strati, 1996b: 100–2). This is also evidenced by what Eric Abrahamson (1996: 126–7) calls 'the management fashion-setting community', referring to the 'interdependent industries that jointly produce fashionable management discourse' on the basis of (a) the 'procurement of new ideas', (b) the 'fashioning of rational and progressive discourse about these ideas', and (c) the 'marketing of this discourse to managers' through consulting firms, business schools and mass media organizations. To be stressed, therefore, is not only the distinction between the designer inspired by the theories debated within his/her professional community and the productive initiatives that his/her client organizations intend to undertake. One must also bear in mind the importance of these negotiative processes in relation to the construction of the global ideologies of which Eco speaks, and in relation to the diverse development of art history and aesthetics to which they may give rise.

In order to provide further illustration of the importance of this latter argument – where aesthetics involve the negotiation of the beautiful, the ugly or the sacred, rather than negotiation exclusively concerned with the 'corporate soul' and the management philosophy – I shall return briefly to the paintings of Caravaggio, resuming a topic already broached in the previous chapter. As said at that time, negotiations between Caravaggio and his ecclesiastical patrons often led to rejection by the latter of his works, in which he depicted religious themes. But, as Ernst Gombrich notes:

To be afraid of ugliness seemed to Caravaggio a contemptible weakness. What he wanted was truth. Truth as he saw it. He had no liking for classical models, nor any respect for 'ideal beauty'. He wanted to do away with convention and to think about art afresh. Some people thought he was mainly out to shock the public; that he had no respect for any kind of beauty or tradition. He was one of the first painters at whom these accusations were levelled [. . .]. (1950; reprinted 1966: 291–2)

We may therefore ask what we would have missed in art history and aesthetics if Caravaggio had lost, that is to say, if his paintings had been burnt instead of being repeatedly rejected and then in the end accepted but at prices much lower than asked by the painter, or if he had surrendered to 'ideal beauty'. Negotiations over organizational aesthetics, too, display this feature: the non-production of painless results in aesthetic terms, and not solely in those of the organizational culture and the symbols of organizational life.

An organization's image as visual display

There is no doubt, write Per Olof Berg and Kristian Kreiner (1990: 41), that organizations grow increasingly concerned with their physical appearance and seek to enhance their 'corporate look' 'in terms of slick, stylish corporate buildings, new office lay-outs and decorations, landscape gardening, graphic designs, corporate "uniforms" and colour codes, visual identities, etc. This apparent "corporate vanity" has infected organizations in most industrial sectors [. . .].'

It has thus become commonplace for managers to talk of 'corporate architecture' when referring to their firm's buildings; or of 'visual identity' when they refer to its visual materials, namely the logo, uniforms, flow-charts, the colour of its offices; or of 'corporate design' when they refer to its products and their packaging, to its internal architecture, or to its physical structures in general.

Newspaper journalists talk about 'offices for the soul' and 'environments that reflect the corporate soul', Berg and Kreiner point out (1990: 52). Architects take pains over how and where to design the 'social main rooms' which identify the organization as a whole for the people who work in it or come into contact with it; places, therefore, which represent the company, its business or its mission, and which are simultaneously able to arouse a sense of belonging to the organization and a sense of community. The architect of an organization's premises, in fact, may make the management philosophy 'visual' and 'available to our senses', by reducing 'pinnacles and towers' or designing the staircase so that it 'encourages ambition' in the organization's members.

The aesthetics of corporate architectures, and more in general of corporate artefacts, reveal the importance ascribed to the visibility of the organization, which is not solely apparent in economic success or the dominance of a particular geographical area, social community or certain markets for products and services, but also in a phenomenon that first appeared after the Second World War and which Fulvio Carmagnola (1989, 1997), on the basis of Sergio Givone's theories, has called 'diffuse aestheticism'. In the case of organizations, aesthetization has penetrated even what is useful and necessary, giving rise to a process that has blurred the sharp distinction drawn by modernity 'between scientific knowledge and the inexact knowledge of the human sciences, in particular of aesthetics and social theory' (Carmagnola, 1997: 365).

The blurring of this distinction has brought to the fore the visual display now so characteristic of organizations. Visual display is 'the other side of the spectacle', writes Peter Wollen (1995: 9); it is 'the side of production rather than consumption or reception, the designer rather than the viewer', and according to Jacques Lacan (1966, 1975) it is 'the best method of concealment'. Thus produced are specific 'signs' which display some characteristics of organizational life while concealing others. The process begins with production of the sign that graphically translates an organization's name into its logo, writes Joan Costa (1992: 218–27), in other words, into an iconic sign and a chromatic connotation which turns the name into something that can be exploited as the public image of the organization's identity.

The visual display of the organization may exhibit or conceal the organizational construction and reconstruction of male and female gender symbologies, as the organizational literature has done by neglecting gender issues (Calàs and Smircich, 1992). This also happens when space is designed in order to prevent the separation of male and female, because, as Mark Wigley tells us (1992: 328), the 'exclusion of sexuality is itself sexual'. Since the earliest of primitive symbols, observes Paola Coppola Pignatelli (1982: 83–4), the circle-sign has represented woman, while the arrow-sign has represented man. The arrow, Coppola Pignatelli continues – drawing on Gilbert Durand's (1963) discussion of *sagitta*, a Latin term whose root is the verb *sagire*, meaning 'perceive rapidly' – is oriented movement, 'the constant search for the goal to be achieved, symbol of velocity, will and power' but which may miss its mark. This mark, by contrast, is at the centre of the circle-sign, which symbolizes harmony and absoluteness, sacredness and totality, heaven and earth. Associated with the two primitive signs of circle and arrow are the spatial archetypes of male and female, and it is important to take account of these to understand the organizational construction of gender symbologies – of the archetypes of femaleness described by Silvia Gherardi (1995: 71–82), namely the Greek female deities who were either virgins or vulnerable goddesses. The spatial archetypes of male and female may emerge in constellations of similar images, argues Coppola Pignatelli (1982: 85), and they may do so 'by homologous convergence in form – obelisk, spire, skyscraper – or content – hut, house, villa, dwelling – or likewise by symbolic analogy – house, boat, automobile'.

In the visual display of an organization's image one may observe the symbolic construction of gender in organizations, noting, for example, the phallocentrism apparent in the relations between sexuality and space which, writes Alessandra Ponte (1992: 305), has distinguished architecture as a discipline since its origins – that is, since the 'foundation of its body (and its body-ness)'. Two-dimensional depictions of intraorganizational and inter-organizational relations also reveal the spatial archetypes of male and female. For instance, Susan Buck-Morss (1995: 111) analyses 'sociograms', or the graphics used to describe a firm's economic performance or the relations among its offices, or with other organizations. The diagram of interorganizational relations may depict these relations as the 'spermlike penetration' of an organization 'into a budding embryo'.

It is therefore important to consider the visual display of organizations as an activity of simultaneous exhibition and concealment which operates on several levels and in various registers. We should not seek to provide a schematic and rational description of this process, which is a process symbolization rooted in aesthetics. It is thus that we may note those forms in which the visual display exhibits 'perverse spaces', as Victor Burgin (1992: 230) observes with reference to those spaces that are designed or represented on the basis of the 'reduction of looking to the visible' and of the objectification–exploitation' register. In other words, we must take care not to reduce the aesthetics of corporate architectures to a rational and systematic representation of the corporate culture and in which the bipolarity between display and concealment is clearly marked out. Instead, we should encourage the emergence – and then observe – the ambiguity, the beauty and also the perversions that may render the visual display of the organization's image incoherent and paradoxical, while also following the process of evocation and analogy elicited by the aesthetics of these non-human elements in both organizational actors and organizational researchers.

The relations between organizational cultures and organizational aesthetics, therefore, are not direct, schematic or linear; above all, they do not move unidirectionally from the corporate culture to the corporate architecture, to the corporate design and to the corporate visual identity. This is very apparent if we consider an organization's visual display as an organizational course of action whose outcomes are hardly prescriptive and not at all prescribable, because discerned in the visible manifestations of organizational life are features which those responsible for the organization's image would prefer to conceal: the firm's graphics reveal sexuality and not just interorganizational action networks; the firm's architectural plan shows its phallocratic culture rather than the layout of its premises; the architecture of its spaces conveys the modernist style rather than the organizational culture.

In the 'coordinated image' of the organization one sees the overlapping and the merging, rather than the orderly accumulation, of technical innovations, of conceptual schemes, of pragmatic knowledge about the use of techniques, and of codification processes which, Giovanni Anceschi (1991: 58) writes, comprise, 'on the one hand, the set of acts – metonymic, metaphorical, but also non-motivated, arbitrary, etc. – which may institute a representance, and on the other the set of conventions and procedures – protective, condensative, etc. – which realize a representation'.

The iconography of an organization reveals a non-virtual organizational life, in that it is experienced as a 'very analogic place', as Nicholas Negroponte (1995: 15) puts it; a world, that is, which

> is not digital at all but continuous. Nothing goes suddenly on or off, turns from black to white, or changes from one state to another without going through a transition.

Indeed, declares Chiara Sebastiani (1997: 241), the virtual space renders the concept itself of 'public sphere' in the collective imagination obsolete, because 'it renders the separation between public and private obsolete': one sees how the multimedia application of information technology – if viewed not as 'technology applied in order to streamline' the organization's bureaucracy but as constituting the space inhabited by the 'public' – 'reveals the largely totalitarian nature of this space in the loneliness, in the standardized and metaphorical language, and in the boundlessness that characterize it', given that 'it is only possible to escape by "de-activating" the network, interrupting all forms of communication'.

Study of the aesthetics of the non-human elements in organizational life shows that, as Matteo Thun (1989: 242) tells us, also the banal objects, the small objects of an organization's visual display, 'help us to develop an awareness of style; they enable us, maybe even compel us, to make personal stylistic preference the basis of our choices'. People's aesthetics are therefore self-referential. They relate, that is to say, to people's sensory faculties and aesthetic judgements, to aesthetic philosophy and to theories of art. They are not the desired outcome of rational action undertaken in pursuit of an organization's ends. When we observe the visual display of an organization in order to understand it through its image, we cannot restrict our observation to whatever is portrayed in the image. That image, *qua* icon, gives rise to a process of association which extends beyond it and in which it operates merely 'as an *aide-mémoire*. It was this that Aristotle recognized,' writes Maurizio Ferraris (1997: 543), 'when he spoke in *De insomniis* of oneiric associations operating not on the basis of formal analogies but through subtle affinities among impressions.'

Management as art

Managing, organizing and participating in organizations should be considered 'as aesthetic phenomena', write Michael Owen Jones, Michael Moore and Richard Snyder (1988: 160–1), because the participants in organizational life 'are craftpersons and aesthetes', and they endeavour 'to perfect form and to seek coherence when organizations are created, changed, or challenged'. The way in which individuals assess their organizational performance is therefore based as much on aesthetic considerations as on technical criteria, even though '[s]ome managers seem to juggle figures, materials, and people as if they were all just raw materials, or perhaps pieces of a puzzle, to be shaped or fitted by strong will and dint of personality into some sort of gestalt' (1988: 161). Yet, whether deliberately considered or deliberately ignored, 'the perceptual and sensory inhere in organizational life', and the appreciation of aesthetics, craftsmanship and artistry is an important feature of the management of everyday organizational life. However, we should remember, Severino Salvemini (1993: 307) points out, 'who the managers are: they are pragmatic and concrete individuals, oriented to visible results, and often educated into rigorous rationality'. Their training is rooted in the dominant paradigms of organization theory, namely universality and generalizability.

Not surprisingly, therefore, given that managers are trained on this model and according to these beliefs, aesthetics is dismissed as 'a weak fact, where weak is synonymous with the decadent, with the superficial, with the affectation associated with taste for taste's sake' (Salvemini, 1993: 307–8). Consequently, a manager who concerns himself or herself with aesthetics is condemned for neglecting the organization's productivity, and for concentrating instead on something 'extraneous to professional norms' and organizational ethics – something that pertains to the person and not to the organization, and which, moreover, lacks maleness and virility. In short, a manager who attends to the aesthetic aspect of organizational life is at the 'stage that precedes the idle *flâneur*, the camp dandy of Oscar Wilde' (Salvemini, 1993: 308). This manager therefore externalizes his/her most intimate feelings and passions, and engages in activities suited to weak individuals who, although they are able to unleash passions, are not able to discipline them as required by the spirit and ethic of managerial work. This, continues Salvemini (1993: 310), is the result of managerial training and of a model of the entrepreneur in which personal feelings are forbidden by 'dry, rational, ascetic training which hinges principally on the force of will and the principles of the Enlightenment'.

A solution to all this might be found by exploring arguments which depict the manager as an artist, as proposed by Vincent Dégot. The starting-point, Dégot writes (1987: 23–4), is the view that

> the manager is himself a creative artist, although not necessarily a solitary figure, since he may belong to a school of thought. He is the one who designs the action taken, even if it is on behalf of others and subjected to certain constraints – e.g. like the retables of the Italian Quattrocento (Braudel, 1979). For the outcome to be considered as a work of managerial art, the manager must be able to leave his personal imprint on it. This does not mean that formal techniques cannot be deployed to analyse the problem and implement the solution. The essential thing is the basic creative design that can be attributed to one individual.

This entails that, first, we must reject the association between 'outstanding managerial work' and economic performance, and, second, that we must adopt criteria which assess managerial works 'by relating them to more local or stylistic trends', Dégot continues (1987: 26), drawing an analogy between organization study and art criticism based on ideas relating to aesthetics and the history of art but 'combined with acquaintanceship with the artists and their works'. This could be followed by classifications of managerial works based on style, genre and importance (1987: 33) so that sharper light is shed on the changes taking place in the criteria used to assess managerial training, managerial performance, and above all on the spirit that imbues it; criteria whereby 'management as it has evolved during the last one or two decades, now looks more like an artistic activity than the rationalistic model which business economists have been trying for so long to impose' (1987: 44–5).

When we study people's creativity, claims Domenico De Masi (1989: xiv), we observe organizational forms very different from those to which we have been accustomed by the dominant Taylorist and Fordist models. If we examine the organizational forms with which European artists and scientists experimented between the mid-nineteenth and mid-twentieth centuries, we find 'original methods for organizing creative work performed collectively', and that these experiments gave rise to 'marvellous concrete examples which, besides synthesizing long historical experience accumulated from building temples, cathedrals and *palazzi*, opening workshops, founding monasteries and academies, also anticipated future forms of post-industrial organization functional to creativity'. Analysis of thirteen groups – for instance the via Panisperna research group in Rome headed by the physicist Enrico Fermi, the Biological School of Cambridge, the Staatliches Bauhaus or the Pasteur Institute – reveals, writes De Masi (1989: xvi), the pre-eminence of the founder-leader, whom the group treated 'with respect and even veneration', and who acted 'as if the organization created by him would die with him'. Also evident is the taste of these groups for the beautiful and their search for beautiful physical settings in which to work, together with their ethical imperatives of anti-bureaucratism and parsimony.

Creativity therefore plays an important part in the constitution of organizations and of the specific forms that they assume. It is a term which has only recently become current and which first appeared in dictionaries only at the end of the last century, writes Alberto Melucci (1994: 11). Nevertheless, it has spread rapidly in the last thirty years. By contrast, the adjective 'creative' has a centuries-long history behind it, and it is usually applied to the skills and abilities involved in creating. The creative process has been analysed by studies conducted in the most diverse areas of human activity, from mathematics to music, and dating back to the reflections of Aristotle and Plato. If one inspects the statements of authors about their creative processes, observes Brewster Ghiselin (1952: 31), one notes that they generally concern 'understanding' of the phenomenon. Taken together, these statements do not constitute a simple 'compendium of fragments' (1952: 11). Instead, they give us 'a feeling for the whole process and a lively sense of the divergences of individual approach and procedure'. More recently, notes Melucci (1994: 11), 'creative' has come to mean 'productive', but also 'imaginative', thereby denoting jobs like those of the 'creatives' in an advertising department, or of designers. Creative work, therefore, is performed by those engaged in inventing and constructing the visual display of organizations.

Dégot's emphasis on the talent of managers and on the putting-to-use of talent in everyday organizational life – as well as his strictures against the intrinsic shortcomings of managerial training founded, to put it *à la* Polanyi, on explicit knowledge – also highlights the creativity of managers, and more in general, the creativity of everyone who takes part in the construction and reconstruction of the everyday life of an organization. Dégot (1987: 23) warns, however, that this is an analogy that should be used with care, given that managerial activity, unlike aesthetic activity, 'does not appear as a permanent activity' of people. However, when it is used, Dégot argues, it shows that managerial training lacks precisely those elements which subsequently prove so distinctive of managerial work in the everyday practice of organizations. Little is known about these elements, and even the scant knowledge that we do possess about them is difficult to organize and manage. Moreover, Hans Joas (1992; Eng. trans. 1996: 4–5) states that models of human behaviour, whether based on rational action or on normatively oriented action, 'ineluctably generate a residual category to which they then allocate the largest part of human action', namely creative activity. The term itself 'life', as in 'philosophy of life', or the concept of 'intelligence' in pragmatism, Joas declares (1992; Eng. trans. 1996: 71), 'are different ways of trying to grasp creativity'.

It is possible to discern in management as art and in the portrait of the manager as an artist – with reference either to all the members of an organization or to only its senior managers – a feature reminiscent of the myth of Leonardo da Vinci and of Renaissance man. In the 'Renaissance tradition', writes Franco Crespi (1996: 185), 'art was the supreme expression, standing at a level higher than religion itself'. The reverse was true after the Reformation, when the modern tradition placed religion above art and asserted the work ethic in organizations, as Aris Accornero points out (1994: 52–8) on the basis of Weber (1904) and the writings of numerous other scholars, notably Raymond Boudon (1984). Religion, rather than art, gave rise to the work ethic which defined the terms of humanity's redemption and self-fulfilment in modernity, just as did the workers' movement and trade unionism (Accornero, 1994: 58).

The myth of Leonardo, writes Elio Franzini (1987: 26), 'arose from consideration of the genius not as an inspired "sorcerer" but as an "artist" able to "invent" according to rules which brought the combined constructive efforts of his faculties to their maximum fruition'. Consequently, there was no magical mixing of universal genius and nature or the complete non-distinction of philosophy, art and science. Herein one grasps the significance of the shift of emphasis in management training and management studies to creativity. The point I would stress, therefore – resuming briefly the arguments of Chapter 2 – is that research into the creativity of human action should not be restricted to the study of lifestyles. For it is 'a provocation, a challenge to sociology's fundamental theoretical concepts,' declares Joas (1992; Eng. trans. 1996: 246), where 'the postmodernism discussion constitutes a radical break with those assumptions concerning rationality and normativity which are enshrined in the basic underlying concepts of sociological theory, and theory of action in particular'.

Awareness of aesthetics and/or aesthetic awareness

This final section of this chapter discusses a number of methodological issues relating to the conduct of empirical research in organizations. It therefore draws together the main threads of the arguments developed in this book, but with particular reference to those set out in this chapter. The themes treated, therefore, will concern the way in which the researcher approaches an organization, focusing on the awareness that s/he acquires of the organizational life under scrutiny. Two sorts of awareness are distinguished: awareness of organizational aesthetics, and therefore recognition of the importance of the aesthetic dimension in organizational life; and aesthetic awareness of organizational life. These two aspects to the study of organizations have given rise to a debate which, sometimes explicitly and sometimes only implicitly, is by now an integral part of the tradition of studies on aesthetics in organizations.

Examined first will be the problem posed by the emotions and feelings for those who carry out empirical research on organizational aesthetics. There then follows a brief discussion of questions relating to the aesthetics of visualizing and of scientific writing, as well as a note on the importance of cultural studies research for the analysis of organizational aesthetics. This will bring us to methodological issues concerning, on the one hand, knowledge of the aesthetic dimension of organizational life and, on the other, aesthetic understanding of it. At this point I shall resume discussion of the study of organizational artefacts, emphasizing that when a researcher conducts such study s/he may assume the guise of an archaeologist or a social historian of art who investigates organizational vestiges in order to identify the social relations and forms of civilization that distinguish the organization in question. The section closes with the methodological principles distinctive of the aesthetic approach: the importance of aesthetic empathic understanding; the connoisseurship exhibited by all participants in organizational life, and also by those who study it; and the importance of the aesthetic categories for empirical research in organizations.

Aesthetics, emotion and sentiment

Feeling anger at the behaviour of a colleague is not to feel an aesthetic sentiment. The feeling of anxiety because the outcome of negotiations is uncertain is not aesthetic. Nor is shock at the result of an organizational meeting. Anger, anxiety, shock or stress, longing for the workday to end:

these are not elements constitutive of the aesthetic dimension of organizational life. They are emotions felt by people in their day-to-day running of organizations, and they evidence the irrationality that constitutes such an essential part of intentional action in organizations (Fineman, 1997: 21), as well as the shortcomings of those studies of organizational meanings that base themselves on what is thought rather than what is felt (Fineman, 1996: 547–52); characteristics, as I have written elsewhere (1999), which constitute the common ground between the tradition of organization studies on emotion in organizations and that on organizational aesthetics. This commonality is further emphasized by 'sentiment' as the aesthetic exhibition which reveals the connection between life and knowledge, and the human nature of the construction and reconstruction of everyday organizational life.

Consider the *pathos* with which, during empirical research in organizations, an event or action may be emphasized by an informant. In what the informant says and how s/he says it, s/he not only provides the researcher with information about organizational processes but also communicates an emotion, a feeling, a sentiment. In my empirical research, when a subject has talked to me about a feeling of pleasure or joy aroused by some or other organizational event, s/he has 'shared' that emotion or emotional state with me. Indeed, the emphasis has provided me with a distinctive 'signal' with which to orient my inquiry (1990: 207). There is sentiment in this emphasis, and it has served to highlight some of the themes discussed while obscuring others.

Sentiment is therefore important for the aesthetic understanding of organizational life because, according to Elio Franzini (1997: 21), it is 'one way in which things, situations and forms offer themselves'. It is neither the event nor the organization that is being talked about; nor is it *per se* the subject of organizational study. A sentiment is 'not a "fact", an abstract object, it is the manifestation of a style, of an intentional attitude'. The sentiment manifest when my informants talked about certain organizational processes did not merely accompany those processes, for 'it did not offer itself "together" with things but "in things" as their specific "expressive quality" or stylistic cipher'. This is the importance of sentiment for the purposes of research into organizational aesthetics: the fact that it is part of the things talked about and part of the things done in organizations.

The study of aesthetics in organizations, therefore, does not examine the causes of sentiment, because sentiment is not an independent effect, distinct and separate from the organizational events talked about. In the course of empirical research, therefore, one seeks to grasp sentiment in its being-in-use, in its *Dasein*, as regards both events and the relation between the organization's members and the researcher. In this case, too, therefore, there emerges the importance of the empathic understanding of organizational life, as well as the fact that empathy itself, as Franzini points out (1997: 277), is a 'sentimental relation with the Other' which 'offers a commonality that constitutes a common ground'.

Aesthetics of visualizing and the anaesthetics of scientific writing

Sentiment therefore characterizes the aesthetic study of everyday organizational life because it is the expressive quality intrinsic to aesthetic phenomena. The same applies to knowing how to 'see' these phenomena, and to knowing how to 'write' about them, without stripping them of their principal dimension, namely their aesthetic dimension.

As I have pointed out on several occasions, those who conduct empirical research in organizations can 'see' what the visual display reveals to their eyes and to those of the other participants in organizational life. They see the building as they enter it, the front door, the organization's logo, the nameplates on the office doors, the uniforms worn by the security staff, the friezes decorating the walls, the plants and ornaments, the bust of the organization's founder, the photographs with the names of the people who work in the organization, the signs for the toilets and emergency exits, the photographs of important moments in the history of the organization. They see all these things simply by entering the organization – obviously if these things are there – but, as I have emphasized in another work (1992: 569), they do not usually mention these aspects of organizational life in their research reports, both because they deem them to be irrelevant and therefore ignore them, and because they do not know how to study them, how to handle them to gain understanding of the organization and how to offer the knowledge acquired to the scientific community and organization students.

During empirical study, however, researchers 'see' certain 'fragments of organizational life', not 'details' of it. I shall dwell for a moment on this distinction in view of its importance for the analysis of organizational aesthetics. Although a fragment is part of a whole, writes Omar Calabrese (1987: 77–8) with reference to the etymology of the term (which derives from the Latin *frangere*), 'its presence is not required for its definition', and its boundaries 'are not "de-limited" but rather "inter-rupted"' because they are formed by chance and not by some objective cause. Indeed, this opposition between chance and cause so sharply differentiates a fragment from a detail that a fragment may be represented by a fractal geometry and a detail by a traditional and regular plane geometry. While researchers conduct their empirical inquiries in organizations, they 'find' fragments of organizational life and, sometimes, 'construct' (by themselves or with the help of members of the organization) organizational icons by introducing, for example, intervals between one event and another in organizational life, between one action and another, between one subject of these actions and another. They thus invent – by themselves or jointly with the organizational actors – frames which mark out and distinguish these fragments of organizational life.

Whether these are fragments of organizational life 'found' in the organizational context in question, or whether they have been 'invented', they provide the basis for the researcher's understanding. In this process, diverse interpretations may arise, and they may usefully draw on studies conducted by visual anthropologists and visual sociologists (Bateson and Mead, 1942; Chalfen, 1987, 1991; Collier and Collier, 1967; Henny, 1986; Hill, 1984; Lomax and Casey, 1998; Mattioli, 1991, 1996; Wagner, 1979), and by semiologists with reference to the problem of iconism (Calabrese, 1985; Eco, 1962, 1968, 1973, 1975; Maldonado, 1979; Mukařovský, 1966; Peirce, 1931–5). More specifically, study of the visual display of organizations may utilize the diverse interpretations of the 'found' and the 'created' fragment proposed by organization scholars, such as those concerning:

(a)   the organization's name as a visual script which has an aesthetic–symbolic effect on the 'seer' (Costa, 1986); the name that becomes the company's emblem and assumes the value of the totem in tribal societies (Stern, 1988); the logo which is an expression both of the organization and of those who take part in the construction of organizational reality and its meanings (Sievers, 1990b);

(b)   the use of photographs of successful products to heighten the sense of belonging to the organization among those who work for it (Bolognini, 1986a); the photographs of customers in annual reports which show specific companies' theories of their customers (Dougherty and Kunda, 1990); the fact that an organization's newsletters and publicity materials document changes in the corporate culture (Schneider and Powley, 1986); the office folklore spread by photocopies which impart a 'patina' and therefore an aesthetic quality (Hatch and Jones, 1997); the fact that corporate architectures serve as 'visual mediators' between the asymmetries of the social structure and the negotiation implicit in cultural and commercial exchanges, translating the abstract into concrete elements of organizational culture (Grafton-Small, 1985); the importance of the aesthetic–narrative choice of the director of a firm's film, which conveys particular readings and representations of organizational life (Bugos, 1996);

(c)   the photo reportage which depicts the researcher's familiarization with a corporate culture (Larsen and Schultz, 1990); the photographs of physical settings which alter their meanings, giving rise to different ways of 'seeing them' and highlighting the performative action of photographic images in the constitution of dialogues among the participants in the knowledge process (Rusted, 1995); the use of computer graphics, diagrams, and pictures in research reports and essays as an alternative to hierarchical thinking, alphabetic writing and verbal reporting (Meyer, 1991);

(d)   the 'vision' of the leader and leadership's style of 'speaking to the eyes' of the participants in organizational life (Guillet de Monthoux, 1996); the suppression of chromatic variety and of the corporality of volumes in organizational space, reflecting the Weberian distinction between organization and the private lives of people who are thus encouraged to be heads rather than bodies (Witkin, 1995: 176–207); the fact that visual cultures are also profoundly influential at the level of metaphorical conceptions of organization, as in the metaphors of 'photographing the organization' or of 'organization as hypertext' (Strati, 1997); the impact of concepts of the beautiful linked to specific management theories, as in the notion of the beauty of the mechanical associated with Taylorism and Fordism (Guillén, 1997).

There is a general remark, however, which applies to a large number of studies on organizational aesthetics, namely that whether they analyse fragments that have been 'found' or deliberately 'created', they omit exploration of the visual, either as an aesthetic fact about the organization or as an aesthetic product of the organization. This also applies to the 'aesthetic' product of the scholar him/herself, in other words, the written report of his/her results. As Fausto Colombo and Ruggero Eugeni (1996) point out, a written text is a visual artefact: which is an issue that links with the theme just discussed of the aesthetics of the visual. Despite the scant influence of the scholar on the visuality of his or her published text, the practical activity of writing is subject to some sort of literary aesthetic, and this applies to writing by organization scholars as well. Surprisingly, this issue has been largely ignored (Van Maanen, 1995) by a scientific community distinguished above all by the fact that 'it writes'; and that it does so according to the aesthetic canons of journals and publishing houses, and in the neutral and ascetic scientific–academic style dictated by the natural sciences and the rationalist and positivist paradigm.

However, this is a consideration that does not apply to organization scholars alone. For instance, research conducted by the present writer (1990: 211–12) in a university department of visual arts showed that these scholars had fashioned their identity as writers of the fruits of their study and research into that of historians and critics of art. This was an identity, for that matter, similar to that envisaged by Barbara Czarniawska (1997: 203–4) for the organization researcher, whom she describes as 'more like a literary critic than a novelist', and who may develop his/her identity as the 'semiotic writer' of his/her studies, given that 'the organizations that the researchers describe are only in a certain sense products of their minds (in the sense that they are responsible for their own texts); the organizations are originally written by organizational actors'.

The relevance of cultural studies research

Cultural studies research is of especial importance for the future development of inquiry into organizational aesthetics. This is an issue, with both theoretical and methodological implications, raised in particular by Brian Rusted (1999), who acknowledges the contribution of culturalist and symbolist theory to analysis of aesthetics in organizations, but points out that scant attention has been paid to the findings of studies conducted within the cultural studies tradition. Following Rusted, there are several lines of research which warrant particular mention, such as:

(a)   the studies of artistic activity by Howard Becker (1974, 1982), who conceives art as collective action involving both the author and other actors like the promoters and distributors of the work of art, and who also seeks to identify the features of groups of artists by using the concept of 'art world', which he shares with Arthur Danto (1964) and George Dickie (1971); he considers how art either criticizes society or integrates with it, on which basis he classifies groups of artists into rebels, naïfs, folk artists and professionals integrated into the constituted social order;

(b)   ethnography-based studies of organizations, like the one conducted by Michael Owen Jones (1987), who combines the ethnographic approach to folk aesthetics with ethnographic research on work in organizations and the material culture of corporate life;

(c)   studies examining organizations which produce culture, art and entertainment, like the studies by Hortense Powdermaker (1950) of Hollywood, or by Gary Alan Fine (1996) of restaurant kitchens and the culinary world; in the latter case, one notes that restaurant products are judged aesthetically, and principally by the intimate sensory faculty of taste – 'intimate' because, as said, it operates internally to the body – as well as by the 'public' sensory faculties of sight and smell and touch. 'Food involves more sensory dimensions than any other art form, except, perhaps, the "art" of love', Fine points out (1996: 13), and this 'aesthetic richness allows vast leeway in choices of food preparation, a diversity that may have hindered the development of a formal aesthetics of cuisine: a theory of eating';

(d)   research that has discussed the theme of political neutrality in aesthetics, like the study by Elizabeth Bird (1979), or which has illustrated the negotiation and conflict aroused in a community when particular importance is ascribed to aesthetics, like Brian Rusted's (1990) study, or which has raised methodological issues concerning empirical research into aesthetics, like John Dorst's (1989) book on the 'written' suburb.

These studies are concerned not with the consumption of the products and events marketed by organizations in the culture industry, but with their production and use in organization. Aesthetics thus belong to the symbolic work of everyday culture, which, as Paul Willis (1990) argues with his concept of 'grounded aesthetics', simultaneously involves both the production of a shared culture, made up of popular representations and of ordinary life, and a critique of the 'hyperinstitutionalization' of art. These are also studies which question the notion of authorship in the production of art and aesthetics, emphasizing instead the interpretation and production of meanings in which, according to Jauss (1982), the user plays an essential and constitutive part in the hermeneutic process which turns collective action into art. In the cultural studies tradition, writes Franco Crespi (1996: 148), scholars refuse to set themselves up as experts. Instead, 'they commit themselves morally to the search for happiness, solidarity and social justice, especially for the marginalized, and they combat every form of authoritarianism both scientific and political'.

As regards the latter point, this book has argued the opposite point of view. It has instead emphasized the connoisseurship of the knowing subject, in relation to both non-human elements and interpersonal relationships. This is the connoisseurship possessed, by virtue of their sensory faculties and their faculty of aesthetic judgement, by all the individuals who take part in the construction, deconstruction, reconstruction or even destruction of organizational life. It is on the basis of connoisseurship that individuals have mastery over their abilities to feel, appreciate and enjoy. It is connoisseurship that enables a factory foreman to choose among his or her fellow-workers, or a chef to choose among the saucepans in his or her kitchen, or a scholar to choose among organizational contexts the one that s/he intends to study. It is connoisseurship – with its tacit rather than explicit knowledge, with its empathic–aesthetic rather than analytic–rational understanding – which enables people to claim the organizational and social legitimacy of their different interpretations of the social construction in which they participate.

The categories of aesthetics

Throughout this book, I have stressed the importance of the aesthetic categories for aesthetic understanding of organizational life. In the previous chapter I dwelt in particular on the category of the beautiful, emphasizing that, in the course of empirical research, it links with other categories like those of the sacred, the picturesque, the tragic or the ugly. I have also said that these are aesthetic categories which we study because they are part of the normal language of organizational actors, so that it is the individuals themselves encountered during research that call our attention to them. They are therefore terms of common currency in everyday organizational life; terms which the researcher may invite subjects to use while describing their usual routines, and which are distinguished by the fact that they have a heritage behind them rooted in philosophy and theories of art, and not, for example, in organization studies.

We may find that one aesthetic category predominates in the everyday language used in organizations, therefore. But we realize that it interweaves with others, albeit in a subtle, indirect and limited manner. Thus the same feature applies to the aesthetic categories as Carlo Sini (1996: 87) points out regarding practices: I do or say something

> within a definite practice – which is already itself a complex pattern of practices – and certainly what I do and say relates to the practice that I am performing. But on the other hand it does not, because the life-contexts in which practices are performed are never exactly the same – even a simple repetition is another occurrence of an action, not the same action repeated – so that what I say and do silently triggers other patterns of practices.

We saw in the previous chapter – for example when the two businessmen were discussing the beauty of their organizations – that when the category of the beautiful was used it was possible to graft onto it those of the picturesque, tragic and sublime. Or we saw in the case of certain employees of the Photographic Company that the category of beautiful used to describe their work and organization merged with those of the sacred, ugly or pathetic. Of course, as I showed in Chapter 4, there are numerous aesthetic categories, but the ones now briefly discussed are those that have most frequently emerged in the course of my own empirical research.

First, *the aesthetic category of the sacred.* This category highlights the marvellous, the inexplicable, unusual and invisible in organizational life. It emphasizes the fact that, in the aesthetic experience of subjects in organizations, reality and fiction are not markedly distinct and separate; indeed, the rational claim that it is possible to distinguish between the real and the non-real is largely an overinterpretation by the knowing subject and, as far as organization studies are concerned, by the scholar. The aesthetic category of the sacred accentuates the representations of what is indivisible, of what is unique, of what is magical and of what arouses reverence and worship – in the same manner, argues Walter Benjamin (1968), as works of art, which have not been produced by techniques that make them infinitely reproducible. The category of the sacred comprises whatever is legendary, fantastic, oneiric, archetypical and mysterious in the organization, whatever relates not to end-directed organizational rationality or to organizational ethics, but to the valency assumed by the divine and inviolable.

Second, *the aesthetic category of the picturesque.* This category highlights the reversal of the terms of the relation between aesthetic experience of organizational life and the evocative process of aesthetic experience to do with what art produces in code. The aesthetic experience is based on visual discoveries made possible by art, Ernst Gombrich points out (1982), so that the aesthetic experience originates from the evocation of whatever it is in art, and in painting in particular, that is familiar to us as enjoyment of something aesthetic. It was Vasari, in mid sixteenth-century Florence, writes Raffaele Milani (1991: 183), who used the term '*alla pittoresca*' for 'the technique of pen drawing which involved the use of flake white highlightings on sheets of paper prepared in tints of varying intensity'. This was a pictorial technique, therefore, which sought to achieve an immediate effect on the observer, but also to evoke 'a mood, an atmosphere, a specific taste, a sensibility' (Milani, 1996: 22), and it became an artistic ideal in eighteenth-century England. The term 'picturesque', Milani tells us (1996: 3), also refers to quaint and unusual landscapes 'with roughly sketched and fanciful touches typified by the idyllic and rustic, and by folk custom', but it was principally used 'in everyday language to describe something vivid and colourful, pleasingly informal and irregular, which aroused aesthetic emotions' and evoked the fascination of places, architectures and landscapes.

Third, *the aesthetic category of the tragic.* This category comprises whatever is 'heroic' in organizational life: that mysterious pleasure which consists of both suffering and the representation of it. The category of the tragic brings out the passions in organizational routine, passions both individual and collective which give rise to organizational conflicts and collective catharsis. Tragedy denotes the heroism of those who challenge the unknown or the inevitable, the threatening and the lacerating, but it does so by emphasizing not the moral but the ludic–aesthetic. The aesthetic pleasure of the tragic, observe Elio Franzini and Maddalena Mazzocut-Mis (1996: 312), derives 'from a game of transpositions and mirrorings, from artistic play which seeks to transcend the terror and horror of existence'. It is driven by the dionysiac transfiguring force 'which enables us to perceive the original joy that also resides in pain and destruction' and which, above all, shows that tragedy must be confronted and transcended through creation.

Fourth, *the aesthetic category of the ugly*. This is a free-standing aesthetic category. It is distinct from the beautiful and therefore not defined from it by default. It arose with mid-nineteenth-century industrialization and denotes the pathology of modern and contemporary civilization and the malaise provoked by it. The ugly is 'an active, dangerous and aggressive power in constant ferment', writes Remo Bodei (1995: 108); 'it does not possess the immobile nature of being but the chameleon nature of becoming'. Bodei identifies various stages in the evolution of the ugly into an autonomous category in aesthetic philosophy, where it now 'grants perhaps even greater dignity to its ancient adversary' (1995: 122), namely beauty, which contains within itself, as essential ambiguity, an irremovable darkness constituted by ugliness. This is perhaps because, Bodei goes on to say (1995: 123–4), ugliness is regarded as less dangerous and less distressing to sensible perception than discordance, dissonance or disproportion. It may also be because of the 'usury' of the sense of ugliness: 'the risks of the impoverishment and standardization of experience' that reside in the withering of the perceptions and emotions, 'in the monotonous repetition of the always-the-same in the phantasmagoric guise of the always-different', or in the 'regressive pleasure of seeing something return that is already well known and therefore gives a sense of security'. Ugliness is not deliberately chosen in organizational life, and this aesthetic category emphasizes – regardless of the beautifying *maquillages* applied by the corporate culture – whatever is shocking, monstrous, dull, impure, horrid, eccentric, disgusting, lascivious and repugnant in the organization. The kitsch represented by the alienation of an organization in which mediocrity and bad taste are celebrated, the banality and artificiality of the camp, or the absence of the sacred and the sublime with the simultaneous presence of the self-seduction and posturing of the fashion industry: these, Milani suggests (1991: 81–2), also belong to this aesthetic category. Involved here are aesthetics 'in the proper sense', points out Ugo Volli (1997: 33–4), that is, a 'perceptive system rather than a value criterion' of distastefulness. The latter, in fact, is 'only secondarily political or social' insubordination of the indomitability of conventions, and this shows, according to Elio Franzini and Maddalena Mazzocut-Mis (1996:

287), that the autonomous aesthetic meaning of the ugly consists in its desecratory thrust.

Fifth, *the agogic aesthetic categories.* These categories concern the rhythm of the activities carried out in an organization, as well as that of organizational phenomena. Rhythm is essential for the coordination of work processes, of the work flow, of initiatives undertaken, and also for the way in which the organization as a whole interacts with other organizations and the rest of society. The category of rhythm brings out the unfolding of a decision-making process or of an official ceremony, the movement of the fingers on a computer keyboard, or that of a queue at a post-office counter, the cadence of coffee-breaks during the workday, or the sequence of advertising campaigns for the organization's products. The unbearable work rate of an organization, its breakdown or its prolongation due to delays in some operation, or alternatively its smooth and easy flow, are highlighted by the agogic categories, which relate to *adagio* or *prestissimo* in music, movement in paintings or sculptures, coordination in the steps of a dance.

Sixth, *the aesthetic category of the comic.* This category concerns the grotesque in organizational life: the irony that it provokes, the laughter that penalizes it, the sarcasm that dismisses it, the sense of humour that attaches labels to it. Grotesque, preposterous, ridiculous: in short, something which is also in certain respects ugly, but whose 'comedy' is highlighted by the aesthetic category of the comic. Thus accentuated are witticisms about colleagues rather than spiteful gossip about them, the jokes played on them rather than malicious pranks, the nicknames applied to them rather than insulting epithets. The aesthetic category of the comic is therefore closely related to that of the ugly, because it, too, has a desecratory thrust, but this is desanctification which does not brand the aspects of organizational life that it brings out as necessarily negative.

Seventh, *the aesthetic category of the sublime.* This category is instead close to that of the beautiful. It concerns the *pathos* of aesthetic feeling evident in the 'rapture' with which someone describes the beauty of his or her work or of the organization to which s/he belongs, or the beauty that is no longer part of his/her work or organization. The aesthetic category of the sublime highlights the beautiful in organizational life, but it does so by imbuing it with mystery, sentiment and turmoil. Rapture and turmoil together characterize a person's intense aesthetic participation in an organizational event, and the *pathos* that it arouses in him/her. The sublime is therefore joy that fills the soul, the tragic sentiment that brings shivers to the body, the imagination and talent that distinguishes the individuality of people in organizations, the evidence of their cognitive boundedness as they seek to understand it by constructing, as Jean-François Lyotard (1991) puts it, a representation of the non-representable. According to Remo Bodei (1995: 82), the aesthetic category of the sublime accentuates the 'form of beauty which requires a noble soul of high-minded moral rectitude' in organizational life. It points up the 'dignity' and the 'nobility of spirit' of those who belong to the organization and bring out its greatness. This greatness is not identified by the category of the sublime in mimetic adherence to an order which already exists and governs the organization, but in the creation of another order, even if it is one difficult to institute and almost impossible to control. The sublime therefore highlights a person's maladjustment to the organizational order, and the fact that this arouses his/her perception of a mismatch between him/herself and the organization, but a mismatch which is lived 'imagining a desperate revenge' (Bodei, 1995: 85). The sublime is therefore a category, write Franzini and Mazzocut-Mis (1996: 291), which denotes 'a "hedonistic" style whose greatness is connected with pleasure. But this is pleasure of a singular kind aroused by the representation of painful and tragic events.'

Finally, *the aesthetic category of the graceful.* This category is the one that most closely concerns the quality of organizational life, because it relates to the elegance of strategic visions, interpersonal relations and work, to the politeness that may strike us as pleasantly surprising and attractive, to the spontaneity and virtuousness of the people who belong to an organization. The category of the gracious accentuates the elegance of behaviour in an organization, of people's clothes, their work settings, the products that they help to create. It refers to the visual and aural pleasure aroused by both people and organizational artefacts, because it brings out the charm of both people and their work, the attractiveness of both people and their activities, the immediacy of both interpersonal relations and the feeling of comfort in a new job. Unlike the other aesthetic categories, the gracious is a category which involves the public senses of sight and hearing, although, Raffaele Milani points out (1991: 103), 'it seems very difficult to extend its attributes to the other senses: taste, touch, smell'. This is a controversial view, however, especially if one thinks of the other categories that the gracious evokes and involves besides the elegant, namely the pleasing (*joli*), the gentle and the pretty.

The social construction of organizational aesthetics

The arguments developed in this chapter have shown the principal research styles used in the analysis of organizational aesthetics. These styles can be distinguished into two broad types:

(a) those which explore organizational aesthetics solely for the purpose of identifying the distinctive features of the organizational cultures of which the aesthetics are part;

(b) those which seek to grasp not only the distinctive features of organizational cultures but also the day-to-day construction and reconstruction of the aesthetics specific to the organizational context being studied.

This distinction emphasizes that, in many studies, awareness of the importance of the aesthetic dimension in organizational life combines with neglect of this dimension, as if it were of little heuristic interest, of little legitimacy in organization theory and management studies, and of scant or no importance for understanding of the researcher's method or of the research process. In other words, one notes the limited awareness among organization scholars that they, too, take part in the social and constructive construction of organizational aesthetics, and that they do so through the creation and development of a tradition of study in organization theory, and through their distinctive research styles. Although styles of empirical research vary considerably, they evidence three principal approaches, which, even if they are not in open conflict, show that methodological incompatibility will grow increasingly likely in this strand of organization studies as it is enriched by specific and situated research. These three approaches are (a) analysis of organizational cultures which observes the 'archaeological' fragments of organizational life; (b) analysis which begins empathically and concludes rationally; and (c) analysis which involves empathic–aesthetic understanding. The empirical research style adopted in order to study organizational aesthetics may therefore be based on the following approaches.

First, *the archaeological approach*. The researcher assumes the guise of an archaeologist, a social historian of art, an art critic who investigates organizational artefacts. This is the most widely used style. It involves identification of 'fragments of organizational life' – which the researcher may both 'find' or 'invent' – and of the organizational cultures that have generated these fragments. As said, on the basis of what the researcher 'sees', 'hears', 'touches', 'smells' and even 'tastes' in an organization (when attending a company dinner or eating in the works canteen), s/he inserts intervals in, and creates frames around, organizational dynamics. At the same time s/he identifies a quantity of organizational artefacts which – examined both separately and jointly, analysed both concretely and in the abstract, judged aesthetically both implicitly and explicitly – furnish the material for his/her interpretations of the predominant or marginal organizational cultures in the organizational context examined. By so doing, writes Per Olof Berg (1987: 25), the researcher essentially undertakes 'an exercise in contemporary archeology, whereby the form and function of objects are analysed in order to find out what information they give about the "civilization" that brought them forth'.

Second, *the empathic–logical approach*. The researcher acts in the twofold guise of a seeker after both empathic and logico-analytic understanding. S/he keeps the three principal phases of research – observation, interpretation and the writing-up of the results – separate and distinct. For those employing this research style, Gagliardi (1996: 577–8) writes, 'it is essential in the first place to abandon oneself to what Kant calls "passive intuition" ' and act 'as if we are there to stay', interrogating ourselves about the sensations aroused within us, and resisting the structuralist temptation to interpret organizational artefacts 'as if they had an intrinsic semiotic status'. The next step, but one which is still part of the first research phase of observation, is 'to "give a name" to our sensations before we become too inured to the aesthetic climate of the setting', and to do so 'in good time' – before, that is, we lose the ability to discern the specificity of the sensations and stimuli to which we have been exposed. During the interpretation stage, emotion and reflection, empathic knowledge and analytical detachment balance each other on the basis of 'a minimum of talent and natural bent' which may also benefit from the 'guidance of able people'. The final report-writing stage, however, involves abandonment of empathic knowledge and its balancing with analytical analysis, so that the researcher can 'rigorously follow logico-analytical methods' embellished by 'a little "eloquence" ' and 'visual reporting'.

Third, *the empathic–aesthetic approach*. The researcher sets out to obtain aesthetic–intuitive information about the organization using the empathic–aesthetic understanding discussed in Chapters 2 and 3. S/he selects the organizational themes to investigate according to aesthetic-based paradigmatic options. S/he activates his/her sensory faculties as s/he enters the organization, forms judgements on the organizational life within it by relying on personal taste, aesthetically enjoys the aesthetic dimension of the organizational setting, and takes part in the negotiative process whereby certain aesthetics prevail over others in that particular organizational context. These are the distinctive features of the aesthetic understanding approach to organizational life. Those who use it:

(a)   immerse themselves in organizational life, activating their perceptive faculties and aesthetic judgement, employing their intuitive and analogic capacities, and also acting, when it is appropriate, as imaginary participant observers;

(b)   observe themselves in this knowledge-gathering process, letting their past experience re-emerge;

(c)   write an 'open text' which describes the active process of reconstructing lived experience and re-evokes this experience according to the aesthetic canons of writing which govern the architecture of the arguments developed.

All three of these research styles seek to gather knowledge about organizational life by studying its aesthetic dimension. The difference among them centres on the researcher's awareness that s/he is taking part in the social construction of organizational aesthetics, and on his/her methodological choice between the assignment of greater or practically no validity to empathic understanding of the meaningful action of people who work in organizations. A further distinction concerns the relations between organizational research, the everyday language of organizational actors and the aesthetic categories. The outline provided above of categories drawn from aesthetic philosophy and the theory of art has had three purposes: first, to show that research into organizational aesthetics may follow a variety of interweaving paths; second, to break down some of the barriers which separate the 'archaeological', 'empathic–logical' and 'empathic–aesthetic' research styles; and, third, to incorporate the aesthetics of empirical research and theoretical analysis into organizational research on organizational aesthetics.

6   Conclusions

If one wants a theme linking all the topics treated in this book on organizational aesthetics, it can be found in a metaphor of which I am especially fond, and which I have taken from visual cultures: the metaphor of the organization as a hypertext (Strati, 1996b, 1997). This is a metaphor based on information technology and on computer graphics, and one which the reader will grasp immediately if he or she thinks back to the computer simulation of the chair discussed in Chapter 1: change a parameter and you have a different chair, change another one and you have yet another chair, until you forget what the original chair was like and are perhaps even unsure whether one actually existed. What the 'original' and 'true' organizational life may or may not have been is not a question that occupies the aesthetic approach to organizations. Instead, the forms in which it can be understood, and which give meaning to the myriad differences of organizational life, these are indeed matters which it finds of central importance.

The metaphor of organization-as-hypertext emphasizes that the endless differentiation of organizational knowledge is a constantly ongoing process in organizations, and that this differentiation does not relate to an original monolithic reality. The metaphor highlights that the endless process of knowledge differentiation in organizations is driven by the intentional action of their members, whose differing understandings of everyday organizational life can be observed in their being put-to-use, in their being practised. The organization–hypertext must be made, brought into being or constructed, and this can only come about through constant interaction between the knowing subject – the creator of the specific chair – and the numerical model – which constitutes the computer-simulation of the chair – through the parameter that s/he selects. Consequently, the linking theme of this book is the thesis that the relations between people and the organizational life of which they are part is the central concern of organizational aesthetics.

According to Gianni Vattimo (1983: 27), the everyday practice of negotiating, deconstructing, destroying, reconstructing and creating in organizations does not produce a 'unitary set'. Instead it generates 'a tight-knit interplay of interferences' which constitute the organization's 'heritage'. This comprises a repertoire of texts 'different' from the organization–hypertext because they have been produced by connoisseurs who put-to-use not only their capacity for rational thought but also their taste, their style, their passion, their feelings, their artistry. This patrimony of artefacts and connoisseurships should be viewed in the light of the organization–hypertext metaphor to grasp not its flow, but its chaotic and fragmentary nature, and to avoid applying definitions to organizational life which stem from 'strong' ontologies: for instance, the organization as a museum for its members' artistry, or the organization as the postmodern arena of the aestheticization of everyday organizational life.

The aesthetic understanding of organizational life does not envisage a metaphysical definition of organization, because its theoretical premises lie in the finiteness itself of aesthetic understanding. It concerns instead the 'refined' corporeality of the people who operate in organizational settings, since it is based on the faculties of sight, hearing, touch, taste and smell, and on the aesthetic judgement. All these faculties are earthbound and socially constructed, and they discriminate among individuals to such an extent that marked inequalities arise among them in the organization. The senses do not tranquillize; rather, they breach the peace. But it is thanks to the senses that 'different' forms of organizational knowledge emerge or disappear in the organization–hypertext.

The aesthetic approach to the study of organizational life therefore does not envisage a 'strong ontology' which defines the true nature of the organization and which has prompted, for example, the debate on whether it should be viewed in terms of 'organization', 'organizations' or 'organizing' (Clegg and Hardy, 1996). Nevertheless, it takes the existence of the sensory faculties and the faculty of aesthetic judgement for granted. That the sensory faculties exist is beyond doubt, whereas the existence of the aesthetic judgement can be questioned on the ground that it is not tied to any of the sensory organs. Moreover, the aesthetic judgement varies greatly among organizational cultures, social cultures and linguistic cultures. To return briefly to the aesthetic categories discussed in Chapter 5, and if we take only the category of the beautiful illustrated in Chapter 4, we find marked differences in the linguistic terms that relate to it. For example, if the English phrase 'I've got a great job' is translated literally into Italian, it does not even bring to mind the aesthetic category of the beautiful. Rather, it evokes the category of the tragic because it denotes a proposition of the kind 'I've got a load of work to do'. 'Definitional difficulties are inherent in languages', Gary Alan Fine observes (1996: 218), and we 'must settle for family resemblances that we hope will serve us well enough, often enough'.

The point is also that there is no ontological explanation for the faculty of aesthetic judgement, or for that of the other senses, even when these faculties are displayed in the practices of organizational actors. It is precisely this feature, in fact, that makes the aesthetic study of organizational life so interesting. However, we can stop ourselves from becoming embroiled in a search for a strong ontology if we imitate Umberto Eco (1997: 102–6) when he discusses Pareyson (1989). Eco reformulates the Heideggerian question of why there is 'being rather than nothingness' and replies: 'Because I say so', that is, because 'it can't be explained'.

But what would happen, then, if we decided to study a factory without any human workers, where everything was coordinated by information technology, by intelligent machines as well as unintelligent ones, highly sophisticated instruments as well as obsolete ones? Would this be an organization devoid of aesthetics? The answer provided by a researcher using the aesthetic approach would not rest on a definition of the organization as ontologically founded on aesthetics, a definition based on the fact that the machinery results from the aesthetic knowledge of the people who constructed them or of the people who installed them in the factory. The only possible answer would take the form of further questions: 'Were you there? What did you see? And tell me, what did you feel when you first set foot in the factory?' It is in being-in-use that organizational aesthetics are observed, and the purpose of the observation is to see whether aesthetic forms of knowledge about organizational life emerge.

The theoretical foundations of the aesthetic approach characterize it as a heuristic approach which seeks to gather dialogic and non-causal knowledge about organizational life. Moreover, although the area of inquiry into the aesthetics of organizational life to which the aesthetic approach belongs has its own research programme, as part of organization theory and management studies, it cannot be used to furnish anthropological or philosophical generalizations. It thus preserves the character that, according to Dan Sperber (1982: 32), ethnographic interpretation should have. These general features of inquiry into organizational aesthetics mean that it has no compulsory points of view, no strong ontologies, no metaphysical definitions of the 'reality' of organizational life. Instead, it directs the organization scholar's attention to organizational aesthetics and sustains the importance of such study in organization theory and management studies. The aesthetic approach, in particular, invites the scholar to take account of his or her own aesthetic knowledge and relate it to the entire complex of research, analysis and the social construction of the scientific community. It does so by stressing that:

(a) a subject of study may be selected on aesthetic grounds;
(b) imaginary participant observation may give rise to research hypotheses;
(c) the aesthetic experiences acquired in organizational contexts may influence the conduct of empirical research;
(d) evocative processes based on aesthetic considerations may focus the researcher's attention when s/he is theory-building, either during field-work or subsequently when analysing its results;
(e) aesthetic canons may influence the topics chosen when writing up the results; and
(f) both the written and verbal texts related to the research can be considered aesthetic products.

However, these connections between aesthetic knowledge and organization theory may be just as much in-use as, obviously, they may not.

References

Abel, Theodore (1953) 'The operation called *Verstehen*', in H. Feigl and M. Brodbeck (eds), *Readings in the Philosophy of Science*. New York: Appleton-Century-Crofts. pp. 677–87.

Abel, Theodore (1967) 'A reply to Professor Wax', *Sociology and Social Research*, 51: 334–6.

Abrahamson, Eric (1996) 'Technical and aesthetic fashion', in B. Czarniawska and G. Sevón (eds), *Translating Organizational Change*. Berlin: de Gruyter. pp. 117–37.

Accornero, Aris (1994) *Il mondo della produzione*. Bologna: Il Mulino.

Ackoff, Russell (1981) *Creating the Corporate Future: Plan or be Planned For*. New York: Wiley

Albertazzi, Liliana (1989) *Strati*. Trent: Reverdito.

Alvesson, Mats and Berg, Per Olof (1992) *Corporate Culture and Organizational Symbolism: An Overview*. Berlin: de Gruyter.

Anceschi, Giovanni (1991) 'Grafica, visual design, comunicazioni visive', in G. Anceschi et al., *Storia del disegno industriale. Vol. III: 1919–1990. Il dominio del design*. Milan: Electa. pp. 56–83.

Arendt, Hannah (1958) *The Human Condition*. Chicago: University of Chicago Press.

Baar, Carl (1967) 'Max Weber and the process of social understanding', *Sociology and Social Research*, 51: 337–46.

Barilli, Renato (1995) *Corso di estetica*. (1st edn 1989). Bologna: Il Mulino. (Eng. trans.: *Course on Aesthetics*. Minneapolis, MN: University of Minnesota Press, 1994.)

Barnard, Chester I. (1938) *The Functions of the Executive*. Cambridge, MA: Harvard University Press.

Barthes, Roland (1957) *Mythologies*. Paris: Seuil. (Eng. trans.: *Mythologies*. London: Granada, 1973.)

Barthes, Roland (1970) *S/Z*. Paris: Seuil. (Eng. trans.: *S/Z*. Oxford: Blackwell, 1990.)

Bateson, Gregory (1972) *Steps to an Ecology of Mind*. New York: Chandler.

Bateson, Gregory (1979) *Mind & Nature: A Necessary Unity*. Isle of Man: Fontana.

Bateson, Gregory and Mead, Margaret (1942) *Balinese Character: A Photographic Analysis*. New York: New York Academy of Science.

Baumgarten, Alexander Gottlieb (1735) *Meditationes philosophicae de nonnullis ad poema pertinentibus*. Halle: Grunert. (Eng. trans.: *Reflections on Poetry*. Edited by K. Aschenbrenner and W.B. Holter. Berkeley, CA: University of California Press, 1954; text and It. trans.: *Riflessioni sul testo poetico*. Edited by F. Piselli. Palermo: Aesthetica edizioni, 1985.)

Baumgarten, Alexander Gottlieb (1739) *Metaphysica*. (7th edn 1779). Halle: Herman (photostat: Olms: Hildesheim, 1963).

Baumgarten, Alexander Gottlieb (1750–8) *Aesthetica I–II*. Frankfurt am Oder: Kleyb (photostat: Olms: Hildesheim, 1986).

Bayer, Raymond (1934) *L'Esthétique de la grâce*. 2 vols. Paris: Alcan.

Beck, Ulrich (1986) *Risikogesellschaft*. Frankfurt-on-Main: Suhrkamp. (Eng. trans.: *Risk Society*. London: Sage, 1992.)

Beck, Ulrich, Giddens, Anthony and Lash, Scott (1994) *Reflexive Modernization: Politics, Tradition and Aesthetics in the Modern Social Order*. Cambridge: Polity Press.

Becker, Franklin D. (1981) *Workspace: Creating Environments in Organizations*. New York: Praeger.

Becker, Howard S. (1974) 'Art as collective action', *American Sociological Review*, 39 (6): 767–76.

Becker, Howard S. (1982) *Art Worlds*. Berkeley, CA: University of California Press.

Benghozi, Pierre-Jean (ed.) (1987) 'Art and organization', Special Issue of *Dragon*, 2 (4).

Benjamin, Walter (1968) 'The work of art in the age of mechanical reproduction', in Walter Benjamin, *Illuminations*, ed. Hannah Arendt. New York: Harcourt, Brace. pp. 219–66.

Berg, Per Olof (1987) 'Some notes on corporate artifacts', *Scos Note-Work*, 6 (1): 24–8.

Berg, Per Olof and Kreiner, Kristian (1990) 'Corporate architecture: turning physical settings into symbolic resources', in P. Gagliardi (ed.), *Symbols and Artifacts: Views of the Corporate Landscape*. Berlin: de Gruyter. pp. 41–67.

Berger, Peter and Luckmann, Thomas (1966) *The Social Construction of Reality*. Garden City, NY: Doubleday.

Biggiero, Lucio (1997) 'Lo spazio', in G. Costa and R.C.D. Nacamulli (eds), *Manuale di Organizzazione Aziendale. Vol. 2: La progettazione organizzativa*. Turin: UTET Libreria. pp. 113–33.

Bird, Elizabeth (1979) 'Aesthetic neutrality and the sociology of art', in M. Barrett, P. Corrigan, A. Kuhn and J. Wolff (eds), *Ideology and Cultural Production*. New York: St Martin's Press. pp. 25–48.

Blau, Judith R. (1984) *Architects and Firms*. Cambridge, MA: MIT Press.

Blau, Judith R. (1988) 'Study of the arts: a reappraisal', *Annual Sociological Review*, 14: 269–92.

Blau, Judith R. (1993) 'What buildings mean and architects say: economy and theory of architecture at a moment of crisis', *Current Research on Occupations and Professions*, Vol. 8. Greenwich, CT: JAI Press. pp. 77–99.

Bodei, Remo (1995) *Le forme del bello*. Bologna: Il Mulino.

Bodei, Remo (1997) *La filosofia del novecento*. Rome: Donzelli.

Bologna, Ferdinando (1992) *L'incredulità del Caravaggio e l'esperienza delle 'cose naturali'*. Turin: Bollati Boringhieri.

Bolognini, Bruno (1986a) 'Images as identifying objects and as organizational integrators in two firms', *Dragon*, 1 (3): 61–75.

Bolognini, Bruno (1986b) 'Il mito come espressione dei valori organizzativi e come fattore strutturale', in P. Gagliardi (ed.), *Le imprese come culture*. Milan: ISEDI. pp. 79–101.

Bonfiglioli, Sandra (1990) *L'architettura del tempo: la città multimediale*. Naples: Liguori.

Bonfiglioli, Sandra (1991) 'Dal tempo lineare all'architettura del tempo', in E. D'Alfonso and E. Franzini (eds), *Metafora mimesi morfogenesi progetto: un dialogo tra filosofi e architetti*. Milan: Guerini e Associati.

Boudon, Raymond (1984) *La Place du désordre*. Paris: Presses Universitaires de France.

Bozal, Valeriano (1996) *Il gusto*. Bologna: Il Mulino.

Braudel, Fernand (1979) *Civilisation matérielle: economie et capitalisme*. Paris: Armand Colin. (Eng. trans.: *Civilization and Capitalism, 15th–18th Century: The*

Perspective of the World. 3 vols. Berkeley, CA: University of California Press, 1992.)

Brown, Richard H. (1977) *A Poetic for Sociology: Toward a Logic of Discovery for the Human Sciences.* Cambridge: Cambridge University Press.

Bruce, Gordon (1995) 'Eschewing design obfuscation', paper presented at the Conference on Organizations, Managers, & Design, Luxembourg.

Bryman, Alan (1989) *Research Methods and Organization Studies.* Boston: Unwin Hyman.

Bryman, Alan and Burgess, Robert G. (eds) (1994) *Analyzing Qualitative Data.* London: Routledge.

Buck-Morss, Susan (1995) 'Envisioning capital: political economy on display', in L. Cooke and P. Wollen (eds), *Visual Display: Culture Beyond Appearances.* Seattle: Bay Press. pp. 111–42.

Bugos, Glenn E. (1996) 'Organizing stories of organizational life: four films on American business', *Studies in Cultures, Organizations and Societies,* 2 (1): 111–28.

Burgin, Victor (1992) 'Perverse space', in B. Colomina (ed.), *Sexuality & Space.* New York: Princeton Architectural Press. pp. 218–40.

Burrell, Gibson (1988) 'Modernism, postmodernism and organizational analysis 2: the contribution of Michel Foucault', *Organization Studies,* 9: 221–35.

Burrell, Gibson and Morgan, Gareth (1979) *Sociological Paradigms and Organizational Analysis.* Aldershot: Gower.

Calabrese, Omar (1985) *Il linguaggio dell'arte.* Milan: Bompiani.

Calabrese, Omar (1987) *L'età neobarocca.* Bari: Laterza. (Eng. trans.: *Neo-Baroque: A Sign of the Times.* Princeton, NJ: Princeton University Press, 1992.)

Calàs, Marta B. and Smircich, Linda (1992) 'Re-writing gender into organizational theorizing: directions from feminist perspectives', in M. Reed and M. Hughes (eds), *Rethinking Organization: New Directions in Organization Theory and Analysis.* London: Sage. pp. 227–53.

Calinescu, Matei (1987) *Five Faces of Modernity. Modernism, Avant-Garde, Decadence, Kitsch, Postmodernism.* Durham, NC: Duke University Press.

Callon, Michel (1991) 'Techno-economic networks and irreversibility', in J. Law (ed.), *A Sociology of Monsters: Essays on Power, Technology and Domination.* London: Routledge. pp. 132–61.

Carmagnola, Fulvio (1989) *La visibilità: per un'estetica dei fenomeni complessi.* Milan: Guerini e Associati.

Carmagnola, Fulvio (1997) 'L'estetica', in G. Costa and R.C.D. Nacamulli (eds), *Manuale di Organizzazione Aziendale. Vol. 2: La progettazione organizzativa.* Turin: UTET Libreria. pp. 357–80.

Cassirer, Ernst (1923–9) *Philosophie der symbolischen Formen, I–III.* Berlin: Bruno Cassirer. (Eng. trans.: *The Philosophy of Symbolic Forms,* I–III. New Haven, CT: Yale University Press, 1955–7; It. trans.: *Filosofia delle forme simboliche, I–III.* Florence: La Nuova Italia Editrice, 1961–4.)

Cassirer, Ernst (1941–2) 'Descartes, Leibniz, and Vico', lecture to the Arbeit Seminar 'Philosophy of History', Yale 1941–2. Reprinted 1979 in: E. Cassirer, *Symbol, Myth and Culture. Essays and Lectures of Ernst Cassirer 1935–1945.* New Haven: Yale University Press.

Cavalli, Alessandro (1969) *La fondazione del metodo sociologico in Max Weber e Werner Sombart.* Pavia: Istituto di Sociologia.

Chalfen, Richard (1987) *Snapshot Versions of Life.* Bowling Green, OH: Bowling Green State University Popular Press.

Chalfen, Richard (1991) *Turning Leaves: The Photograph Collections of Two Japanese American Families.* Albuquerque, NM: University of New Mexico Press.

Changeux, Jean-Pierre (1994) *Raison et plaisir.* Paris: Jacob.

Chisholm, Roderick (1979) 'Verstehen: the epistemological question', *Dialectica*, 33 (3–4): 233–46.

Clegg, Stewart R. and Hardy, Cynthia (1996) 'Introduction: organizations, organization and organizing', in S.R. Clegg, C. Hardy and W.R. Nord (eds), *Handbook of Organization Studies*. London: Sage. pp. 1–28.

Clegg, Stewart R., Hardy, Cynthia and Nord, Walter R. (eds) (1996) *Handbook of Organization Studies*. London: Sage.

Cohen, Anthony P. (1985) *The Symbolic Construction of Community*. London: Ellis Horwood and Tavistock Publications.

Collier, John and Collier, Malcom (1967) *Visual Anthropology*. Albuquerque, NM: University of New Mexico Press.

Collingwood, R.G. (1946) 'Human nature and human history', in R.G. Collingwood, *The Idea of History*. Oxford: Oxford University Press. Reprinted 1994 in: M. Martin and L.C. McIntyre (eds), *Readings in the Philosophy of Social Science*. Cambridge, MA: MIT Press. pp. 163–72.

Colombo, Attilio, Merlo, Lorenzo, Migliori, Nino and Piovani, Alberto (eds) (1979) *Fotografia giapponese dal 1848 ad oggi*. Bologna: Galleria d'Arte Moderna.

Colombo, Fausto and Eugeni, Ruggero (1996) *Il testo visibile: teoria, storia e modelli di analisi*. Rome: La Nuova Italia Scientifica.

Cooley, Charles Horton (1926) 'The roots of social knowledge', *American Journal of Sociology*, 12: 59–79.

Cooley, Charles Horton (1930) *Sociological Theory and Social Research*. New York: Holt, Rinehart and Winston.

Cooper, Cary L. and Jackson, Susan E. (eds) (1997) *Creating Tomorrow's Organizations: A Handbook for Future Research in Organizational Behavior*. Chichester: Wiley.

Cooper, Robert (1989) 'Modernism, postmodernism and organizational analysis 3: the contribution of Jacques Derrida', *Organization Studies*, 10: 479–502.

Cooper, Robert and Burrell, Gibson (1988) 'Modernism, postmodernism and organizational analysis: an introduction', *Organization Studies*, 9: 91–112.

Cooper, Robert and Law, John (1995) 'Organization: distal and proximal views', *Research in the Sociology of Organizations*, 13: 237–74.

Coppola Pignatelli, Paola (1982) *Spazio e immaginario: maschile e femminile in architettura*. Rome: Officina.

Corigliano, Emma (1991) *Tempo spazio identità: No Place Like Home*. Milan: Angeli.

Coser, Lewis A. (1971) *Masters of Sociological Thought*. New York: Jovanovich.

Costa, Giovanni and Nacamulli, Raoul C.D. (eds) (1997) *Manuale di Organizzazione Aziendale. Vol. 2: La progettazione organizzativa*. Turin: UTET Libreria.

Costa, Joan (1986) 'Toward a signaletic symbology of identity in corporate communication', *Dragon*, 1 (5): 5–16.

Costa, Joan (1992) *Imagen pública: una ingenería social*. Madrid: Fundesco.

Crespi, Franco (1996) *Manuale di sociologia della cultura*. Bari: Laterza.

Croce, Benedetto (1902) *Estetica come scienza dell'espressione e linguistica generale*. Bari: Laterza. Reprinted 1990, Milan: Adelphi. (Eng. trans.: *Aesthetic*, ed. D. Ainslic. London: Macmillan, 1909, 2nd complete edn 1922.)

Czarniawska, Barbara (1997) *Narrating the Organization: Dramas of Institutional Identity*. Chicago: University of Chicago Press.

D'Agostini, Franca (1997) *Analitici e continentali: guida alla filosofia degli ultimi trent'anni*. Milan: Cortina.

Danto, Arthur (1964) 'The artworld', *Journal of Philosophy*, 61 (4): 571–84.

Dean, James W. Jr, Ramirez, Rafael and Ottensmeyer, Edward (1997) 'An aesthetic perspective on organizations', in C. Cooper and S. Jackson (eds), *Creating Tomorrow's Organizations: A Handbook for Future Research in Organizational Behavior*. Chichester: Wiley. pp. 419–37.

Dégot, Vincent (1987) 'Portrait of the manager as an artist', *Dragon*, 2 (4): 13–50.

De Masi, Domenico (1989) 'Introduzione', in D. De Masi (ed.), *L'emozione e la regola: i gruppi creativi in Europa dal 1850 al 1950*. Bari: Laterza.

De Masi, Domenico (ed.) (1993) *Verso la formazione del post-industriale*. Milan: Angeli.

Derrida, Jacques (1967a) *De la Grammatologie*. Paris: Minuit. (Eng. trans.: *Of Grammatology*, Baltimore: Johns Hopkins University Press, 1974.)

Derrida, Jacques (1967b) *L'Écriture et la différence*. Paris: Seuil. (Eng. trans.: *Writing and Difference*, Chicago: University of Chicago Press, 1978.)

Dewey, John (1925) *Experience and Nature*. Reprinted 1958, New York: Dover.

Dewey, John (1934) *Art as Experience*. New York: Putnam's Sons.

Dickie, George (1971) *Aesthetics: An Introduction*. New York: Pegasus.

Dilthey, Wilhelm (1887) *Die Einbildungskraft des Dichters: Bausteine für eine Poetik*, in W. Dilthey, *Gesammelte Schriften*, Vol. VI. Stuttgart: Teubner. (Eng. trans.: 'The Imagination of the Poet: Elements of a Poetics', in R.A. Makkreel and F. Rodi (eds), *Wilhelm Dilthey: Selected Works*, Vol. V, Princeton, NJ: Princeton University Press, 1985, pp. 29–173; partial It. trans.: 'Creazione poetica', in S. Zecchi and E. Franzini (eds), *Storia dell'estetica*. Bologna: Il Mulino, 1995, pp. 740–5.)

Dilthey, Wilhelm (1914–36) *Gesammelte Schriften*. Stuttgart: Teubner. (Eng. trans.: *Selected Works*. Princeton, NJ: Princeton University Press, 1979– .)

Dorfles, Gillo (1967) *L'estetica del mito: da Vico a Wittgenstein*. Milan: Mursia.

Dorst, John (1989) *The Written Suburb: An American Site, an Ethnographic Dilemma*. Philadelphia: University of Pennsylvania Press.

Dougherty, Deborah and Kunda, Gideon (1990) 'Photograph analysis: a method to capture organisational belief systems', in P. Gagliardi (ed.), *Symbols and Artifacts: Views of the Corporate Landscape*. Berlin: de Gruyter. pp. 185–206.

Doxtater, Dennis (1990) 'Meaning of the workplace: using ideas of ritual space in design', in P. Gagliardi (ed.), *Symbols and Artifacts: Views of the Corporate Landscape*. Berlin: de Gruyter. pp. 107–27.

Dray, William (1957) 'The rationale of actions', in W. Dray, *Laws and Explanation in History*. Oxford: Clarendon Press. Reprinted 1994 in: M. Martin and L.C. McIntyre (eds), *Readings in the Philosophy of Social Science*. Cambridge, MA: MIT Press. pp. 173–80.

Durand, Gilbert (1963) *Les Structures anthropologiques de l'imaginaire*. Paris: Presses Universitaires de France.

Eco, Umberto (1962) *Opera aperta*. Milan: Bompiani. (Eng. trans.: *The Open Work*. Cambridge, MA: Harvard University Press, 1989.)

Eco, Umberto (1968) *La struttura assente*. Reprinted 1983, Milan: Bompiani.

Eco, Umberto (1973) *Segno*. Milan: ISEDI.

Eco, Umberto (1975) *Trattato di semiotica generale*. Milan: Bompiani. (Eng. trans.: *A Theory of Semiotics*, Bloomington: Indiana University Press, 1976.)

Eco, Umberto (1997) 'Brevi cenni sull'essere', in F. Barone, C. Bernardini, E. Berti, R. Bodei, U. Eco, D. Losurdo and F. Volpi, *Metafisica: il mondo nascosto*. Bari: Laterza. pp. 99–139.

Evered, Roger and Louis, Meryl R. (1981) 'Alternative perspectives in the organizational science: "inquiry from the inside" and "inquiry from the outside"', *Academy of Management Review*, 6 (3): 385–95.

Featherstone, Mike (1991) *Consumer Culture and Postmodernism*. London: Sage.

Ferraris, Maurizio (1996) *L'immaginazione*. Bologna: Il Mulino.

Ferraris, Maurizio (1997) *Estetica razionale*. Milan: Cortina.

Ferry, Luc (1990) *Homo Aestheticus: l'invention du gout à l'âge démocratique*. Paris: Grasset & Fasquelle. (Eng. trans.: *Homo Aestheticus: The Invention of Taste in the Democratic Age*. Chicago, IL: University of Chicago Press, 1993.)

Fine, Gary A. (1996) *Kitchens: The Culture of Restaurant Work*. Berkeley, CA: University of California Press.

Fineman, Stephen (1996) 'Emotion and organizing', in S.R. Clegg, C. Hardy and W. Nord (eds), *Handbook of Organization Studies*. London: Sage. pp. 543–64.

Fineman, Stephen (1997) 'Emotion and management learning', *Management Learning*, 28 (1): 13–25.

Franzini, Elio (1987) *Il mito di Leonardo: sulla fenomenologia della creazione artistica*. Milan: Unicopli.

Franzini, Elio (1991) *Fenomenologia: introduzione tematica al pensiero di Husserl*. Milan: Angeli.

Franzini, Elio (1995) *L'estetica del settecento*. Bologna: Il Mulino.

Franzini, Elio (1997) *Filosofia dei sentimenti*. Milan: Mondadori.

Franzini, Elio and Mazzocut-Mis, Maddalena (1996) *Estetica: i nomi, i concetti, le correnti*. Milan: Mondadori.

Fukasawa, Naoto (1995) 'The theory of HARI in design', paper presented at the Conference on Organizations, Managers, & Design, Luxembourg.

Gadamer, Hans-Georg (1960) *Wahrheit und Methode*. Tübingen: Mohr. (Eng. trans.: *Truth and Method*. New York: Sheed & Ward, 1975; It. trans.: *Verità e metodo*. Milan: Bompiani, 1983, 7th edn 1990.)

Gadamer, Hans-Georg (1977) *Die Aktualität des Schönen: Kunst als Spiel, Symbol und Fest*. Stuttgart: Phillip Reclam Jr. (Eng. trans.: 'The relevance of the beautiful: art as play, symbol, and festival', in H.-G. Gadamer, *The Relevance of the Beautiful and Other Essays*. Cambridge: Cambridge University Press, 1986. pp. 3–53.)

Gagliardi, Pasquale (1990a) 'Artifacts as pathways and remains of organizational life', in P. Gagliardi (ed.), *Symbols and Artifacts: Views of the Corporate Landscape*. Berlin: de Gruyter. pp. 3–38.

Gagliardi, Pasquale (ed.) (1990b) *Symbols and Artifacts: Views of the Corporate Landscape*. Berlin: de Gruyter.

Gagliardi, Pasquale (1996) 'Exploring the aesthetic side of organizational life', in S.R. Clegg, C. Hardy and W.R. Nord (eds), *Handbook of Organization Studies*. London: Sage. pp. 565–80.

Geertz, Clifford (1973) *The Interpretation of Cultures: Selected Essays*. New York: Basic Books.

Georgiou, Petro (1973) 'The goal paradigm and notes toward a counter paradigm', *Administrative Science Quarterly*, 18 (3): 291–310.

Gherardi, Silvia (1995) *Gender, Symbolism and Organizational Cultures*. London: Sage.

Gherardi, Silvia and Strati, Antonio (1988) 'The temporal dimension in organization studies', *Organization Studies*, 9 (2): 149–64.

Ghiselin, Brewster (1952) 'Introduction', in B. Ghiselin (ed.), *The Creative Process: A Symposium*. New York: Penguin. pp. 11–31.

Giddens, Anthony (1990) *The Consequences of Modernity*. Cambridge: Polity Press.

Giddens, Anthony (1991) *Modernity and Self-Identity*. Cambridge: Polity Press.

Givone, Sergio (1988) *Storia dell'estetica*. Bari: Laterza.

Gombrich, Ernst H. (1950) *The Story of Art*. Reprinted 1966, London: Phaidon.

Gombrich, Ernst H. (1982) *The Image and the Eye: Further Studies in the Psychology of Pictorial Representation*. Oxford: Phaidon.

Gombrich, Ernst (1995) *Shadows: The Depiction of Cast Shadows in Western Art*. London: National Gallery Publications.

Grafton-Small, Robert (1985) 'Making meaning concrete: exchange processes and the cultural determination of physical space', *CEBES Journal*, 1 (1): 62–75.

Grafton-Small, Robert and Linstead, Stephen (1985) 'Bricks and bricolage: deconstructing corporate image in stone and story', *Dragon*, 1: 8–27.

Gross, Edward (1969) 'The definition of organizational goals', *British Journal of Sociology*, 20: 277–94.

Guillén, Mauro F. (1997) 'Scientific Management's lost aesthetic: architecture, organization, and the Taylorized beauty of the mechanical', *Administrative Science Quarterly*, 42: 682–715.

Guillet de Monthoux, Pierre (1996) 'The theatre of war: art, organization and the aesthetics of strategy', *Studies in Cultures, Organizations and Societies*, 2 (1): 147–60.

Haraway, Donna J. (1985) 'A manifesto for cyborgs: science, technology, and socialist feminism in the 1980's', *Socialist Review*, 80: 65–107.

Haraway, Donna J. (ed.) (1991) *Simians, Cyborgs and Women: The Reinvention of Nature*. London: Free Association Books.

Hassard, John (1993) *Sociology and Organization Theory: Positivism, Paradigms and Postmodernity*. Cambridge: Cambridge University Press.

Hassard, John and Parker, Martin (eds) (1993) *Postmodernism and Organizations*. London: Sage.

Hatch, Mary Jo (1987) 'Physical barriers, task characteristics, and interaction activity in research and development firms', *Administrative Science Quarterly*, 32: 387–99.

Hatch, Mary Jo (1990) 'The symbolics of office design: an empirical exploration', in P. Gagliardi (ed.), *Symbols and Artifacts: Views of the Corporate Landscape*. Berlin: de Gruyter. pp. 129-46.

Hatch, Mary Jo (1997) *Organization Theory: Modern, Symbolic, and Postmodern Perspectives*. Oxford: Oxford University Press.

Hatch, Mary Jo and Jones, Michael Owen (1997) 'Photocopylore at work: aesthetics, collective creativity and the social construction of organizations', *Studies in Cultures, Organizations and Societies*, 3 (2): 263–87.

Hauser, Arnold (1955) *Sozialgeschichte der Kunst und Literatur*. Munich: Beck. (Eng. trans.: *The Social History of Art*. 4 vols. London: Routledge, 1951; It. trans.: *Storia sociale dell'arte*. 2 vols. Turin: Einaudi, 1956.)

Heidegger, Martin (1954) *Vorträge und Aufsätze*. Pfullingen: Neske.

Hempel, Carl G. (1942) 'The function of general laws in history', *Journal of Philosophy*, 39: 35–48. Reprinted 1994 in: M. Martin and L.C. McIntyre (eds), *Readings in the Philosophy of Social Science*. Cambridge, MA: MIT Press. pp. 43–53.

Henny, Leonard (ed.) (1986) 'Theory and practice in visual sociology', Special Issue of *Current Sociology*, 3 (34).

Hill, Michael (1984) *Exploring Visual Sociology*. Monticello, IL: Vance Bibliographies.

Hulsker, Jan (1980) *The Complete Van Gogh: Paintings, Drawings, Sketches*. Oxford: Phaidon.

Husserl, Edmund (1907) 'Ein Brief für Hugo von Hofmannsthal', edited by R. Hirsch in 'Edmund Husserl und Hugo von Hofmannsthal: eine Begegnung und ein Brief', in C.-J. Friedrich and B. Reifenberg (eds) (1968), *Sprache und Politik: Festgabe für Dolf Sternberger zum sechzigsten Geburtstag*. Heidelberg: Verlag Lambert Schneider. pp. 108–15. (It. trans.: 'Una lettera di Husserl a Hofmannsthal', ed. G. Scaramuzza, *Fenomenologia e scienze dell'uomo*, 1985, 1 (2): 203–7.)

Husserl, Edmund (1913) *Ideen zu einer reinen Phänomenologie und phänomeno-logischen Philosophie*, ed. by M. Biemel (1950), *Husserliana III*. The Hague: Nijhoff. (Eng. trans.: *Ideas Pertaining to a Pure Phenomenology and to a Phenomenological Philosophy*, 2 vols, The Hague: Nijhoff, 1973; It. trans.: *Idee per una fenomenologia pura e per una filosofia fenomenologica*. Turin: Einaudi, 1965.)

Husserl, Edmund (1920–6) *Analysen zur passiven Synthesis*, ed. by M. Fleischer (1966), *Husserliana XI*. The Hague: Nijhoff.

Hutcheon, Linda (1989) *The Politics of Postmodernism*. London: Routledge.

Izzo, Alberto (1994) *Storia del pensiero sociologico*. Bologna: Il Mulino.

Jameson, Frederic (1991) *Postmodernism, or, the Cultural Logic of Late Capitalism*. Durham, NC: Duke University Press.

Jauss, Hans Robert (1982) *Ästhetische Erfahrung und literarische Hermeneutik*. Frankfurt-on-Main: Suhrkamp Verlag. (Eng. trans.: *Question and Answer: Forms of Dialogic Understanding*. Minneapolis, MN: University of Minnesota Press, 1989; It. trans.: *Esperienza estetica ed ermeneutica letteraria*. 2 vols. Bologna: Il Mulino, 1987/8.)

Joas, Hans (1992) *Die Kreativität des Handelns*. Frankfurt-on-Main: Suhrkamp Verlag. (Eng. trans.: *The Creativity of Action*. Cambridge: Polity Press, 1996.)

Jones, Michael Owen (1987) *Exploring Folk Art: Twenty Years of Thought on Craft, Work, and Aesthetics*. Ann Arbor, MI: UMI Research Press.

Jones, Michael Owen (1996) *Studying Organizational Symbolism*. Thousand Oaks, CA: Sage.

Jones, Michael Owen, Moore, Michael D. and Snyder, Richard C. (eds) (1988) *Inside Organizations: Understanding the Human Dimension*. Newbury Park, CA: Sage.

Kaghan, William and Phillips, Nelson (1998) 'Building the Tower of Babel: communities of practice and paradigmatic pluralism in organization studies', *Organization*, 5 (2): 191–215.

Kant, Immanuel (1790) *Kritik der Urteilskraft*. In I. Kant, *Werke in zwölf Bänden*, Vol. X, ed. by W. Weischedel. Frankfurt-on-Main: Suhrkamp, 1968. (Eng. trans.: *The Critique of Judgement*. Oxford: Oxford University Press, 1952.)

Knorr-Cetina, Karin (1994) 'Primitive classification and postmodernity: towards a sociological notion of fiction', *Theory, Culture & Society*, 11: 1–22.

Kronhausen, Phyllis and Kronhausen Eberhard, (1968–70) *The Complete Book of Erotic Art, I–II*. New York: Bell.

Kuhn, James W. (1996) 'The misfit between organization theory and processional art: a comment on White and Strati', *Organization*, 3 (2): 219–24.

Kuhn, Thomas (1962) *The Structure of Scientific Revolutions*. Chicago: University of Chicago Press.

Lacan, Jacques (1966) *Écrits*. Paris: Seuil.

Lacan, Jacques (1975) *Le Séminaire. Livre I: Les écrits techniques de Freud*. Paris: Seuil. (Eng. trans.: *The Seminar of Jacques Lacan. Book 1: Freud's Papers on Technique 1953–1954*. Cambridge: Cambridge University Press, 1988.)

Lalo, Charles (1927) *Notions d'esthétique*. Paris: Alcan.

Langer, Susanne K. (1942) *Philosophy in a New Key*. Cambridge, MA: Harvard University Press.

Langer, Susanne K. (1953) *Form and Feeling: A Theory of Art*. New York: Scribner's Sons.

Langer, Susanne K. (1967) *Mind: An Essay on Human Feeling*. Baltimore: Johns Hopkins University Press.

Larsen, Janne and Schultz, Majken (1990) 'Artifacts in a bureaucratic monastery', in P. Gagliardi (ed.), *Symbols and Artifacts: Views of the Corporate Landscape*. Berlin: de Gruyter. pp. 281–302.

Lash, Scott (1993) 'Reflexive modernization: the aesthetic dimension', *Theory, Culture & Society*, 10: 1–23.

Latour, Bruno (1991) 'Technology is society made durable', in J. Law (ed.), *A Sociology of Monsters: Essays on Power, Technology and Domination*. London: Routledge. pp. 103–31.

Latour, Bruno (1992) 'Where are the missing masses? Sociology of a few mundane Artifacts', in W. Bijker and J. Law (eds), *Shaping Technology-Building Society: Studies in Sociotechnical Change*. Cambridge, MA: MIT Press. pp. 225–58.

Linstead, Stephen and Hopfl, Heather (eds) (1999) *The Aesthetics of Organization.* London: Sage.

Lipps, Theodor (1897) *Raumästhetik und geometrisch-optische Täuschungen.* Leipzig: Barth.

Lipps, Theodor (1903–6) *Ästhetik: Psychologie des Schönen und der Kunst, I–II.* Hamburg and Leipzig: Voss.

Lipps, Theodor (1913) *Zum Einfühlung.* Leipzig: Engelmann. (Partial It. trans.: 'Empatia e godimento estetico', in G. Vattimo (ed.), *Estetica moderna.* Bologna: Il Mulino, 1977. pp. 179–91.)

Lomax, Helen and Casey, Neil (1998) 'Recording social life: reflexivity and video methodology', *Sociological Research Online,* 3 (2).

Lyotard, Jean-François (1991) *Leçons sur l'analytique du sublime.* Paris: Galilée. (Eng. trans.: *Lessons on the Analytic of the Sublime.* Stanford, CA: Stanford University Press, 1994.)

Maldonado, Tomás (1979) 'Does the icon have a cognitive value?', in S. Chatman, U. Eco and J.-M. Klinkenberg (eds), *A Semiotic Landscape: Proceedings of the First Congress of the International Association for Semiotic Studies, Milan, June 1974.* The Hague: Mouton. pp. 774–6.

Mangham, Iain L. and Overington, Michael A. (1987) *Organizations as Theatre.* Chichester: Wiley.

March, James (1988) *Decisions and Organizations.* Oxford: Basil Blackwell.

Marquard, Odo (1989) *Aesthetica und Anaesthetica: Philosophische Überlegungen.* Paderborn: Schoningh.

Martin, Jane R. (1969) 'Another look at the doctrine of *Verstehen*', *British Journal for the Philosophy of Science,* 20: 53–67.

Martin, Joanne and Frost, Peter (1996) 'The organizational culture war games: a struggle for intellectual dominance', in S.R. Clegg, C. Hardy and W.R. Nord (eds), *Handbook of Organization Studies.* London: Sage. pp. 599-621.

Mattioli, Francesco (1991) *Sociologia visuale.* Turin: Nuova ERI.

Mattioli, Francesco (1996) 'La sociologia visuale: qualche risposta a molti inter-rogativi', in C. Cipolla and A. de Lillo (eds), *Il sociologo e le sirene: la sfida dei metodi qualitativi.* Milan: Angeli. pp. 390–408.

Melucci, Alberto (1994) 'Creatività: miti, discorsi, processi', in A. Melucci (ed.), *Creatività: miti, discorsi, processi.* Milan: Feltrinelli. pp. 11–32.

Merton, Robert K. (1968) *Social Theory and Social Structure.* New York: Free Press (1st edn 1949).

Meyer, Alan D. (1991) 'Visual data in organizational research', *Organization Science,* 2 (2): 218–36.

Milani, Raffaele (1991) *Le categorie estetiche.* Parma: Pratiche Editrice.

Milani, Raffaele (1996) *Il Pittoresco: L'evoluzione del Gusto tra classico e romantico.* Bari: Laterza.

Mukařovský, Jan (1966) *Studie z estetiky.* Prague: Odeon.

Negroponte, Nicholas (1995) *Being Digital.* New York: Alfred A. Knopf.

Ottensmeyer, Edward (1996a) 'Too strong to stop, too sweet to lose: aesthetics as a way to know organizations', *Organization,* 3 (2): 189–94.

Ottensmeyer, Edward (ed.) (1996b) 'Essays on aesthetics and organization', *Organization,* 3 (2).

Outhwaite, William (1975) *Understanding Social Life: The Method Called Verstehen.* London: Allen & Unwin.

Pareyson, Luigi (1943) *Studi sull'esistenzialismo.* Florence: Sansoni.

Pareyson, Luigi (1954) *Estetica. Teoria della formatività.* Turin: Giappichelli. Reprinted 1988, Milan: Bompiani.

Pareyson, Luigi (1971) *Verità e interpretazione.* Milan: Mursia.

Pareyson, Luigi (1989) *Filosofia della libertà.* Genoa: Il Melangolo.

Peirce, Charles S. (1931–5) *Collected Papers*, Vols 1–8. Cambridge, MA: Harvard University Press.

Perniola, Mario (1997) *L'estetica del novecento*. Bologna: Il Mulino.

Perrow, Charles (1972) *Complex Organizations: A Critical Essay*. Glenview, IL: Scott, Foresman.

Pfeffer, Jeffrey (1982) *Organizations and Organization Theory*. Marshfield, MA: Pitman.

Polanyi, Michael (1945) 'The Autonomy of Science', *The Scientific Monthly*, 60: 141–50. Reprinted 1974 in: M. Polanyi, *Scientific Thought and Social Reality: Essays by Michael Polanyi*, ed. by F. Schwartz, *Psychological Issues*, 8 (4), Monograph 32. New York: International Universities Press. pp. 15–33.

Polanyi, Michael (1946) *Science, Faith and Society*. London: Oxford University Press.

Polanyi, Michael (1954) 'On the introduction of science into moral subjects', *Cambridge Journal*, 7 (Jan.): 195–207. Reprinted 1974 in: M. Polanyi, *Scientific Thought and Social Reality: Essays by Michael Polanyi*, ed. by F. Schwartz, *Psychological Issues*, 8 (4), Monograph 32. New York: International Universities Press. pp. 82–97.

Polanyi, Michael (1961a) 'Knowing and Being', *Mind*, 70 (280): 458–70.

Polanyi, Michael (1961b) 'Faith and reason', *Journal of Religion*, 41: 237–47. Reprinted 1974 in: M. Polanyi, *Scientific Thought and Social Reality: Essays by Michael Polanyi*, ed. by F. Schwartz, *Psychological Issues*, 8 (4), Monograph 32. New York: International Universities Press. pp. 116–30.

Polanyi, Michael (1962) *Personal Knowledge*. London: Routledge & Kegan Paul (1st edn 1958).

Polanyi, Michael (1966) *The Tacit Dimension*. Garden City, NY: Doubleday.

Polanyi, Michael (1969) *Knowing and Being: Essays by Michael Polanyi*, ed. by M. Grene. Chicago: University of Chicago Press.

Polanyi, Michael (1974) *Scientific Thought and Social Reality: Essays by Michael Polanyi*, ed. by F. Schwartz, *Psychological Issues*, 8 (4), Monograph 32. New York: International Universities Press.

Ponte, Alessandra (1992) 'Architecture and phallocentrism in Richard Payne Knight's theory', in B. Colomina (ed.), *Sexuality & Space*. New York: Princeton Architectural Press. pp. 273–305.

Powdermaker, Hortense (1950) *Hollywood: The Dream Factory*. Boston: Little, Brown.

Putnam, Linda, Phillips, Nelson and Chapman, Pamela (1996) 'Metaphors of communication and organization', in S.R. Clegg, C. Hardy and W.R. Nord (eds), *Handbook of Organization Studies*. London: Sage. pp. 375–408.

Rafaeli, Anat and Pratt, Michael G. (1993) 'Tailored meanings: on the meaning and impact of organizational dress', *Academy of Management Review*, 18 (1): 32–55.

Ramirez, Rafael (1987) 'An aesthetic theory of social organization', *Dragon*, 2 (4): 51–63.

Ramirez, Rafael (1991) *The Beauty of Social Organization*. Munich: Accedo.

Read, Herbert (1955) *Icon and Idea*. London: Faber & Faber.

Reed, Michael (1992) *The Sociology of Organizations: Themes, Perspectives and Prospects*. New York: Harvester Wheatsheaf.

Restaino, Franco (1991) *Storia dell'estetica moderna*. Turin: UTET.

Ricolfi, Luca (1997) 'La ricerca empirica nelle scienze sociali: una tassonomia', in L. Ricolfi (ed.), *La ricerca qualitativa*. Rome: La Nuova Italia Scientifica.

Rossi, Arcangelo (1988) 'Prefazione all'edizione italiana', in M. Polanyi, *Conoscere ed essere: saggi*, ed. by M. Grene. Rome: Armando.

Rusted, Brian (1987) ' "It's not called show art!": aesthetic decisions as organizational practice', *Dragon*, 2 (4): 127–36.

Rusted, Brian (1990) 'Housing modifications as organizational communication', in P. Gagliardi (ed.), *Symbols and Artifacts: Views of the Corporate Landscape.* Berlin: de Gruyter. pp. 85–105.

Rusted, Brian (1995) 'Framing a house, photography and the performance of heritage', *Canadian Folklore Canadien*, 17 (2): 139-58.

Rusted, Brian (1999) ' "Cutting a show": grounded aesthetics and entertainment organizations', in S. Linstead and H. Hopfl (eds), *The Aesthetics of Organization.* London: Sage.

Salvemini, Severino (1993) 'Formatore debole/formatore forte', in D. De Masi (ed.), *Verso la formazione del post-industriale.* Milan: Angeli. pp. 305–11.

Sassoon, Joseph (1990) 'Colors, artifacts, and ideologies', in P. Gagliardi (ed.), *Symbols and Artifacts: Views of the Corporate Landscape.* Berlin: de Gruyter. pp. 169-84.

Schein, Edgar H. (1984) 'Coming to a new awareness of organizational culture', *Sloan Management Review*, 25 (4): 3–16.

Scherer, Andreas Georg (1998) 'Pluralism and incommensurability in strategic management and organization theory: a problem in search of a solution', *Organization*, 5 (2): 147–68.

Schleiermacher, Friedrich Daniel Ernst (1959) *Hermeneutik.* Heidelberg: Carl Winter Universitätsverlag. (Eng. trans.: *Hermeneutics: The Handwritten Manuscripts.* Atlanta, GA: Scholars Press, 1978.)

Schneider, Susan C. and Powley, Ellen (1986) 'The role of images in changing corporate culture: the case of A.T.&T.', *Dragon*, 1 (2): 5–44.

Schütz, Alfred (1962) *Collected Papers*, Vol. I. The Hague: Nijhoff.

Schütz, Alfred (1964) *Collected Papers*, Vol. II. The Hague: Nijhoff.

Schwartz, Howard and Jacobs, Jerri (1979) *Qualitative Sociology: A Method to the Madness.* New York: Free Press.

Scialpi, Antonio (1979) 'La *Einfühlungstheorie*', *Rivista di Estetica*, 1: 67–84.

Scriven, Michael (1971) 'Verstehen Again', *Theory and Decision*, 1: 382–6.

Sebastiani, Chiara (1997) 'Spazio e sfera pubblica: la politica nella città', *Rassegna Italiana di Sociologia*, 38 (2): 223–43.

Sievers, Burkard (1990a) 'The diabolization of death: some thoughts on the obsolescence of mortality in organization theory and practice', in J. Hassard and D. Pym (eds), *The Theory and Philosophy of Organizations: Critical Issues and New Perspectives.* London: Routledge. pp. 125–36.

Sievers, Burkard (1990b) 'Curing the monster: some images of and considerations about the dragon', in P. Gagliardi (ed.), *Symbols and Artifacts: Views of the Corporate Landscape.* Berlin: de Gruyter. pp. 207–31.

Simmel, Georg (1907) 'Die Ruine: ein ästhetischer Versuch', *Der Tag*, 96. Reprinted in G. Simmel (1918) *Philosophische Kultur. Gesammelte Essais.* Leipzig: Kröner Verlag. (It. trans.: 'La Rovina', *Rivista di Estetica*, XXI (8) 1981. Reprinted 1996 in: P. Panza (ed.), *Estetica dell'architettura.* Milan: Guerini e Associati. pp. 159-66.)

Sini, Carlo (1992) 'Il pensiero e il simbolo', in S. Zecchi (ed.), *Estetica 1992: Forme del simbolo.* Bologna: Il Mulino. pp. 93–113.

Sini, Carlo (1996) *Gli abiti, le pratiche, i saperi.* Milan: Jaca Book.

Smircich, Linda (1983) 'Concepts of culture and organizational analysis', *Administrative Science Quarterly*, 28: 339-58.

Smircich, Linda, Calàs, Marta and Morgan, Gareth (eds) (1992) 'New intellectual currents in organization and management theory: theory development forum', Special Issue of *Academy of Management Review*, 17 (3).

Souriau, Étienne (1929) *L'Avenir de l'esthétique.* Paris: Alcan.

Sparti, Davide (1992) *Se un leone potesse parlare: indagine sul comprendere e lo spiegare.* Florence: Sansoni.

Sparti, Davide (1995) *Epistemologia delle scienze sociali*. Rome: La Nuova Italia Scientifica.

Sperber, Dan (1974) *Le Symbolisme en général*. Paris: Hermann. (Eng. trans.: *Rethinking Symbolism*. Cambridge: Cambridge University Press, 1975.)

Sperber, Dan (1982) *Le Savoir des anthropologues*. Paris: Hermann (Eng. trans.: *On Anthropological Knowledge: Three Essays*. Cambridge: Cambridge University Press, 1985).

Steele, Fred I. (1973) *Physical Settings and Organization Development*. Reading, MA: Addison-Wesley.

Stern, Stephen (1988) 'Symbolic representation of organizational identity: the role of emblem at the Garrett Corporation', in M.O. Jones, M.D. Moore and R.C. Snyder (eds), *Inside Organizations: Understanding the Human Dimension*. Newbury Park, CA: Sage. pp. 281–95.

Stewart, David (1956) *Preface to Empathy*. New York: Philosophical Library.

Strati, Antonio (ed.) (1985) *The Symbolics of Skill*. Trent: Dipartimento di Politica Sociale, Quaderno 5/6.

Strati, Antonio (1990) 'Aesthetics and organizational skill', in B.A. Turner (ed.), *Organizational Symbolism*. Berlin: de Gruyter. pp. 207–22.

Strati, Antonio (1992) 'Aesthetic understanding of organizational life', *Academy of Management Review*, 17 (3): 568–81.

Strati, Antonio (1995) 'Aesthetics and organization without walls', *Studies in Cultures, Organizations and Societies*, 1 (1): 83–105.

Strati, Antonio (1996a) 'Organization viewed through the lens of aesthetics', *Organization*, 3 (2): 209–18.

Strati, Antonio (1996b) *Sociologia dell'organizzazione: paradigmi teorici e metodi di ricerca*. Rome: La Nuova Italia Scientifica. (Eng. trans.: *Researching Organizations: Theoretical Paradigms and Methodological Choices*. London: Sage, forthcoming.)

Strati, Antonio (1997) 'Organization as hypertext: a metaphor from visual cultures', *Studies in Cultures, Organizations and Societies*, 3 (2): 307–24.

Strati, Antonio (1999) 'The aesthetic approach in organization studies', in S. Linstead and H. Hopfl (eds), *The Aesthetics of Organization*. London: Sage.

Strauss, Anselm (1993) *Continual Permutations of Action*. New York: Aldine de Gruyter.

Thun, Matteo (1989) 'Banal design', in V. Fischer (ed.), *Design Now: Industry or Art*. Munich: Prestel. pp. 241–8.

Tucker, Kenneth H. (1996) 'Harmony and transgression: aesthetic imagery and the public sphere in Habermas and poststructuralism', *Current Perspectives in Social Theory*, Vol. 16. Greenwich, CT: JAI Press. pp. 101–20.

Turner, Barry (1988) 'Connoisseurship in the study of organizational cultures', in A. Bryman (ed.), *Doing Research in Organization*. London: Routledge. pp. 108–22.

Turner, Barry (ed.) (1990) *Organizational Symbolism*. Berlin: de Gruyter.

Van Evra, James W. (1971) 'On Scriven on "Verstehen"', *Theory and Decision*, 1: 377–81.

Van Maanen, John (ed.) (1979) 'Qualitative methodology', Special Issue of *Administrative Science Quarterly*, 24 (4).

Van Maanen, John (1995) 'Style as theory', *Organization Science*, 6 (1): 133–43.

Van Maanen, John and Barley, Stephen R. (1984) 'Occupational communities: culture and control in organizations', in B.M. Staw and L.C. Cummings (eds), *Research in Organizational Behavior*, Vol. 6. Greenwich, CT: JAI Press. pp. 287–366.

Vattimo, Gianni (1977) 'Introduzione', in G. Vattimo (ed.), *Estetica moderna*. Bologna: Il Mulino. pp. 7–46.

Vattimo, Gianni (1983) 'Dialettica, differenza, pensiero debole', in G. Vattimo and P.A. Rovatti (eds), *Il pensiero debole*. Milan: Feltrinelli. pp. 12–28.

Vico, Giambattista (1725) *Principi di una scienza nuova*. Naples: Mosca. 3rd edn 1744. (Eng. trans.: *The New Science of Giambattista Vico*, ed. by T.G. Bergin and M.H. Fisch, Ithaca, NY: Cornell University Press, 1968.)

Volli, Ugo (1997) *Fascino: Feticismo e altre idolatrie*. Milan: Feltrinelli.

Wagner, Jon (ed.) (1979) *Images of Information*. Beverly Hills, CA: Sage.

Wax, Murray J. (1967) 'On misunderstanding Verstehen: a reply to Abel', *Sociology and Social Research*, 51: 323–33.

Weber, Max (1904) *Die protestantische Ethik und der Geist des Kapitalismus*, in M. Weber (1922), *Gesammelte Aufsätze zur Religions-soziologie*. Tübingen: Mohr. (Eng. trans.: *The Protestant Ethic and the Spirit of Capitalism*, London: Routledge & Kegan Paul, 1976.)

Weber, Max (1922) *Wirtschaft und Gesellschaft. Grundriß der verstehenden Soziologie*. Tübingen: Mohr. (Eng. trans.: *Economy and Society*. Berkeley, CA: University of California Press, 1978.)

White, David A. (1996) ' "It's working beautifully!": philosophical reflections on aesthetics and organization theory', *Organization*, 3 (2): 195–208.

Wigley, Mark (1992) 'Untitled: the housing of gender', in B. Colomina (ed.), *Sexuality & Space*. New York: Princeton Architectural Press. pp. 327–89.

Willis, Paul (1990) *Common Culture*. Boulder, CO: Westview Press.

Witkin, Robert W. (1990) 'The aesthetic imperative of a rational–technical machinery: a study in organizational control through the design of Artifacts', in P. Gagliardi (ed.), *Symbols and Artifacts: Views of the Corporate Landscape*. Berlin: de Gruyter. pp. 325–38.

Witkin, Robert W. (1995) *Art and Social Structure*. Cambridge: Polity Press.

Wollen, Peter (1995) 'Introduction', in L. Cooke and P. Wollen (eds), *Visual Display: Culture Beyond Appearances*. Seattle: Bay Press. pp. 9–13.

Wright, George H. von (1980) *Freedom and Determination*. Helsinki: Philosophical Society of Finland.

Zecchi, Stefano (1978) *La fenomenologia dopo Husserl nella cultura contemporanea. Sviluppi critici della fenomenologia*. Florence: La Nuova Italia Editrice.

Zecchi, Stefano (1990) *La bellezza*. Turin: Bollati Boringhieri.

Zecchi, Stefano (1995) *Il brutto e il bello: nella vita, nella politica, nell' arte*. Milan: Mondadori.

Zecchi, Stefano and Franzini, Elio (eds) (1995) *Storia dell'estetica*. Bologna: Il Mulino.

Zey-Ferrel, Mary (1981) 'Criticisms of the dominant perspective on organizations', *The Sociological Quarterly*, 22 (Spring): 181–205.

Zolberg, Vera L. (1990) *Constructing a Sociology of the Arts*. Cambridge: Cambridge University Press.

Index

formal organizations, 87–8
fragments, 180–1, 189
Franzini, Elio, 60–1, 83–5, 114, 119, 126–7,
138–9, 154, 155, 177, 179, 186, 188
Frost, Peter, 6
Fukasawa, Naoto, 170
functionalism, 5–6, 162, 168

Gadamer, Hans-Georg, 78, 106–7, 134, 135–6,
138, 145
Gagliardi, Pasquale, 3, 6, 157, 158–60, 162,
189
Geertz, Clifford, 7
gender symbologies, 172–3
Georgiou, Petro, 86
Gherardi, Silvia, 6, 166, 172
Ghiselin, Brewster, 176
Giddens, Anthony, 5
Givone, Sergio, 172
'global ideology', 164, 165, 170
gnoseology, lower-order, 108
goal paradigm, 86–7, 91
Gombrich, Ernst, 150, 170–1, 185
gracious (aesthetic category), 115, 118, 119,
188
Grafton-Small, Robert, 6, 181
grandiose/grandiosity, 104–6, 119, 149
Gross, Edward, 86
grotesque, 12, 117, 118, 119, 187
Guillén, Mauro F., 182
Guillet de Monthoux, Pierre, 181

Haraway, Donna, 3
Hardy, Cynthia, 192
Hassard, John, 3, 4, 157
Hatch, Mary Jo, 166–7, 168, 181
Hauser, Arnold, 133
hearing, 1–2
Hegel, Georg Wilhelm Friedrich, 60
Hegelian logic, 77
Heidegger, Martin, 5
Hempel, Carl G., 58, 63
Henny, Leonard, 181
hermeneutics, 8, 53, 59, 78–80, 85, 183
'heuristic acts' 98, 99
heuristic process, 11, 14, 15, 16, 52, 64–5, 94,
113, 193
dominant feature, 72–3, 74
hierarchy, organizational, 2, 37–9
Hill, Michael, 181
history/historicism, 58, 60, 62
Hopfl, Heather, 157
Hulsker, Jan, 25
human
artistry of, 162–78
experience, 79, 81–2,
human sciences, 59, 61

humanist philosophy, 85
Husserl, Edmund, 5, 82–3, 84, 85, 97, 105,
127, 151
Hutcheon, Linda, 4
hybridization process, 30, 121, 122
hypertext metaphor, 8, 182, 191–3

iconography, 43, 44–5
ideal-type organization, 3–4, 5, 57
idealism, 60, 62
identity (organizational), 6, 40–1
image, 11–12, 145, 154–5
corporate, 6, 167, 171, 173–4
digitization, 30, 31
as visual display, 171–4
imagined participant observation, 11–18, 70
individual artefacts, 33–4
induction, 93
inductive logic, 63, 74
'informal organizations', 87
instrumental rationality, 56–7
intellectual
analysis of meaningful action, 50, 56
beauty, 51, 99
knowledge, 23, 26, 38–9, 46, 94, 95, 97–8,
106–8, 113
intentional action, 1, 49, 50, 85, 87
empathic understanding, 7, 8, 68–74, 111
pathos of, 51–67, 72, 74, 92, 111, 116, 179
skills and, 92, 94–5, 97
understanding of, 77, 79–80, 117–19
intentional consciousness, 84
interpretation, 55–6, 59–60, 66, 78–80, 105
intracultural level (*Verstehen*), 65
intuition, 11, 63–6, 68, 85, 139, 189
Izzo, Alberto, 60, 153

Jackson, Susan E., 157
Jacobs, Jerry, 53, 58, 62
Jameson, Frederic, 5
Jaspers, Karl, 59, 63
Jauss, Hans Robert, 3, 137, 138, 183
jewel analogy, 125, 126, 127–8, 130
Joas, Hans, 177, 178
Jones, Michael Owen, 6, 137, 157, 174, 181,
183

Kaghan, William, 3
Kant, Immanuel, 107, 108–10, 152, 189
katharsis, 137
kitsch, 12, 186
Knorr-Cetina, Karin, 1
knowing subject, 13, 83, 105–6, 112, 113, 121,
137, 138, 184
knowledge
causal, 58, 60, 62, 64, 85
differentiation, 8, 191–2

knowledge, *cont.*
  digital/analogic, 174
  empathic, 57–71, 105
  evocation of, 11–18 *passim*
  finiteness of, 81–8, 111
  -gathering, 11, 15, 40, 46, 54, 67–9, 74, 97, 111, 133, 190
  intellectual, 23, 26, 38–9, 46, 94–5, 97–8, 106–8, 113
  non-causal, 8, 58, 102–14, 193
  personal, 92–101, 112
  rational, 23, 26, 39, 46, 94, 95, 108, 134
  tacit, 8, 88–101, 108, 110–13, 184
  see also aesthetic knowledge; scientific knowledge
Kreiner, Kristian, 164, 165, 171
Kritik der Urteilskraft (Kant), 108–9
Kronhausen, Eberhard, 45
Kronhausen, Phyllis, 45
Kuhn, James, 113
Kuhn, Thomas, 50–1, 93
Kunda, Gideon, 181

Lacan, Jacques, 172
Lalo, Charles, 119
Langer, Susanne K., 154–5, 159, 160–1
language, 62, 65, 100–1, 136, 192
  ordinary aesthetic, 115–22
Larsen, Janne, 181
Lash, Scott, 5
Latour, Bruno, 2–3, 159
Law, John, 3
leadership style, 162–81
Leonardo da Vinci, 177
Linstead, Stephen, 6, 157
Lipps, Theodore, 61, 105
lived experience, 21, 59, 60, 81, 150, 161
logic, 7, 8, 13, 85
logica poetica, 139–55
logical empiricism, 62
logical positivism, 93, 98
logico-rational model, 7, 8, 13
logo, 6, 7, 159, 171, 172, 181
logos, 49, 154
Louis, Meryl R., 3
lower-order gnoseology, 108
Luckmann, Thomas, 1
Lyotard, Jean-François, 187

MacIver, Robert M., 63
Madonna (portrait), 44, 132–3
Magna Graecia, 119, 122, 125, 130
Maldonado, Tomás, 181
management, 6
  as art, 174–8
  organizational form/feeling, 160–2
managerial practices, 6

Mangham, Iain L., 157
maquillages, 42, 186
March, James, 4
Marquard, Odo, 81
Martin, Jane R., 58
Martin, Joanne, 6
mastery, 96, 101
material artefacts, 30–3, 165
Mattioli, Francesco, 181
Mazzocut-Mis, Maddalena, 60, 84, 114, 119, 186, 188
Mead, Margaret, 181
meaning, 4
  corporate (designing), 166–9
  -event, 137
meaningful action, 63–4, 116, 132, 152
  empathic understanding, 8, 49–50, 53–7, 91, 190
  rational analysis, 50, 106, 113
  tacit knowledge, 8, 91, 94–5, 97, 110–11
meetings (use of chairs), 34–7
Melucci, Alberto, 176
memory, organizational, 43–4
mental states, 63, 66, 120
Merleau-Ponty, Maurice, 97
Merton, Robert K., 3
metaphor, 152–3
  artefact as, 37–9, 40
  organization-hypertext, 8, 182, 191–3
  of organizational time, 165–6
metaphysics, 60, 80–2, 84, 153, 154, 192–3
Methodenstreit, 49, 62, 74
Meyer, Alan D., 181
Milani, Raffaele, 185, 186, 188
modernity, 4–5
Moore, Michael, 6, 174
moral judgement, 108–9
moralization of organizational life, 110–14, 131
Morgan, Gareth, 3, 157
Mukařovský, Jan, 181
music, 1–2
'mythic space', 168
mythos, 152–3, 154
myths/mythical thinking, 53, 151–5

Nacamulli, Raoul C.D., 157
Narahara, Ikko, 45
natural sciences, 50, 51, 53, 58–9, 62, 85, 97, 98, 153–4, 182
negotiation process, 2, 28–30, 34–5, 39, 46, 75, 102–3, 105, 112–14, 169–71
  ordinary language and, 117–22, 184, 192
Negroponte, Nicholas, 174
neo-idealism, 62
neo-Kantianism, 62
neo-positivism, 64, 93